TOWARD A PSYCHOLOGY OF
READING AND LANGUAGE

TOWARD A PSYCHOLOGY OF
READING AND LANGUAGE

*Selected Writings of
Wendell W. Weaver*

EDITED BY

ALBERT J. KINGSTON

Athens
THE UNIVERSITY OF GEORGIA PRESS

Library of Congress Catalog Card Number: 75–3816
International Standard Book Number: 0–8203–0386–0

The University of Georgia Press, Athens 30602

Set in 10 on 12 point Times Roman type
Printed in the United States of America

CONTENTS

428.4
W36t
(1975)

FOREWORD

It is with a mingled sense of regret and pleasure that I write these comments upon the scholarly works of Wendell Weaver. Wendell was both a personal friend of mine and a professional colleague. Our association began in 1961 at the annual meeting of the National Reading Conference when he presented a paper based upon his dissertation which had been inspired, in part, by my earlier work on the cloze procedure. Our friendship and my high regard for his towering intellectual capabilities grew over the years. Later, when he became president of the National Reading Conference and I served as president-elect, we struggled together in our attempts to work in administrative roles for which we had little training or experience. When his short professional career was suddenly and tragically terminated by his death in 1971, it was a great shock to me personally. The world had lost a brilliant scientist and scholar whose impact upon the expansion of knowledge was prevented from developing to its fullest potential. I lost a friend and colleague with whom I shared many personal, scientific, and professional interests.

It is indeed gratifying to know that this excellent selection of Wendell Weaver's papers will be published by the University of Georgia Press. It is my sincere hope this book will find its way into the hands of many graduate students and scholars who have not known of his important work and into others' hands who, like myself, have read many of his papers. Although I have studied most of these publications, I find that I learn much upon second or even third reading of these scholarly contributions, a reaction to an important characteristic of Wendell Weaver's thought. His unique mind stretched across the boundaries of disciplines that place constraints upon the understanding of most scholars and students. Thus, he achieved insights that few in his area of study could equal. At the same time, the originality of his thought tended to interfere with adequate communication upon first hearing or reading. Like a Bach fugue, his ideas present something new upon each successive exposure to the subtle complexities. For these reasons, there is a great need to have a collections of Weaver's thoughts and findings in one publication. This book will allow all readers to understand more fully the major thrust of his intellectual contributions through careful study of each paper in its relationship to his other papers. Through careful reading and rereading of this carefully selected sample of his scholarly works, there is much to be learned that cannot be grasped from studying his individual publications in other contexts.

Weaver's work was the antithesis of the noncumulative research and theory of many specialists in the areas of language and reading. There are several major themes that run throughout both his theoretical and empirical studies. These themes are basic to a full understanding and appreciation of his work. First, he always viewed reading as an aspect of language and cognition. Second, he organized and interpreted research in intimate relationship to theory. Third, his research on language and reading was based upon a multidisciplinary synthesis of significant theory and findings from the basic sciences of psychology and linguistics. Fourth, he developed much of his research and theory from the perspective of a communications model. Fifth, he devoted much attention to the separate but interacting lexical and structural elements in language and reading. Sixth, he made use of the cloze procedure as a basic research tool in much of his work throughout his brief professional career. To my knowledge, no other student of language and reading has developed his thinking so completely from the vantage point of this particular framework. The papers in this collection represent a good sample of the development and frequent "recapitulation" of these important motifs. Therefore, in my judgment, this book represents a novel as well as a highly significant contribution to the understanding of language and reading.

Many, if not most, of Weaver's papers were addressed to a relatively small number of people in the areas of educational psychology and reading. Many who have heard him speak at meetings undoubtedly failed to grasp the subtleties of his thought. Countless others in the broader disciplines of psychology, linguistics, and education have probably never heard of his work. Scholars in the diverse fields of verbal learning, tests and measurements, and psycholinguistics have much to learn from his contributions. For both those who have heard him speak and have read his papers and for others who are not familiar with his publications, this book of readings will offer revealing insights into little-known areas on the edge of knowledge. Wendell Weaver's thought was well ahead of his time. Even his early writings offer much to contemporary thought. In my perhaps not unbiased opinion, the publication of these papers constitutes a major contribution to the academic community. Although Wendell Weaver is no longer with us, his thoughts live on and provide him with a well-deserved immortality.

Earl F. Rankin
Director of Graduate Studies in Reading,
University of Kentucky;
President, National Reading Conference

PREFACE

During the past twenty years there has been increasing interest among behavioral scientists in the domain of verbal behavior. Language, thought by most to be species-specific to man as to the processes by which it is encoded and decoded, is a genuine challenge to those seeking to better understand human behavior. Not only has the study of language itself fascinated men for years, but how we learn and how we use language and its relationship to intelligence and cognition continue to challenge our best thinkers. Linguists and philosophers long have speculated upon and studied the many-faceted dimensions of language. Recently a small group of cognitive psychologists have devoted increased attention to language acquisition and use. Impetus has been given to the problem by an increased awareness that thousands of American school children have difficulty in mastering written language. Millions of dollars have been spent in the past two decades in hopes of discovering clues which will result in improved reading pedagogy. Wendell Weaver was one of those who sought to understand how humans acquired and utilized language. Unlike many psychologists, he did not study language by means of serial learning, paired associates, or word association experiments. During his student days at the University of Georgia, he became fascinated with the cloze procedure, developed by Wilson Taylor, while reading Earl Rankin's work at the University of Michigan. During the following twelve years of his life he was to utilize the cloze in the majority of experiments. In his doctoral dissertation he used the cloze to examine differences in oral and written language and throughout his life continued to experiment with variations of the technique. He varied the number and type of word classes, deleted, experimented with pre- and postcloze procedures (i.e., alternated mutilated with nonmutilated passages in their presentation), examined the differences in aural and written cloze, and tested the reliability and validity of the technique under a variety of conditions. Toward the end of his life he became interested in using cloze procedure as a teaching technique with first graders and also sought to use it as a means for establishing a basic appraisal method for assessing the language progress of primary-grade children.

Weaver's interest in written language led him to study the role played by language in reading. Many of his papers were aimed at trying to understand the linguistic and psychological nature of the reading process. Unlike some who work in this area, he eschewed expansive, high-blown theories. Rather he favored systematic experiments designed to explain specific aspects of language and reading.

Wendell Weaver had a comparatively short academic career. He received the Ed.D. degree at the University of Georgia in 1961 and joined the psychology faculty of Campbell College in Buies Creek, North Carolina. In 1966 he returned to the University of Georgia as associate professor of educational psychology. Shortly after he was appointed to the graduate faculty and in 1969 was promoted to professor. His research rapidly brought him recognition, and in 1969 he was elected vice-president of the National Reading Conference, an organization of reading specialists, psychologists, and linguists interested in the study of reading. He became president in 1971. He also served as a reviewer-evaluator in the consortium of specialists organized at Rutgers University during the years 1970–71 which searched the literature for the purpose of defining promising models for future research.

Wendell Weaver was not a highly organized person. He was a big man who loved to sit up late at night with a few colleagues and favored students and theorize about the nature of language and cognition. He did not keep extensive personal records. Even after he discovered that he was ill, he made little or no effort to put his personal or professional records in order. Putting together these papers was thus a major job, for nowhere did a complete bibliography or vitae exist. Indeed this lack of organization was characteristic of the man because he did not seek kudos and personal recognition. To him the major purpose of research was the act of discovery or knowing. He did not, as lesser men sometimes do, parade or display his academic accomplishments. It may be that some of Weaver's papers have been overlooked. In fact some of the titles listed under other papers at the end of the book were not included in the list of his collected works because only notes or rough drafts were discovered among Weaver's papers. In such cases every effort was made to determine that a paper actually was presented despite its loss. The writer, however, had close personal and professional ties with Weaver and was familiar with his more recent works. Many of Weaver's former colleagues and students were contacted for help in tracking down papers and for suggestions concerning which papers they felt should be included in the book.

Major problems in any book of readings are first the selection of which papers to include and how to organize those selected. In choosing papers for inclusion in this work, a number of criteria were employed. First efforts were made to choose representative papers, particularly those which were not printed but rather were presented orally at professional meetings. Secondly, an attempt was made to present earlier as well as later papers in order to present a longitudinal view of Weaver's systematic research efforts. Finally, the papers selected tend to be from sources which had specialized and limited readership. It is hoped that by assembling them in a single book greater readership will be attained.

The book itself is organized into two major parts. Section I, titled "Theoretical Papers on the Nature of Reading and Language," consists of ten articles of an expository nature. These papers either were delivered at meetings attended by persons largely interested in reading or were published in journals sponsored by reading organizations. Those familiar with reading will recognize that several papers were considered to be landmarks when they first were published.

Section II, titled "Empirical Investigations of Language and Reading," consists of fifteen papers and an abstract of Weaver's unpublished doctoral dissertation. The papers reveal Weaver's continued interest in the cloze procedure. In his doctoral dissertation he sought to examine differences in the way college students handled cloze techniques in oral and written language. In other papers he studied the effect of cloze deletions under many varied conditions. Also included in this section are several studies in which Weaver and A. C. Bickley probed the degree to which reading test items convey meaning to the reader. These papers have provoked favorable comment and have stimulated a number of subsequent investigations.

Many people helped with this project. I particularly wish to thank Dr. E. Paul Torrance, head of the Department of Educational Psychology at the University of Georgia, for his encouragement and advice. Dr. Stanley Ainsworth, as associate dean for graduate studies in the College of Education, University of Georgia, provided financial support for the project. Dr. A. C. Bickley of Francis Marion College, Dr. J. Jaap Tuinman of Simon Frasier University, Dr. Leslie E. Figa of Francis Marion College, and Dr. James A. Dinnan of the University of Georgia offered genuine assistance in the finding and selection of manuscripts and papers. Dr. Earl Rankin of the University of Kentucky, a pioneer researcher in the exploration of the cloze, gave valuable advice concerning the organization of the book and contributed the forward.

Finally, I wish to thank the officers of the College Reading Association, the International Reading Association, the National Reading Conference, the American Psychological Association, and the Southeastern Psychological Association for permission to reproduce the papers. Appreciation is also due the editors of the *Journal of Social Psychology*, the *Journal of Psychology*, *Perceptual Motor Skills*, and the *Journal of Communication* who gave reproduction permission.

A. J. K.

I

THEORETICAL PAPERS
ON THE NATURE OF READING
AND LANGUAGE

This section consists of ten papers of a theoretical and expository nature. In each paper Weaver examines one aspect either of language or of reading. In the first paper, which Weaver presented at the National Reading Conference in 1961, he seeks to relate the findings of those who had studied auding to the process of reading. The second paper, "On the Psychology of Reading," also was presented at the National Reading Conference. In this work Weaver defines the problems involved in developing a viable psychology of reading. The third article, "Theoretical Aspects of the Cloze Procedure," represents a serious attempt to analyze the way in which cloze technique disrupts normal language. This paper was presented in 1964 and published in 1965 at a time when the cloze procedure was just beginning to become popular as a research technique.

In "The Retrieval of Learning Sets by the External Display of Learning Materials," Weaver and Bickley examine certain visual and perceptual aspects of reading. This paper was presented at the National Reading Conference in 1966 and published in 1967.

The three following papers, "The Word as a Unit of Language," "Questioning in Content Reading," and "Psychological Examinations of Newer Dimensions of Linguistics and Their Implications for Reading," were published in 1967 in the "Research for the Classroom" feature of the *Journal of Reading*. A major purpose of this feature was to introduce classroom teachers of reading to some of the newer theoretical developments in the study of the reading process. In the first paper, "The Word as a Unit of Language," Weaver pointed out that linguists analyze language by using many systems or constructs other than "words" or vocabulary. His gentle suggestion that reading teachers may overstress the importance of vocabulary and word recognition was acclaimed by many. This work has been widely cited by subsequent researchers. "Questioning in Content Reading" introduced reading teachers to Rothkopf's technique of interspersing questions in prose writing. As the name implies, the next paper, "Psychological Examinations of Newer Dimensions of Linguistics and Their Implications for Reading," represented an attempt to bridge the findings of psycholinguistics and linguistics and the pedagogy of reading.

Weaver presented "Linguistic Assumptions and Reading Instruction" at the National Reading Conference in 1968. In this paper he examined five linguistic assumptions which reading specialists apparently accepted. Even today his cautions are worthy of notice. "The Contribution of Research to Reading Theory" was first presented as a lecture at the Temple University Symposium on a Theory of Reading organized by Carl A. Lefevre and later published in the *Journal of Reading Behavior*. Weaver later developed some of the ideas introduced in this paper in one not included in this collection because of its specialized nature. Students might, however, be interested in reading Weaver's "Discussion of Professor Neal F. Johnson's Paper" as a follow-up.

In 1970–71 Weaver served as a reviewer evaluator for the Targeted Research and Development Program in Reading supported by the U. S. Office of Education and under the aegis of Rutgers University. The thrust of the project was to search the literature in order to identify models which might prove helpful in explicating reading theory and pedagogy. (I was fortunate in serving as a member of the advisory board of the project.) "Modeling the Effects of Oral Language upon Reading Language" grew out of this stimulating project. The paper was included in the final report of the project and presented at a special symposium of the International Reading Association. Subsequently it was reprinted in the *Reading Research Quarterly*. Essentially the article suggests that Tolman's sign theory may be helpful in understanding the nature of reading, and it offers fourteen propositions to demonstrate the point.

The final paper in this section, "Oral and Oral-Written Language Measures with First Grade Pupils," demonstrates the interest Weaver developed during the last few years of his life in trying to measure the oral language abilities of first graders and to establish similar or common measures of written language abilities. The reader will note that we still lack proper terminology for even describing the problem adequately. While we have clearly differentiated terms to describe specific aspects of oral language—e.g., speaking, listening—we find such vague terms as visible language, oral-written, reading, written, and so on employed by various researchers. The paper included in this selection describes a number of attempts to find a common basis for measuring the child's oral language prior to his development of basic reading skills and his reading proficiencies during the first year of learning.

The Predictability of Omissions in Reading and Listening

Colin Cherry put forth the view of language as a set of constraints, and theorizes that these constraints may be profitably categorized as operating at two levels of redundancy—semantic and syntactic. It is not difficult to grasp the idea of semantic redundancy as a repetition or association of the denotations and connotations of words. Syntactic redundancy is a more subtle concept. Cherry says, "Syntactic redundancy implies additions to a text; something more is said or written than is strictly necessary to convey the message" (1).

Researchers in the field of mechanical translation of language have made a similar dichotomy. For instance, Reifler says, "Understanding the import of a message . . . is either of a non-grammatical or of a grammatical nature" (2). Reifler thus finds a grammatical dimension of understanding. C. C. Fries asserts that an utterance is not understandable without both structural (or syntactic or grammatical meaning) and lexical (or semantic, non-grammatical meaning); yet he views these two categories as distinct. Fries states, "Certain types of analysis are possible without knowing the lexical meanings of words or what the sentence is about" (3). Other investigators have found lexical elements to be relatively independent of the structural. Richens and Booth say, "Generally . . . in straightforward descriptive writing, the mere sequence of words, without any knowledge of syntax at all is sufficiently revealing" (4). Thus, there is wide agreement that there are two distinct elements in language, with certain styles of language demanding more or less of one element than another.

Rankin has shown that a noun-verb deletion using the cloze procedure removes more lexical meaning from a passage than structural meaning, and that an "every *n*th word" deletion reduces the structural meaning more than it reduces lexical meaning. Using the cloze procedure in this fashion it is possible to examine experimentally relationships between these two language categories (5).

Weaver has shown that structural redundancy is significantly higher in the reading situation than in the listening situation, while lexical

Published originally in *Problems Programs and Projects in College-Adult Reading*, E. P. Bliesmer and R. C. Staiger, eds. The Eleventh Yearbook of the National Reading Conference, 1962. Reprinted with the permission of the National Reading Conference.

redundancy is similar in these situations. This relationship was obtained even though the subjects were allowed as many repeats of the materials listened to as they desired (6). This implies that redundancy is not only a function of the language, but involves the characteristics of the various communication channels of the organism. A knowledge of the nature of this redundancy would seem to provide clues to basic information-processing activities of the organism; certainly the observed differences in these redundancies raise interesting questions about the operation of human coding processes.

The total capacity of the human nervous system is enormous. Von Neuman estimated the nervous system contains 10^{10} neurons. No computer conceived contains anywhere near this number of parts. Computers are constructed with maximum storage capacities of several million bits (one bit is the information contained in a binary decision—a yes or no answer to a question). This is far from the storage capacity of the human organism.

The capacity of the eye and ear as receptors is also quite large. Jacobson estimated the informational capacity of the eye as 4,300,000 bits per second and the informational capacity of the ear as 10,000 bits per second. Although this means a 430-fold difference in the capacity of eye and ear, both receptors have a large capacity nevertheless (7).

With such potential capacity, one is quite unprepared for the difference in the amount of information which is transmitted by the human organism. Quastler and Wulff estimated that the maximum rate of informational transmission of impromptu speech is about 26 bits per second. They also estimated a maximum silent reading processing rate of 44 bits per second (8). It is the rare investigator who finds the human informational transmission rate higher than 50 bits per second.

One of the "bottle-necks," if such be a proper term, to more rapid information processing is the immediate memory. This is a very narrow gate through which we pass information to the enormous capacity of long-term memory. A relatively reliable cue to the mentally deficient is the inability of the individual to repeat a group of three or four digits immediately on hearing them. On the other hand, the brightest individuals rarely can repeat over nine digits correctly. The average immediate memory span for digits is seven and the limits of this ability tend to cluster closely around this figure—as Miller says, 7 plus or minus 2. Why such a restricted apperture for such a large reservoir?

Miller has shown that the retention of digits and letters of the alphabet is a function of the length of the material to be retained rather than its informational content. He also concluded that long-term memory processes are of the same nature as the immediate memory in regard to the characteristic unit to be processed—that is, the storage capacity is determined by the length of the material to be retained in long-term memory (9).

Using this approach one may view the immediate memory as a register on which is recorded an encoding problem. If we are to keep the material presented to the immediate memory it must be re-grouped, or as Miller says "chunked." This "chunking" operation is the task of our central processing and is a complexed, time-consuming operation which causes the time delay in transmission.

The findings of Miller raise other problems however. If language is constrained by length rather than by informational content, why must it be so redundant? Shannon has estimated that the English language is as much as 75% redundant (that is, the language could be written and spoken with only 25% of the symbols now in use) (10). We have input capacities measured in millions and thousands of bits, but this capacity can only be completely processed in tens of bits. If this system is not informationally controlled, would not redundancy act to increase the burden on central processing? The fact of redundancy in the language and in the sensory reception of it and the fact that length of the material, rather than informational richness, constrains retention arouses the idea that perhaps a reduction of redundancy occurs in the human coding operation. In a psychophysical context, H. B. Barlow has hypothesized that just such a phenomenon occurs (11).

There is a rather large amount of evidence that lexical redundancy is tied to a relatively narrow context. Kaplan found that when subjects were presented contexts of different numbers of words and asked to identify nouns, verbs, and adjectives embedded in the context, "a context of one or two words on each side of the key word had an effectiveness not markedly different from that . . . when . . . the whole sentence . . . surrounded the word" (12). Structural elements, on the other hand, are scattered throughout a message, implicit in its word order, tacked on to its lexical units, and coded into "lexical-appearing" units which defy denotation (e.g., "the"). Edward Sapir, for instance, found ten different syntactical relationships scattered throughout the simple sentence, "The farmer kills the duckling" (13). There are strong common sense grounds for assuming that an entire message is not stored. One does not reproduce previously received messages verbatim; in fact, the common characteristics of reproduced messages is that they contain idosyncracies of the transmitter, rather than being exact reproductions of the original input to the transmitter. It is as if one were dealing with two elemental units in the language situation; one the lexical, for storage and retention; the other structural, a plan for storage and retention. The more redundant elements of the language then would not be involved in storage; retention would involve lexical elements primarily which can be shown to consist of short contextual units.

It is possible to view the highly redundant structural element as the "program" for the individual's coding. That is, the reader or listener expects to hear or read and to process routinely in terms of this expectation. Unfamiliar structural elements would increase the central processing load because these elements could not be handled routinely. This would tend to decrease the rate of processing. Using another strategy, the individual might process unfamiliar structural elements rigidly in terms of his expectations introducing distortions. The reader as encoder has advantages over the listener because he has spacial and sequential cues; he has the ability and opportunity to repeat selectively; and he has the permanent structure of the language before him to compare to his own structuring. The listener may limit his structural processing to the relatively small complex of the lexical (as the cloze procedure seems to force him to do) in which case he would seem to miss widely-spaced contextual elements, but a strategy also seems plausible of coding large amounts of the context into informational rich "chunks" ignoring the details. The reader should be able to encode both if his internal structuring (i.e., the way he *produces* language sequences) is not inflexibly incompatible with the language he is receiving. Structural redundancy is needed then to decode messages and to encode messages because it "programs" the lexical elements not because it reduces the information burden. The idea of structure as a recoding plan would seem to fit hypotheses of Barlow concerning serial reduction of redundancy. Barlow makes the following points:

1. The coding out of redundancy lends itself to subdivision.

2. Small parts of the input, selected by spatial and temporal contiguity, may be dealt with in isolation then brought together for more complex forms of decoding.

3. If this coding were successful channel capacity would be reduced in the channel acting as input to the next stage.

4. This would be advantageous because the difficulty in selecting a code is related to the number of possible codes, which in turn is dependent upon channel capacity, not the amount of information the channel is carrying (11).

It is interesting to note that this view is in accord with Miller's finding concerning the constraining effect of length. The channel capacity of immediate memory (or better for these purposes "immediate input") is small and this limits the coding rather than the amount of information involved. Reading, in the case of the proficient reader, generally allows better encoding than listening, because there is a better matching, in an engineering sense, of "immediate input" to central processing.

REFERENCES

1. Cherry, Colin, *On Human Communication.* New York: The Technology Press of Massachusetts Institute of Technology and John Wiley & Sons, 1957.

2. Reifler, Erwin, "The Mechanical Determination of Meaning." In William N. Locke and A. Donald Booth (Eds.), *Machine Translation of Languages.* New York: John Wiley & Sons, 1955.

3. Fries, C. C., *The Structure of English.* New York: Harcourt, Brace and Company, 1952.

4. Richens, R. H., and A. D. Booth, "Some Methods of Mechanized Translation." In William N. Locke and A. Donald Booth (Eds.), *Machine Translation of Languages.* New York: John Wiley & Sons, 1955.

5. Rankin, E. F., Jr., "An Evaluation of the Cloze Procedure as a Technique for Measuring Reading Comprehension." Unpublished Ph.D. dissertation. Ann Arbor, Michigan: University of Michigan.

6. Weaver, W. W., "An Examination of Some Differences in Oral and Written Language Using the Cloze Procedure." Unpublished Ed. D. dissertation. Athens, Georgia: University of Georgia.

7. Miller, G. A., "Human Memory and the Storage of Information," *IRE Transactions in Information Theory,* 1956, Vol. IT-2, No. 3, pp. 128–137.

8. Quastler, H., and V. J. Wulff, "Human Performance in Information Transmission." Part One: Simple Sequential Routinized Tasks. (Manuscript). Quoted in Fred Attneave, *Applications of Information to Psychology.* New York: Henry Holt, 1959.

9. Jacobson, Homer, "The Informational Capacity of the Human Eye," *Science,* 113; 463–471, 1951; and "Information and the Human Ear," *Journal of the Acoustical Society of America,* 23:463–476, 1951.

10. Shannon, C. E., "Prediction and Entropy of Printed English," *Bell System Technical Journal,* 30:56–64, 1951.

11. Barlow, H. B., "Possible Principles Underlying the Transformations of Sensory Messages," Rosenblith, Walter A. (Ed.), *Sensory Communication.* New York: John Wiley & Sons, 1961.

12. Kaplan, Abraham, "An Experimental Study of Ambiguity in Context." Mimeographed, 18 pp. November 30, 1950. Microfilm, Papers on Mechanical Translating, Roll 799. Cambridge, Massachusetts: Massachusetts Institute of Technology, 1950.

13. Sapir, Edward, *Language,* New York: Harcourt, Brace and Company, 1921, 1949.

On the Psychology of Reading

In the Eleventh Yearbook, Kingston (8, p. 20) defined reading as "a process of communication by which a message is transmitted graphically between individuals." The treating of language processes as parts of a communication system analogous to a mechanical system is an outgrowth of advances in communications engineering. These concepts of communications theory, especially their mathematical elaboration, do not always fit well the psychological situations but the implications of the ideas are so intriguing and seem to have such potential for explanation that many psychologists have not been able to leave them alone.

The most common classification of communications systems involves five components—a source, a transmitter, a channel, a receiver, and a destination. Here, I refer to the operations of the source and the transmitter as encoding and to the operations of the receiver and the destination as decoding. Our system of graphic symbols encoded into and decoded out of the neurophysiological code of the organism is the coding operation. The graphic symbols themselves are the external display, and the figure and ground, in the case of reading, is the channel. By the psychology of reading I mean the scientific study of graphical decoding operations in the human organism.

Such a scientific psychology of reading is difficult to come by. Not the least of the problems of the psychological thinker is the pervasive idea that reading is a human sort of thing of such a nature that it is unpredictable, unmechanical, even unmeasurable. This attitude is expressed in many ways, some subtle, some not so subtle as the following:

> I think that I shall never see
> A calculator made like me.
> A me that likes Martinis dry
> And on the rocks a little rye.
> A me that looks at girls and such,
> But mostly girls, and very much.
> A me that wears an overcoat
> And likes a risky anecdote.
> A me that taps a foot and grins

Published originally in *New Concepts in College-Adult Reading,* E. L. Thurston and L. G. Hafner, eds. The Thirteenth Yearbook of the National Reading Conference, 1964. Reprinted with the permission of the National Reading Conference.

> Whenever Dixieland begins.
> They make computers for a fee,
> But only moms can make a me (10, p. 111).

A cognition involving not only a psychological but also a biological half-truth. Such sentiments are not at all proper for a psychologist studying reading, for here the search is explicitly for the predictable, the mechanical, the measurable. Other considerations are for philosophy or for art. As a psychologist one does not concern himself with the whole person, but only with that part of the person which with simplification can be shown to exhibit lawful behavior.

Not only must the psychologist ignore popular assumptions that the reading process is scientifically unanalyzable but he must overcome biases in his own training. Reading processes are largely covert. Since the introspectionists, psychologists have not been comfortable with covert processes.

The psychologist does not feel uncomfortable in dealing with the auditory display, which we call speech, for he treats the display as an overt behavior directly related to the source. Thus Skinner (11) labels speech, and other overt acts, as verbal behavior but excludes listening from this category. If we consider carefully, however, we see that speech and writing are but the *end* products of an encoding operation: they are not complete displays of that operation. They are only the part of the encoding operation which has potential for subsequent decoding operations. There is no reason to assume that we can learn more about the total speech or writing act from the external display of speech or writing than we can learn about reading or listening from the same external display. In studying any part of the language process the psychologist has been restricted largely to the message in transit from one organism to another. There seems no virtue in considering these messages in transit as outputs only. As elements in the channel of communication these messages are at once both output and input. It seems valid to look either way along the channel of communication, back to the source of the message, or forward to the destination of the message. In either case, the primary interest of the psychologist is not in the message in transit, but in the originator and destination of the message.

Whatever inferences psychologists make from the vantage point of the channel of communication, the inferences are directed toward those "black boxes" we call human organisms. The "black box" is another term originating in engineering. It describes a problem situation which contains an unknown "machine" with input and output connections. The problem solver may vary the characteristics of the input and measure the effects on the output. He cannot open the box. From his knowledge of what went in and his measurement of what comes out he is to deduce the internal operations performed in the box.

The psychologist dealing with his problem cannot be sure of the operations that are "really" performed in the box. He can only be sure that he has an analogue. Although he is in contact with the covert only by inferences he is able to draw from the overt certain assumptions that must be maintained if the psychologist is to remain scientific. How easy it is to stray from these assumptions is illustrated by this quotation from Wendell Garner's otherwise insightful book *Uncertainty and Structure as Psychological Concepts.*

> The signification of a word is the actual identifying relation, and it cannot exist in lesser or greater degree. It is simply a statement of the nature of a relation and while the nature of the relation can be changed, this change is qualitative and cannot be quantified. To a child, the signification of the word *honesty* may be very simple, while to an adult it may be very complex. But this change is not one of quantity of signification, but rather of quality (6, p. 142).

Now whatever the signification of a word is, as psychologists we should assume it is a state of the organism and as such must be a physical state, in principle reducible to quantity or form, or to sequences of quantity or form. That is, in the broadest sense it must be quantifiable unless extra-scientific assumptions are made.

Because the obvious approach to all language study is along the channel of communication with its "public" content, the psychologist studying reading shares an interest in language in transit with several other disciplines. Discoveries in these related fields while providing many analyses suggestive to psychological thinking, may also distort the proper psychological approach to reading. The linguists, for example, share several concerns with the psychologist. There is a basic difference however in the direction of the effort exerted. The linguist is not ordinarily interested in the question, "What does this language sample imply about the source or the destination of the message?" He asks rather, "What does this language sample imply about language samples in general?" The linguist ordinarily assumes that his task is accomplished when he demonstrates the lawfulness of the language display itself.

A recent examination of reading from the linguistic point of view while appearing to contribute to reading instruction could misdirect the psychologist. In his book *Linguistics and Reading* (4), C. C. Fries develops the position that reading is a substitution of a printed display for the previously learned sounds of the language. The assumption is that, organismically, graphic symbols encode verbal symbols. As the sounds have been related previously to semantic structures the semantic structures already learned are transferred directly to the written cues. The thesis implies that anyone who can talk can read and those who talk but do not read are the victims of inadequate instruction in transferring graphic symbols into sound symbols. For all I know this is an acceptable hypothesis, but the point here is that Fries gives the impression he is dealing with linguistic fact while he is actually stating an untested neurophysiological hypothesis. Accepting the hypothesis is tantamount to saying the psychology of reading is the psychology of speech once the word is matched with the sound it represents.

Fries goes on to draw the implication that the teacher of reading is not concerned with "meaning" as such. Perhaps it would be fairer to say Fries believes the "meaning" is already there, as a result of previous verbal experiences, so the reading teacher does not need to be concerned. Whether this absence of concern for meaning is proper for the teacher of reading or not, the psychologist interested in decoding operations of the organism is concerned. He assumes meaning must be represented in organic tissue or be a result of states of the organism. Just as the structures which make reading possible are coded organic structures, the structures which make meaning possible are coded organic structures. The reading process is not completed until the organism has determined if the message has meaning; I use this phraseology advisedly.

Meaning, as I think of the term, is the result of the application of prior codings of the organism to the present decoding task. The prior codings of the organism do not seem entirely dependent on input sources external to the organism. That is, the internal system seems to be productive of new input to the system. External inputs into the system are interpreted by previous external inputs plus internal reorganizations which have occurred.

A message is communicated as the coding of the message approaches relevant coded structures within the organism. Communication by reading depends upon equivalent states in source and destination. Under certain circumstances a message may be meaningful without communicating. The written display may activate structures in the receiver not congruent with structures the same coding activates in the source. These activated structures are under the control of the internal organization of the destination rather than under the control of the organization of the source of the message. The popular terms for this condition are "misreadings" or "variant readings."

There is no theory of language worthy of the name. Until there is, of course, there will be no adequate theory of reading. As one looks at reading research for aid in framing such a theory he gets the impression of intense interest and activity but little consistency of direction. Traditional approaches have been barren as far as theory is concerned; current approaches are "far out" and who can tell what will become of them. The approach I prefer is based on a result that keeps cropping up in many studies, in many disciplines.

Language, on the one hand, is highly redundant. By developmental criteria, the structure of language is easily learned. The redundancy of a third reader is about the redundancy of a simple adult text. The redundancy of a fifth reader approaches the redundancy in average adult texts (1). The three-year-old fashions many structurally correct sentences. Certain language elements are tied down early, and these elements tend to remain invariant. They seem to function in some fashion as a frame on which to hang other elements carrying lexical information.

On the other hand, abundant stores of lexical information take much longer to acquire. The lexical unit is many times unique to a context but the most infrequently used item of information once learned can be made to appear at the appropriate time though kept under cover for years.

This sort of dichotomy of language elements has been widely noted. Colin Cherry views language as a set of constraints and theorizes that these constraints may be categorized as operating at two levels of redundancy—syntactic and semantic (2). Researchers in the field of the mechanical translation of language usually refer to the dichotomy as grammatical and nongrammatical (e.g., 9). John Chotlos (3) examining distributions in the light of Zipf's harmonic equation concludes, using a mathematical argument, that the words of a language should be divided into two categories, structural words which form the core or framework of the language, and content and action words that have directly or indirectly an extensional reference. The linguist, Fries (5), uses the terms I adopted for this paper, structural and lexical, and considers it possible to study each in isolation.

In attempting research in this area a few assumptions about how decoding processes operate have had to serve as my theory. When there is no king in Israel every man does as he desires. I assume that language elements in a neurophysiological code entering the central nervous system perform different functions. One of these functions is a control function involving relating incoming elements to elements already present in the internal environment of the organism. This control function seems to be a property of the structure of the language.

I imagine the structural part of language to be in a different system from the lexical elements of language. One bit of evidence here is that structural units are not stored with lexical units; at least, we have great difficulty in repeating intact long language sequences in the exact order in which they were presented.

I have operated with the view that language codes for the organism a progression from points of high redundancy to points of low redundancy. Points of high redundancy are points of control (i.e., these points provide directions for reorganizing and storing lexical elements). The points of high redundancy may be a few nouns for the beginning decoder— function words, punctuation, word order, and position of language element in context for the sophisticated decoder. The points of low redundancy are points of lexical information—the content or the semantic focus of the message. The analogy to the computer program is obvious. The program controlling the operation must be determined at any point in time, yet flexibility can be built into the system, even to the point of having the program alter itself. Not that the organism performs as the computer, but that the computer performs, under certain conditions, as a very insensitive and rigid, but logical organism. We can determine more accurately the nature of this simpler operation. Such a dialectic between organism and computer seems to hold much promise both for the formulation of theory and for the testing of hypotheses.

I am not recommending these assumptions to others. To date all of us have apparently missed the mark so widely that more searching among alternative formulations seems appropriate. The psychology of reading is in part beneficiary, in part victim, of the utilitarian background of the research effort: beneficiary in having a large number of people who care, who would like to see something accomplished; victim because practicality is not a prolific breeder of the imaginative. William Blake once said, "What is now proved was once only imagined." Reading theory exemplifies lack of imagination, of looking beyond what "is" to what "might be." Imagination in science must eventually be criticized by experiment, but without imagination experiment cannot come into being. We have many models and we have many investigations, but no model plus extensive fitting of the data to the model. A scientific psychology of reading can only come into being from people with a point of view who research the point of view long enough to determine its explanatory efficiency.

REFERENCES

1. Carterette, Edward C. and Margaret Hubbard Jones. "Redundancy in Children's Texts," *Science.* 140: 1309–1311, 21 June, 1963.
2. Cherry, Colin. *On Human Communication,* New York: The Technology

Press of Massachusetts Institute of Technology and John Wiley & Sons, 1957.

3. Chotlos, John W., "A Statistical and Comparative Analysis of Individual Written Language Samples," *Psychological Monographs,* Vol. 56, No. 244, 1944.

4. Fries, Charles C., *Linguistics and Reading,* New York: Holt, Rinehart and Winston, Inc., 1962.

5. Fries, Charles C., *The Structure of English,* New York: Harcourt, Brace and Company, 1952.

6. Garner, Wendell R. *Uncertainty and Structure as Psychological Concepts.* New York: John Wiley and Sons, Inc., 1962.

7. Glanzer, Murray, "Grammatical Category: A rote learning and word association analysis," *Journal of Learning and Verbal Behavior,* 1: 31–41, 1962.

8. Kingston, Albert J. "Some Thoughts on Reading Comprehension," in Emery P. Bliesmer and Ralph C. Staiger (Eds.), *Eleventh Yearbook of the National Reading Conference,* Milwaukee: National Reading Conference, 1962, 20–23.

9. Reifler, Edwin, "The Mechanical Determination of Meaning," in William N. Locke and A. Donald Booth (Eds.), *Machine Translation of Languages.* New York: The Technology Press of the Massachusetts Institute of Technology and John Wiley & Sons, Inc., 1955, 136–164.

10. Schenck, H. Jr., *"Me," The Best from Fantasy and Science Fiction:* Ninth Series. New York: Doubleday. Copyright 1959 by Mercury Press, Inc. Reprinted from *The Magazine of Fantasy and Science Fiction.*

11. Skinner, B. F. *Verbal Behavior.* New York: Appleton-Century-Crofts, 1957.

Theoretical Aspects of the Cloze Procedure

CLOSURE AND CLOZE

Taylor (18) in his doctoral dissertation which introduced the cloze procedure as a technique for the investigation of language phenomena proposed two rationales for the procedure. One was based on the Gestalt concept of closure, the other on ideas of communications theoreticians and engineers and popularly called "information theory." The relationship of Gestalt ideas of closure to the cloze procedure seems a very tenuous one. It is based more or less on the rather obvious observation that there is a gap to be filled in and the equating of the subject's response to this gap with the Gestalt description of the perception of a non-symmetrical, incomplete situation. The true Gestaltist has always concentrated on the perceptual and has invariably considered closure a literal closing. There is no evidence that subjects close cloze units in this literal fashion. The term "cloze" is misleading as a designation of this procedure primarily because it arouses in the thinker the more common constructs of Gestalt psychology which have always been difficult to apply to verbal situations. In an exhaustive review of the literature concerning closure and the cloze procedure Rankin (14, p. 20) states, "All of this suggests that making cloze responses is primarily a cognitive rather than a perceptual task." Gestalt explanations have not been very successful with cognitive processes.

If one adopts a rather deviant view of closure, deviant at least from the point of view of the Gestaltist, he may think of the restructuring operations of closure as a coding operation. Miller (9, p. 235) argues that, "when the field theorist talks about 'restructuring' we can often substitute the word 'recoding.'" Cloze lends itself very well to a description as a coding operation. Furthermore if one defines closure in this manner many of the constructs of information theory are available to aid in the analysis. By defining closure in some probabilistic fashion (e.g., using informational analogies) our descriptions are improved and experimental testing becomes more feasible.

Published originally in *The Philosophical and Sociological Basis of Reading,* E. L. Thurston and L. E. Hafner, eds. The Fourteenth Yearbook of the National Reading Conference, 1965. Reprinted with the permission of the National Reading Conference.

LANGUAGE ORGANIZATIONS AND
THEIR COMPONENTS

It should be noted at the outset that the operations which a subject performs in completing cloze units go beyond those phenomena investigated in communications engineering. Informational analysis for the communications engineer involves only the statistical rarity of signs. The human communicator is certainly using signs but in a manner that goes far beyond their probabilities of occurrence. It is well to keep in mind from the beginning that the cloze procedure is related not only to language but also to thought, and I, for one, assume no simple relationship between language and thought.

I have always found it impossible to attempt to analyze the cloze procedure without having in mind some concept of how language operates in general. The concept of language in the background of this paper is that language is generated from a preestablished "plan." By "plan" I have in mind Miller's et al. (10, p. 16) concept of "any hierarchical process in the organism that can control the order in which a sequence of operations is to be performed." The plan for a specific language is learned, but I assume many genetically based elements in the organization of the human nervous system which make language possible—otherwise one could teach an ape to speak. There is a plan for generating language, or as I say here, encoding; there is another plan for interpreting language input—decoding. The plans for encoding and decoding may have many similarities, but there are also basic differences. For example, Miller, Pribram, and Galanter (10, p. 145) writing of such plans for speaking remark, "The plan of the sentence, it seems, must be determined in a general way before it is differentiated into the particular words that we are going to utter." Evidence from the use of the cloze procedure suggests, however, that plans for interpretation of speech operate over very small segments of the text—four or five words on each side of a particular deletion—and thus must proceed from the particular to the general (8).

My idea of decoding plans is that they proceed sequentially, yet at each language unit in the sequence there is a parallel process going on (11). Perhaps a rather simple table will make clearer what I am saying. Assuming that the planning process is word by word (which is unlikely) one might represent a particular sentence as shown in Table 1.

The planned sequence is 1, 2, 3, 4, 5. Our subject is presented with a sentence to read: "Red has more good shoes." These words are in storage with other words, but they are related by many kinds of categories. Here we are considering only the grammatical category. I assume that reading for the practiced reader is a maximum-cue, over-practiced recognition routine. There is little uncertainty involved in this situation. Reading

Table 1.

1	2	3	4	5
Don	Brought	His	Black	Bread
He	*Has*	*More*	Cheap	Sheep
Red	Left	No	*Good*	*Shoes*
Slim	Loves	Some	Wet	Socks
Who	Took	The	Wrong	Things

reaction times are very rapid, only slightly slower than disjunctive reactions. If one examines intonation patterns for pauses (pauses have been shown to be related to points of high information) he finds only very short pauses typical of the task of phoneme production and phrase integration during reading.

The cloze procedure disrupts this decoding process with an instruction for a decision process requiring more or less elaborate search procedures by the organism—at least more elaborate than the ongoing recognition process. There seems to be a shift from some sort of matching process to some sort of search procedure. One might represent this change on Table 1 by leaving out the italics in the second position for example. The subject now has no direct cue to the language element which should occupy this space in his plan. I submit he must search for it, that is to say he must survey certain categories of language elements for the most probable one, and the products of his searching will give the experimenter cues to his language processes. At one point in the processing of language materials, then, our subject is reading; at another point he is producing a word to fit a certain context. The procedures relevant to decoding are appropriate on the one hand, and the procedures relevant to encoding on the other. The cloze procedure enlists the subject in an hierarchical process which goes beyond the ordinary demands of reading.

I am viewing the cloze procedure as a phenomenon related to the production of components to fit a language organization. The implications of modern grammars such as the structural grammar of Fries (3) and the generative grammar of Chomsky (2) assume, at least implicitly, a language process moving in at least two dimensions—a sequence, moving in English from left to right, or from first to last in time; and a "choice" structure moving perpendicularly at every language unit in the sequence.

Goldman-Eisler (4) has demonstrated that pauses in sentences indicate a consistent expanding and contracting of information over the sentence, and I have shown this phenomenon using Shepard's "word-guessing" technique, which I consider a variation on the cloze procedure. Here are the data, for example, from six subjects per word who were instructed to "guess all the different words you can think of which 'make sense' in the empty blank in this sentence." The subjects were given five minutes to produce words.

These data indicate the size of the vertical distribution when the sequential and semantic constraints of the sentence are involved. Note that the same constraint is not operating when the context is only on one

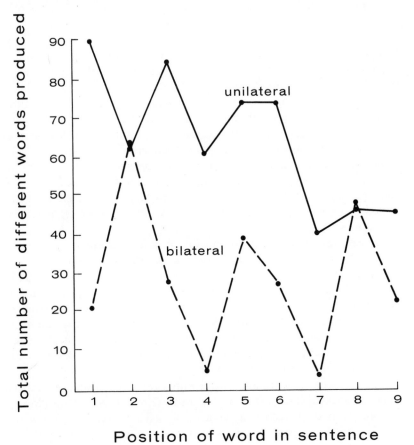

Figure 1.
Decrease in constraint from the bilateral to the unilateral situation

side of the gap in the text. Constraints of the unilateral text computed on the left side of the cloze unit, then independently on the right side of the cloze unit sum to an amount very close to the bilateral constraint. This is one argument for the position that the sentence to be encoded is planned as an entity, not bit by bit. Notice that in the bilateral condition (context on either side of the cloze unit) there is a movement from a large number of "types," to a small number of "types," back to a large number of "types," etc. I have shown this same effect in sentence sizes from 6 to 18 words. Generally, words at the points of low information are structural words, and words at the points of high information are lexical words. One possible explanation is that structural words form restricted, short categories and thus are rapidly exhausted, while lexical words form long, practically inexhaustible categories.

The cloze procedure then, does not always produce the same type distribution. Rankin (15) adapted the cloze procedure to Fries' division of language into structural and lexical elements. Incidentally this is one of the most used divisions in studies using the cloze procedure and Rankin is rarely credited with this important and original distinction. The structural deletion is, of course, confounded with the lexical because of the usual method used in forming the structural cloze. I think of both structural and lexical deletions as a removing of a member of a category. This is the whole implication of applying informational measures to the words filled in cloze units. The implicit assumption is that at this particular point in a language passage there is a distribution from which a particular language element is to be selected. The size of this distribution is the measurement we are seeking.

Further support for a dichotomizing of language into structural and lexical categories has come from certain studies of aphasia. Jones and Wepman (7) in their classification of aphasics according to the nature of the speech difficulty have designated a "syntactic" aphasia and a "semantic" aphasia. Some 40 percent of a sample of over one hundred patients exhibited syntactic aphasia; over 50 percent of another sample of 168 aphasics exhibited semantic aphasia. Syntactic aphasia is characterized by the misuse, or more often, the omission of function words and grammatical inflections. Speech tends to be telegraphic and little of its melody is retained. Many substantive words are retained, and certain well practiced phrases and short routine sentences are available. The following is a sample of the speech of a syntactic aphasic: "Cards . . . It's a 'cards' . . . four men . . . game . . . money table . . . money and cigarettes . . . everything . . . fun cards. That's all . . . cards money . . . fun."

The semantic aphasic on the other hand has great difficulty with substantives (except the most frequent and general). Long pauses are often found when the aphasic is trying to recall such words. They retain the use of function words and often retain highly frequent substantives also. To a large extent they maintain the sequential characteristics of speech-flow, melody, pitch changes, and grammatical structure. A sample of the speech of a semantic aphasic follows: "Well, I would say . . . ah . . . prak . . . ah . . . parkenkawr . . . dray men are spey. They are the ticks and the, ticks . . . five tars . . . in that what I'm wrong."

STRUCTURAL AND LEXICAL DIFFERENCES

While there are both syntactic and semantic constraints affecting both structural and lexical language elements there is a high degree of correlation between the structural and the syntactic and the lexical and the semantic. This may be illustrated using diagrams of the type used in generative grammars. Let us consider this sentence presented to subjects with only itself as context:

They _____ going to town.

In a sample of individuals asked to fill in this blank with all the possible words which would fit it, every individual included the word "are." The next most common word was "were." Eighty per cent of the words given followed the structural pattern shown in Figure 2.

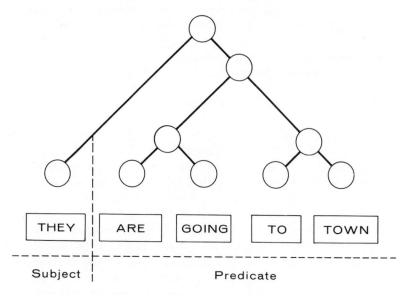

Figure 2. Diagram of sentence with auxiliary and verb

The constraint for these subjects was primarily the constraint of syntactic agreement. With this amount of context few subjects saw the possibility of using "going" as a direct object and shifting the word in the second slot from an auxiliary to a main verb.

Now consider this increased context:

The young boys went downtown their first day in the new town. They were chased home by a gang of roughnecks—rock-throwing roughnecks. The next day they tried again, the same thing happened, and again the next day. They _____ going to town.

The most frequent word with which the subjects now filled in the blank was "stopped." The next most frequent word was "quit." The sentence was restructured by the subjects as follows:

The auxiliary has practically disappeared; in fact, in only eight per cent of the responses is any type of primarily structural element inserted in the blank. With the constraining context, the subjects have now retrieved words which are congruent with the semantics of the situation.

The rate of production of words is much faster with the increased context, in this case, than it is without the context. This is contradictory to Shepard's (17) finding that constraint varies directly with the amount of context. It is true that when random language passages are used the size of the distribution of subjects' guesses decreases with the amount of context. In this situation, however, one must consider the size of the category to be searched. An examination of our Figure 2 indicates here that the constraint in this situation is imposed by the main verb. Most subjects select a plan to supply an auxiliary. They are thus selecting from a relatively small distribution, i.e., the distribution of auxiliaries. Even though the sentence without other context gives a wide latitude for meaning, most subjects become entangled with a plan to supply the grammatically correct auxiliary.

In the condition represented by Figure 3 the semantic constraints pattern the choice of a plan and the search for a main verb is the obvious strategy. The category of main verbs is much larger than the category of auxiliaries. With the additional context the auxiliary has been rejected as a candidate for filling in the cloze unit because it has little probability in the light of the semantic structure of the context.

Structural elements in the language are ordinarily short, very high frequency units. Zipf (23) some years ago demonstrated that when the rank order of a word is plotted against the frequency of the word on a logarithmic scale the result is an exponential curve with a slope of −1. Miller (9) says of this formula that it explains too much to be completely false and too little to be completely true. It may be that parts of the

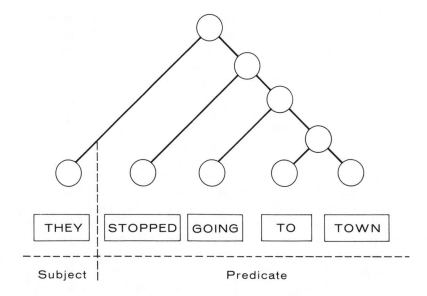

Figure 3. Diagram of sentence with verb and object

language act require an ergodic, stochastic process while other parts require planned, teleologic processes. The operation of this type of system might be to run off a highly probable, i.e., highly redundant, matrix in which to embed low-redundant elements retrieved from a relatively independent system. In this system the function words might be expected to distribute stochastically; the lexical elements would not exhibit this characteristic. The Zipf data lends some credence to this idea.

It is my conception that the structural elements in the language are not stored in the same sense that lexical elements of the language are stored. The structure of the language appears to me as primarily for encoding. It thus forms a matrix within the language producer, very closely correlated with the matrix in other language producers—this is one of the things we mean by the high frequency of structural elements—but nevertheless this matrix is *not* transmitted from encoder to decoder.

The same system could be used to strip redundancy from input language. As the very frequent language structure matches with the language input from the external environment, only the discrepancies, the uncertainties in the incoming message, require further processing. This is a common principle of communication theory. Storage of such frequent elements coming from the external environment would be extremely inefficient and would seem to greatly overload the capacity of the organism. I have commented before that this idea of the effect of structure on decoding seems to fit the hypothesis of Barlow concerning the serial reduction of redundancy (20). If our idea of permanent memory is anywhere near correct, entire language units are not stored; they are recoded (chunked). I have shown that function words in the recall of stories and scientific material conform more closely to the distributions of function words in the individual's spontaneous production than they do to the distribution of function words in the original materials. Lexical elements, on the other hand, conform very closely to the lexical elements in the original materials. I have also investigated the effect of function word position on rate. Using the technique of Pierce and Karlin (13) and lists of prepositional phrases and their reversals (e.g., phrases of the type "of the dog," as opposed to phrases of the type "the dog of") it may be demonstrated that prepositional phrases are read significantly faster when information, frequency of component words, number of syllables, and familiarity are controlled. I assume this to mean that words following the structural units are "expected" to require interpretation or storage. Structural elements give cues to the proper process. When these expectations are violated, longer latencies are evidenced.

Lexical deletions using the cloze procedure involve the language units designated by traditional grammars as nouns, main verbs, sometimes adjectives, and more rarely adverbs. If we have subjects guess all the words which will "make sense" at these particular loci, we get long lists of words, so long in fact that if the adjustment of both experimenter and subject is to be preserved, a time limit is imposed and the extent of the list estimated by the rate of production.

Taylor (19), the originator of the cloze procedure, conducted a study in which he deleted words according to an "any" or "hard" procedure which corresponds to our present dichotomy of structural-lexical, respectively. Structural cloze was correlated significantly closer to the *Air Force Qualification Test* than lexical cloze, but lexical cloze was a significantly better predictor of achievement. Taylor also noted that structural cloze was a better measure of readability. I became interested in the theoretical implications of this finding. I divided two forms of the *Davis Reading Test* into four equal segments and made up structural and lexical deletions of alternate paragraphs (every 10th word) in each of the four groups of four sections. I assumed that the test authors had arranged the material within the sections on some difficulty scale and the Flesch and Dale-Chall formulas confirmed this. I then gave another form of the *Davis Reading Test* to all the subjects who completed the cloze blanks. The results appear in Figure 4.

When the structural deletion scores for the entire group are used there is an indication of a gradual increase in difficulty of the material. The

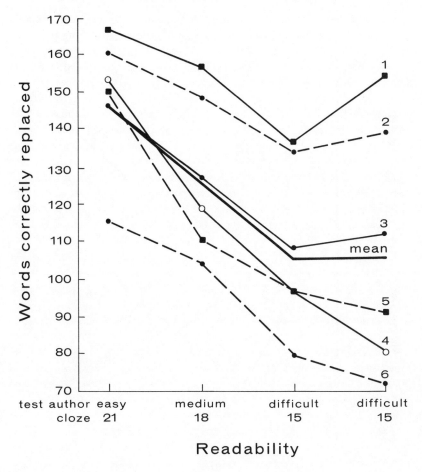

Figure 4. Readability measures vs. Davis Reading Test raw scores (Davis Reading Ability Raw Score: 1. 60–69, 2. 50–59, 3. 40–49, 4. 30–39, 5. 20–29, 6. 10–19)

subjects who determine this effect, however, are the subjects who score lowest on the reading test. Generally, the poorer the subject on the reading comprehension test, the more efficient he is as a measure of readability. I take this to imply that readability as measured by the cloze procedure is measured primarily through *lack* of redundancy reducing capabilities of the subjects. Since this redundancy reducing capacity is easy by every developmental standard, and, if Shannon's (16) calculations are correct, tends even for the best redundancy reducers to approach a limit somewhere between 50 and 75 percent redundancy, one would

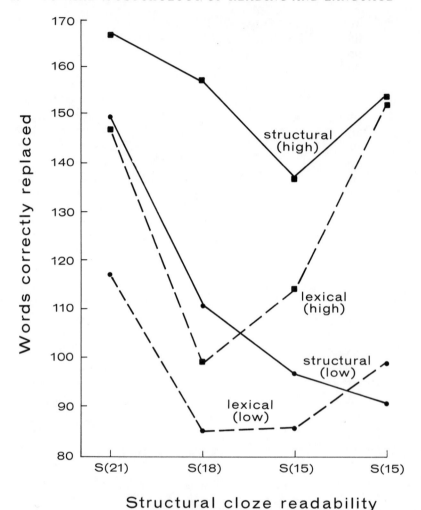

Figure 5. Lexical and structural deletions of subjects
with high and low reading ability on a structural difficulty scale

expect only the most inefficient performers to exhibit great deficiency in
it. In fact, one of the great mysteries of language is just this—that its
structural elements are acquired so early and so easily that as Carterette
(1) shows the fifth grade reader has already attained the redundancy
characteristics of "average" adult prose though its lexical elements show
no such maturity.

. When we look at the results of the lexical deletions in the same study another difference in structural and lexical distributions is evident.

The reproductions of these lexical units from materials of varying difficulty do not give us consistent measurements of this difficulty. In fact, the lexical deletions actually reduce the efficiency of structural cloze as a readability measure. There is certainly no simple relationship between the two deletions. I take it that a "correct" response to lexical cloze units depends to a great extent upon the semantic constraints of the context. The completion of lexical units is tied in, therefore, to the cognitive and affective systems of the organism. A proper interpretation then must involve some understanding of the formation and retention of concepts, problem-solving strategies, categorization, and heuristically organized retrieval schemes. This is nothing less than a rather complete psychology of language and thought so for now we will follow the technique of the heroine of *Gone with the Wind* and "think about that tomorrow."

SEEKING AND FINDING

I have never thought of the cloze procedure as anything other than a search procedure. Perhaps it's just the contiguity of working as a computer programmer and writing a dissertation on the cloze procedure during the same period of time, but I am convinced that it is more than that coincidence. The data have demonstrated time and time again that subjects act as if variable numbers of words are available at various points in a sentence. The longer the list of words which these subjects emit, the longer period of time it takes other subjects to supply a word to fill the same blank, if we run those subjects against time. Taylor (18) demonstrated that the single guess predictability of a word in a bilaterally distributed context is correlated −.87 with a probability measure of the distribution of all the subjects' responses. The more frequently subjects correctly filled in a cloze unit, the smaller the size of the distribution at that particular unit, i.e., the fewer word types.

Goldman-Eisler (5) deleted sentences at points which had previously been shown to have high hesitation pauses and low hesitation pauses and instructed subjects that they were to read the sentences aloud and substitute for the blanks words most suitable to the context. She demonstrated that the amount of information which a word contains (information computed by the Shannon letter-guessing technique) is related directly to the length of the pause before the reader fills in the blanks; the shortest hesitations occur when the words contain the least amount of information.

Claude Shannon's (16) original estimate of the redundancy of English was made by having subjects guess which letter of the alphabet (including the printer's space) came next in some meaningful language series. Shepard (17) has demonstrated that a technique of having subjects guess, for a five-minute period, all the words which will "make sense" in a deleted unit will produce a measure of information based on *rate* of responding closely approximating the Shannon results. This study assumes that words are obtainable from single categories, e.g. famous artists, in such a manner that the rate will decline regularly from time period to time period as the category is exhausted. The assumptions also imply that any one element must be searched out from the total list of elements and that the length of the search will depend upon the number of elements involved in the category.

Other investigators using methods not directly related to the cloze procedure and its variations have assumed that some form of search procedure best characterizes the data on retrieval of information. Yntema (12), studying search processes, begins with a finding of Broadbent that when lists of two different digits presented to the ears simultaneously (one digit in one ear, another digit in the other) are recalled by the subject they are recalled by the side of the head to which the digits are presented, i.e., all digits presented to the left ear are reported, then all digits presented to the right ear. If a subject is required to report digits pair by pair—the first two digits, then the second pair, then the third—he makes more mistakes. Yntema arranges materials in the following fashion:

No crossings		One crossing		Two crossings	
L	R	L	R	L	R
bet	7	3	part	0	good
sage	1	worse	8	roam	2
jack	4	house	6	5	coil

There were three conditions for the subjects. First, reporting by simultaneous pairs—for the no crossings condition, for example, this would mean reporting bet, 7; sage, 1; jack, 4. Next reporting by ears—for the no crossing condition this would mean reporting bet, sage, jack; 7, 1, 4. Finally, reporting by type of material—for the one crossing condition this would be 3, 8, 6; part, worse, house.

If the task is really a search problem, retrieval by type of material should be about as easy as retrieval by ears. The crossings are organized in such a fashion that a list with no crossing should be particularly easy for the subject to handle when he is instructed to report by ears or by type of material if a search procedure is involved. A search organized in this way would be organized on two redundant principles, that is, whether the items are words or digits, and whether they are heard on the left or on the right. Both of these criteria are met by the data as illustrated in Figure 6.

Retrieval by types is the easiest of the three tasks and the difficulty increases with the number of crossings.

There have been several attempts to simulate storage and retrieval processes, and from some of these attempts have come estimates of the efficiency of search procedures to simulate human verbal behavior in certain selected tasks. An example of such attempts is one by Hunt (6). Hunt programed a digital computer to simulate a "keeping-tract of verbal categories" task. The results of the computer program were correlated over all the psychological conditions which had been previously

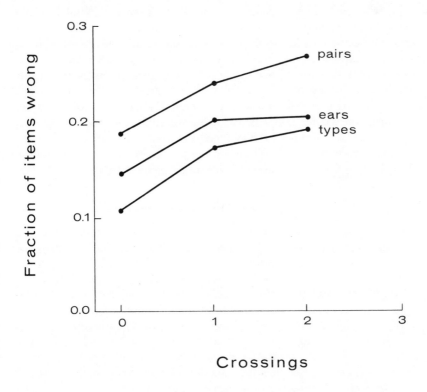

Figure 6. Errors in recall of different stimuli presented to the ears simultaneously (Douwe B. Yntema, "Recall as a form of data processing")

investigated by Yntema and Mueser (22) using human subjects. There was a correlation of .80 between the "search-type" program of Hunt and the data of Yntema and Mueser.

In many of the studies of searching procedures, and invariably in studies using the cloze procedure, the search has been considered as some sort of logical, exhaustive process. This assumption is almost certainly *not* true of human search procedures. It is easy to show that exhaustive search procedures would be much more time consuming than any human being could afford, and the illogicalness of many of our search efforts is obvious. That the human organism's searching is planned in some heuristic fashion seems much closer to the evidence. Contrary to Dewey's ideas, in such complex tasks as problem-solving the array of solutions to the problem are not lined up and then the most probable solution chosen by some logical procedure. For example, Newell, Shaw, and Simon (12) considered the set of all possible sequences of expressions in propositional logic which might have occurred in the second chapter of Whitehead and Russell's *Principia Mathematica.* Using computers to generate all the possible sequences it would take hundreds of thousands of years to compute all the results. By operating heuristically the problem solver always runs the risk he will discard the correct solution along with the millions of irrelevant ones. On the other hand, given the astronomical combinations and permutations of things, human processing systems perform remarkable tasks. Most of our speculations concerning search procedures in this paper have assumed a logically exhaustive process. It is obvious, however, that we consider the psychological data that this can only be a first approximation to the situation in reality.

SUMMARY

The sequential nature of language in its external display is so obvious that we have rarely considered that language production and interpretation within the central nervous system may not be, indeed probably is not, in the same form. If input language sequences were maintained intact, for example, there is no apparent reason they could not be reproduced intact—yet ordinarily they cannot be. Also, if input language sequences were maintained intact, it is difficult to see how individual language "styles" could develop. We know that long messages, beyond eight or nine digits and beyond twenty-five words or so, ordinarily cannot remain intact because they exceed the capacity of immediate memory, and of necessity must be processed as parts of the sequence.

Reading involves different levels of processing of this sequence. It may proceed at a very superficial level in relation to meaning. One can read, i.e. transduce, pages without getting any meaning from them as almost any reader who has tried to read under conditions of great fatigue or anxiety can testify. At another level reading may offer no problems of interpretation. The reader is entirely familiar with the sequence and the vocabulary. He is simply matching internally distributed signs with the external elaboration. At still another level the sign system represented by the external reading display finds no ready correlates in the organism, or as in the case of the cloze procedure there are gaps in the external display which the organism must supply from his store of rules and signs of the language.

The cloze procedure spreads before the subject a language sequence in a relatively normal form. At some points in the sequence, however, rather than a sign to recognize and match, there is a gap in the sequence. Where most reading input supplies a certain, direct cue to the matching mechanisms of the organism, the cloze procedure requires an analysis, a search, of a distribution of probable elements in order to arrive at a "most likely" one in the light of the reduced cues which are presented.

The implications of the cloze procedure go far beyond its use as a measurement device. In the midst of a subject's decoding operations, it imposes a precise productive operation. Because of the constraints involved it enables us to get a close-up view of what is occurring at particular points in a language passage. Certainly it is true that this view may be distorted by the eccentricity of the task imposed on the subject, but this is true of practically all laboratory techniques. The cloze procedure opens up for us the opportunity to examine syntactic and semantic effects of context on particular language units. We are on the way toward developing differentials between the syntactic and the semantic, using the cloze procedure—if finally realized this would be a major methodological advance. The potential of the cloze procedure has been widely recognized in such diverse areas as those of reading comprehension, achievement testing, aptitude testing, classification of brain injury, readability studies, and studies of suicide. I hope to make the point here that the cloze procedure and its variations carry major theoretical implications for a psychology of language and thought.

REFERENCES

1. Carterette, Edward C. and Margaret Hubbard Jones, "Redundancy in Children's Texts," *Science.* 140:1309–1311, 21 June, 1963.

2. Chomsky, Noam, *Syntactic Structures,* 's-Gravenhage: Mouton, 1957.

3. Fries, C. C., *The Structure of English,* New York: Harcourt, Brace and Company, 1952.

4. Goldman-Eisler, Frieda, "The Predictability of Words in Context and the Length of Pauses in Speech," *Language and Speech,* 1: July-September, 1958.

5. Goldman-Eisler, Frieda, "Speech Production and the Predictability of Words in Context," *Quarterly Journal of Experimental Psychology,* 10: May, 1958.

6. Hunt, Earl B., "Simulation and Analytic Models of Memory," *Journal of Verbal Hearing and Verbal Behavior,* 2: July, 1963.

7. Jones, L. V. and J. N. Wepman, *Studies in Aphasia: An Approach to Testing,* Chicago: Univ. of Chicago Industrial Relations Center, 1961.

8. Kaplan, Abraham, "An Experimental Study of Ambiguity in Context," *Microfilm, Papers on Mechanical Translating, Roll 799.* Cambridge: Massachusetts Institute of Technology, 1950.

9. Miller, G. A., *Language and Communication,* New York: McGraw-Hill, 1951.

10. Miller, George A., Eugene Galanter, and Karl H. Pribram, *Plans and the Structure of Behavior,* New York: Henry Holt and Company, 1960.

11. Miller, G. A., "Some Psychological Studies of Grammar," Presidential Address, Eastern Psychological Association, Atlantic City, N. J., 1962.

12. Newell, Allen, J. C. Shaw, and Herbert A. Simon, "Empirical Exploration of the Logic Theory Machine: A Case Study in Heuristic," *Proceeding of the Western Joint Computer Conference,* Los Angeles: 218–230, February, 1957.

13. Pierce, J. R. and J. E. Karlin, "Reading Rates and the Information Rate of a Human Channel," *Bell System Technical Journal,* 497–516, March, 1957.

14. Rankin, Earl F., Jr., "Closure and the Cloze Procedure," *The Third Yearbook of the North Central Reading Association,* Minneapolis: University of Minnesota, 1964.

15. Rankin, Earl F., Jr., "An Evaluation of the Cloze Procedure as a Technique for Measuring Reading Comprehension," Unpublished doctoral dissertation, University of Michigan, 1957.

16. Shannon, C. E., "Prediction and Entropy of Printed English," *Bell System Technical Journal,* 30:50–64, 1961.

17. Shepard, Roger N., "Production of Constrained Associates and the Informational Uncertainty of the Constraint," *American Journal of Psychology,* 218–228, June, 1963.

18. Taylor, W. L., *Application of 'Cloze' and Entropy Measures to the Study of Contextual Constraint in Samples of Continuous Prose.* Unpublished doctoral dissertation, University of Illinois, 1954.

19. Taylor, W. L., "Cloze Readability Scores as Indices of Individual Differences in Comprehension and Aptitude," *Journal of Applied Psychology,* 41:19–26, 1957.

20. Weaver, Wendell W., "The Predictability of Omissions in Reading and Listening." In Emery P. Bliesmer and Ralph C. Staiger (Eds.), *Eleventh Yearbook of the National Reading Conference.* Milwaukee: The National Reading Conference, Inc., 1962.

21. Yntema, Douwe B., "Recall as a Form of Data-Processing," paper read at

Psychology Section of American Association for the Advancement of Science, Philadelphia, December 29, 1962. (Preprint.)

22. Yntema, D. B. and Mueser, G., "Remembering the Present States of a Number of Variables," *Journal of Experimental Psychology,* 60:18–22, 1960.

23. Zipf, G. K., *Human Behavior and the Principle of Least Effort,* Cambridge: Addison-Wesley, 1949.

The Word as the Unit of Language

Language analysts have long recognized that language has more than one subsystem. Hockett (7) categorized this characteristic of language as a "universal" and described the phenomenon as an enormous number of language elements of low frequency of occurrence "mapped" onto a small number of language elements of very high frequency of occurrence.

Teachers of reading have focused their attention on the "enormous numbers of language elements of low frequency of occurrence." This usually takes the form of emphasis on "vocabulary" or "comprehension." Kingston (12) reviewed the manner in which the concept "vocabulary" is usually applied and brings into question the unitary nature of this concept. Rankin (19) reviewed studies of reading comprehension and concludes that generally two factors, vocabulary and reasoning, define the concept. While the studies reviewed do not imply independence, in the sense of complete separation of function, they do indicate sources of variation which are not identical. Vocabulary is generally thought of as a language variable, while reasoning is usually connected with the conceptualization process "behind" the word. The experience of teachers of reading seems to lead to a concentration of instructional procedures directed toward amelioration of difficulties in these areas, with the preponderence of attention given to the language rather than to the concept. Thus, teachers have emphasized the "word" and especially the "content" word.

In more elaborate analyses of the reading process—as, for example, readability studies—the word still tends to be the unit. In the Flesch formula the syllables counted are bounded by the printer's space, though there is sound transfer across this space. The average sentence length measured in words is another part of the measure. In the Dale-Chall formula the number of words which correspond to a list of high frequency "lexical" words is a major characteristic. When the "cloze procedure" is used as a readability measure, again the word is the unit of analysis.

The teacher of reading does not usually spend very much time in teaching grammar. Since grammatical relationships tend to be revealed particularly by the "function" words of the language, the question of the relationship of reading instruction to the language characteristic Hockett

Published originally in the *Journal of Reading*, 1967, 10, 262–268. Reprinted with the permission of the International Reading Association.

describes as "a small number of language elements of very high frequency of occurrence" has received little formal consideration. Researchers and practitioners seem to have little communication about this problem. One reason, perhaps, is that a distinct factor measuring grammatical ability has not been isolated from reading tests. This could be an artifact related to the traditional form of the reading test. A summary not far from the truth is that teachers of reading have ignored structure and emphasized "meaning" while linguists have ignored "meaning" and emphasized structure.

There seems to be no question among reading teachers that the word is an important language unit. The objective appearance of the letters, bounded by the printer's space, possibly contributes to the proposition that doubting the existence of words, linguistically and psychologically, is a distortion of the *facts* of perception. The concept "word," however, has had a difficult time among students of language. Linguists have always rejected it in favor of units for which precise definitions have been constructed, such as "phoneme" and "morpheme." Psychologists attempted to get around the "word"-"concept" interaction by the use of nonsense syllables. When it was discovered that nonsense syllables also varied in "meaning," psychologists studying association began to investigate processes involved when one word was used to stimulate recall of another. In these studies, however, many classes of words (all the "function" word classes) were excluded. More recently the relatively new approaches of communications theory (the ideas came into psychology in the early 50s) and transformation linguistics (Chomsky published his first work which influenced psychology generally in 1957) have again brought the word into question as a unit of language.

While studying the characteristics of immediate memory, Miller (16) found that symbols drawn from 2, 4, 8, 16, and 32 different possibilities were not retained differentially. Since the amount of "information" involved in the selection of items from each of these distributions is 1, 2, 3, 4, and 5 binary decisions (bits), respectively, an informational analysis would predict that long strings of words drawn from the first distribution, for example, and containing only one bit of information, would be recalled as readily as half that number of items drawn from the second distribution, above, and therefore containing twice the amount of information as in the first distribution. In Miller's study, however, only the length of the sequence to be retained made a difference. He hypothesized that this limitation on length imposed by immediate memory implied that language was made informationally "rich" in small numbers of different units by telescoping units—e.g., words—together in some fashion. He called this process "chunking." There is regrouping, then, according to this explanation, of individual words into larger units than words.

The body of research related to this hypothesis is extensive and will not be reviewed here. The unitizing process, however, which was integral to Miller's idea was emphasized by new theories of the organization of language which were springing up at this time. These linguistic theories triggered a whole set of psychological research which is probably at its peak, measured by volume, today. The theories of Noam Chomsky (2) have been particularly influential.

The unit of language in this system is the phrase structure, a set of "rules" by which basic sentences (kernal strings) are derived. From these kernal strings all other sentence forms are obtained by transformation. The implication, then, is that a sentence is not produced word by word, but rather, kernal string by kernal string. Psychologists, studying this model based on a logical analysis of language, have attempted to demonstrate the "psychological reality" of the immediate constituents of kernal strings. Three different traditional psychological methodologies have yielded similar evidence.

Fodor and Bever (5) observed that clicks which were sounded within immediate constituents were perceived by the subjects to occur, not in this objective locale, but at the nearest boundary of the immediate constituent. Johnson (8), using a paired-associates learning task with numbers as the stimulus number and sentences as the response member, showed that errors of recall for parts of immediate constituents were significantly greater than errors of recall of entire constituent phrases. Weaver and Garrison (21), using prepositional phrases and their reversals (e.g., "of the dog," "the dog of"), found that latencies of reading lists of the phrases of the type "the dog of" were greater than reading phrases of the type "of the dog" when information and frequency of occurrence of the phrases were controlled. These three studies imply that the several words making up the phrase are operating as units which are perceived, learned, and processed while being read, as units.

Other studies have attempted to find evidence in behavior for Chomsky's idea that all sentence transformations—e.g., active to passive, declaration to question, affirmative to negative—are based on an underlying kernal from which the various sentence forms are constructed. The method has many variations, but the general idea is to use Chomsky's model to deduce the number of steps of the transformations. For example, only one transformation is required to convert a kernal into a negative, while two steps are required to convert the same kernal into the passive-negative. If we measured the speed of converting a kernal, then, into a negative, it should be faster than the speed required to convert the same kernal into the passive-negative. This is essentially the technique used by Miller (17) to demonstrate that various transformations could be arranged around a cube and the speed of reaction to the transformation predicted by counting the number of transformations involved.

Miller's experiment has been repeated several times by other investigators, usually with variations in procedure, and the original results have been modified in a number of ways. Clifton, Kurcz, and Jenkins (4) found differences for different transformations, but disagreed about the order of the transformations. Mehler's (14) study supported Miller's order of the complexity of the transformation. Clifton and Odom (3) investigated other patterns of grammatical relationships derived from Katz and Postal (11), similar, but different from Chomsky's model, and found that their obtained pattern was congruent with the hypothesized one. The volume of this type of study is very large at present, and since it is being performed by sympathetic people they generally get sympathetic results. A dependable evaluation will have to await the perspective of time.

One characteristic of all the studies reported above is that none of them involves the understanding of the sentences used in the experiments. When this variable is added, the situation becomes much more clouded.

Gough (6) added a semantic variable of affirmation-negation and found that the relationship between reaction-time and sentence complexity became confused. Martin and Roberts (13) define structural embedding in an original way and concluded that the kind of sentence affected recall, but not in the manner a transformation model would predict. Slobin (20) used pictures which were either reversible or nonreversible (in the latter case the object of action could not normally serve as subject) and concluded that all the factors which he considered—syntactic, semantic, and pragmatic—were needed to account for the performance.

In an attempt to apply Chomsky's concepts directly to reading, Morton (18) used statistical approximations to English consisting of "200-word passages of zero- to sixth-order inclusive, of eighth-order approximations, and a 430-word passage of prose." He instructed subjects to read the passages aloud. He concludes that "many of the errors" are consistent with a transformational grammar. He speculates that continuous prose is analysed by kernal sequences and then resynthesized into "thought units." The syntactic and semantic systems are thus thought of as separate. The study is not very instructive, however, about what is happening in the reading process when the text is intact, rather than distorted, for in this study only one intact text is used as a control.

It will be seen then that the Chomskian-type language description proposes a very abstract "unit" of language. It can be dealt with very rigorously, linguistically, because the analyzer has an extended, fixed body of material from which he can derive "rules" that appear inherent in the material. Psychologically, the unit is much more ephemeral. It is very much like Miller, Pribram, and Galanter's "plan" (15). It is a very close relative of the *Bewusstseinslagen* of the Wuerzburgers—i.e., an unanalyzable attitude, categorized by the linguists into a rational set of "rules" which the organism "acts upon" but does not "know."

Whatever this unit is, it is not the word. In fact, a part of this theory not discussed here is that the word is also put together, by some sort of hierarchical process, from smaller parts. When combined with other language elements, its characteristics are different—e.g., its associational nature changes (9).

Although this research is voluminous, if one does not restrict himself to particular applications, it offers very little, if anything, at present in the way of practical direction of instruction. One reason for this lack of practicality is that the developing organism does not need to learn the structural aspects of language in any formal sense, because he already has learned what he needs to know. Jones and Carterette (10) have shown that the structural element, as measured by redundancy, in children's free reading choices at the first, third, and fifth grade levels is more like the adult level than are their basal readers. In another study, Carterette and Jones (1) show that by the fifth grade level even the basal reader has attained adult structural characteristics. The small number of very frequent elements and their orders are learned early; there is little change after age five except in compounding and subordinating large units. From then on structure appears very loosely related to age level—a necessary factor, but sufficient to explain little of the multitudinous variations in the ability to use language. Almost everyone seems to have, by typical socialization experiences, enough language "structure" to read. The content causes the difficulty.

To summarize, there is an apparent contradiction in the attitude of the teacher toward the word as a unit of language and that of the linguist and certain psychologists who base their experiments on the logical analyses of the linguists. There is little expressed doubt by the teacher of reading that the word is other than it appears—a definitive language unit, the attainment of which leads to the learning of the particular segment of behavior implied by the word. An insidious effect seems to result when the further assumption is made that there is a simple one-to-one relationship between learning a word and learning a concept.

The linguist, generally, begins with the assumption that language may be analyzed separately from "meaning," and he rejects the concept of the word as a unit. He, thus, is able to develop an elegant, that is, internally consistent, model of language. Nevertheless, there is much more "pragmatic" evidence that the approach of the reading teacher leads to improvement in language and conceptualization in students. There are few applications of linguistic findings to the teaching of language to a native speaker or writer, and even fewer to the teaching of listening and reading.

The findings of psychologists and linguists are interesting and important in their own right. They meet the criteria of "basic" research, and it seems that in a healthy relationship between "basic" and "applied" there should be a preponderance of the "basic" from which to choose the applications. In the scientific enterprises of the West what is "basic" today has a pronounced tendency to become "applied" tomorrow. The reading instructor realized many failures in attempting to teach reading. It is possible that in individual cases there is a deficiency, even in the adolescent and the adult, in the "natural" unitizing skills. With the further unraveling of these complex relationships by the researcher, there is always the potential for uncovering the particular process which is awry in the inadequate reader. A scientifically accurate psychology of language could truly revolutionize the teaching of reading.

REFERENCES

1. Carterette, Edward C. and Margaret Hubbard Jones. "Redundancy in Children's Texts," *Science,* 140 (June 21, 1963), 1309–1311.

2. Chomsky, Noam. *Syntactic Structures* ('s Gravenhage: Mouton, 1957).

3. Clifton, Charles Jr. and Penelope Odom. "Similarity Relations among Certain English Sentence Constructions," *Psychological Monographs,* 80, #5, (No. 613, 1966).

4. Clifton, C. J., I. Kurcz, and J. J. Jenkins. "Grammatical Relations of Sentence Similarity," *Journal of Verbal Learning and Verbal Behavior,* 4 (April, 1965), 112–117.

5. Fodor, J. A. and T. G. Bever. "The Psychological Reality of Linguistic Segments," *Journal of Verbal Learning and Verbal Behavior,* 4 (October, 1965), 414–420.

6. Gough, P. B. "Grammatic Transformations and Speed of Understanding," *Journal of Verbal Learning and Verbal Behavior,* 4 (April, 1965), 107–111.

7. Hockett, Charles F. "The Problem of Universals in Language," *Universals of Language,* ed. by Joseph H. Greenberg (Cambridge: The MIT Press, 1963), pp. 1–22. Reprinted in Hockett, *The View from Language: Selected Essays, 1948–1974* (Athens: The University of Georgia Press, 1977), pp. 163–186.

8. Johnson, Neal. "A Model of Sentence Generation," Paper presented at symposium on *Psychological Aspects of Language Structure* (APA, Los Angeles, 1964).

9. Johnson, Neal F. "The Influence of Associations between Elements of Structured Verbal Responses," *Journal of Verbal Learning and Verbal Behavior,* 5 (August, 1966), 369–374.

10. Jones, Margaret Hubbard and Edward C. Carterette. "Redundancy in Children's Free-Reading Choices," *Journal of Verbal Learning and Verbal Behavior,* 2 (December, 1963), 480–493.

11. Katz, J. J. and P. M. Postal. *An Integrated Theory of Linguistic Description* (Cambridge: MIT Press, 1964).

12. Kingston, Albert J. "Vocabulary Development," *Journal of Reading,* 8 (March, 1965), 265–271.

13. Martin, Edward and Kelyn H. Roberts. "Grammatical Factors in Sentence Retention," *Journal of Verbal Learning and Verbal Behavior,* 5 (June, 1966), 211–218.

14. Mehler, Jacques. "Some Effect of Transformations on the Recall of English Sentences," *Journal of Verbal Learning and Verbal Behavior,* 2 (November, 1963), 346–351.

15. Miller, George A., Eugene Galanter and Karl H. Pribam. *Plans and the Structure of Behavior* (New York: Henry Holt, 1960).

16. ———. "Human Memory and the Storage of Information," *IRE Transactions on Information Theory, IT-2,* #3 (September, 1956), 129–139.

17. ———. "Some Psychological Studies of Grammar," *American Psychologist,* 17 (November, 1962), 748–762.

18. Morton, John. "A Model for Continuous Language Behavior," *Language and Speech,* 7, Part I (Jan.-Mar., 1964) 40–70.

19. Rankin, Earl F. "The Definition of Reading Comprehension," *College and Adult Reading,* North Central Reading Association Yearbook, 1, (Univ. of Minnesota, 1962), 15–31.

20. Slobin, Dan I. "Grammatical Transformation and Sentence Comprehension in Childhood and Adult," *Journal of Verbal Learning and Verbal Behavior,* 5 (June, 1966), 210–277.

21. Weaver, Wendell W. and Nelson Garrison. "The Coding of Phrases: An Experimental Study," *Journal of Communications,* 16 (September, 1966).

Psychological Examinations
of Newer Dimensions of Linguistics and
Their Implications for Reading

During the last decade teachers of reading have been caught up in the furious activity of that branch of study designated (for want of a better term) psycholinguistics. Devine (1) has competently reviewed studies by linguists and English educators dealing in detail with linguistic research. This review is concerned with the implications of linguistic research and theory for the *psychological* study of the reading process.

One of the reasons teachers of reading have paid so little attention to linguistic findings is the confusion caused by the multitude of conflicting voices speaking on the problems. One reason this conflict is so pronounced is that educators, linguists, psychologists, anthropologists, sociologists, and others have become interested in the problems of language and are attempting to analyze language from the parochial point of view of their own disciplines. While no one wants to eradicate this interest, it is not a situation that lends itself to clear directives for translating theory and research findings into practice.

Limiting the discussion to the term "psycholinguistics" is no real solution to the problem, for a number of groups from linguists to psychological verbal behaviorists have applied the term (or had it applied) to what they are doing.

Within linguistics there are individuals who lean heavily on an empirical description of how language operates. Since this group depends upon individual producers and interpreters of the language, the psychological part of the term "psycholinguistics" seems to fit very well. Another group of linguists generally subscribes to a transformational grammar of the type initiated by Noam Chomsky in his 1957 book, *Syntactic Structures* (2), and is concerned primarily with linguistic theory. As Wardhaugh (3) says, these "theories say nothing about performance, that is, how human beings actually generate or interpret sentences." Generative-transformational grammatical theories depend upon so-called "underlying facts" of language which according to these theories cannot be derived directly from language performance of individuals, but only, it

(Co-authored with Albert J. Kingston.) Published originally in the *Journal of Reading*, 1967, 11, 238–242. Reprinted with the permission of the International Reading Association.

would seem, from abstractions derived from the body of verbal language materials. These theorists go on to posit what the language structure of the organism must be like in order to generate all the variety potentials present in the language. The psychological part of the term "psycholinguistics" in this case is defined in a rather deviant manner to say the least. Nevertheless, this type of linguistic theory has triggered extensive research endeavors by psychologists seeking to show that these proposed linguistic variables are causative of a number of kinds of behavioral variation.

Descriptive linguists who deal most directly with empirical linguistic findings have had the most impact on the teaching of reading. Fries in his book *Linguistics and Reading* (4) emphasized the relationship between speech and writing (some linguists think "overemphasized") in terms of grapheme-morpheme correspondencies. He criticized, extensively, the misuse of the term "phonics" and attempted to develop discrimination among the terms "phonics," "phonetics," and "phonemics" and their implications for reading. In *Linguistics and the Teaching of Reading* (5), Lefevre emphasized the importance of sentence patterning, intonation contours and other such concepts coming directly from established linguistics research findings, providing information to correct a number of inadequacies in reading instruction based on faulty linguistic knowledge. Goodman (6) has also pursued this line of attack, stressing the inadequacy of the words as a unit of language. He is concerned with the fact that context imposes a set of variations on any word, and demonstrates in a number of examples that semantics is dependent upon the structure of the language.

All these linguists are united in viewing the unit of language as larger than the word. With his concepts "structural meaning" and "lexical meaning" Fries (7) develops a dichotomy by which he incorporates word units into a higher system. Lefevre and Goodman see the sentence as the unit of language. This point of view is common to most of the linguists mentioned in this review, and the contention that teachers of reading do not share this point of view is their major criticism of teachers of reading. Briggs (8) attempts to bring the viewpoints of these linguists together and discusses the patterns of the language and the potential for the teaching of these patterns to improve reading.

Fries' work has led to a number of psychological experiments but Fries' theories do not allow the experimenter to move far from the word as the unit of language, probably because of the influence of the rather static concept of "form class." The ideas of Lefevre and Goodman have a much wider potential for analyzing larger units of language. On the other hand, this work suffers from the paucity of the psychological research on such questions as "What is the relationship between temporal patterning as the reader derives it from the printed page and the reader's comprehension of the material?" Linguistic findings alone cannot determine such crucial psycholinguistic relationships.

The potential for psychological research on temporal patterning seems enormous. Brown and Bellugi (9) have shown that temporal patterning occurs in earliest language learning and affords the best explanation to date for the ability of the child to attend to the words of the language carrying the highest information loads. Temporal patterning in this case wins out over that other ubiquitous language variable—frequency. Jenkins, Foss, and Greenberg (10) found that relations between sounds that are said to be regular within linguistic theory systematically influence the learning of stimuli and responses which involve these sounds. Epstein (11) found that structured materials were distinguished from unstructured materials by the fact that the former is marked by a temporal schema. O'Connell, Turner, and Onuska (12) found that intonation facilitated recall in all learning conditions using nonsense syllables but structure was effective in facilitating recall only with intonation.

A number of psychological findings based on a transformation idea of linguistics were reviewed earlier (13). Hypotheses derived from transformational grammars remain a popular source of research. Coleman (14) showed that four levels of grammaticalness constructed by using rules of a generative grammar with an accumulation of rules through the various levels, showed that learning under these conditions was a function of grammatical level. In another paper, Coleman (15) showed that active-verb transformations were easier to learn than their nominalizations, actives were easier to learn than their passives, and nonembedded sentences were easier to learn than their embedded counterparts, all of which would be predicted by a transformational grammar.

Schlesinger (16) found that eye-voice span was related to syntactical constituents of sentences. Odom and Johnson (17) found that hearing subjects' recall of material conformed to phrasal segments, while the recall of non-hearing subjects was not facilitated by phrasal segments. Schlesinger also reports an unpublished study of Roger Wales (18) in which sentences were presented in a format with "cuts" at the end of a syntactic constituent as contrasted with "cuts" within the syntactic constituent, e.g.,

(1) The very old man
     was always sitting down
     on one of the big chairs.
(2) The very old man was always sitting
     down on one of the big chairs.

Sentences were significantly easier to learn when presented as in (1) than when presented as in (2).

Some points of transformational theory have been controverted by recent studies. Segal and Martin (19) found that the subjects of sentences were ranked most important (for semantic reference) followed by verbs and direct objects no matter what transformation was involved. Martin and Roberts (20) found that retention was related to phrase structure analyses of sentences and a counting of the grammatical commitment (the effect of one word in sequence on the word or words following it) of each word in the sentence, but that the recall was not related to the kind of sentence in the systematic way predicted by the transformational grammar model. Roberts (21) showed that subjects receiving various kinds of associational and grammatical treatments were not making transformational errors in their recall, but, rather, errors connected with association condition and grammatical type—interacting in some cases, not interacting in others.

Wardhaugh (3), in an excellent review, notes that transformation-generative grammarians have used the sentence framework for their study and that some important transformationalists see no need for going beyond the sentence. On the other hand, the tagmemicists, another group of linguists, see Pike (22) and Becker (23), are interested in larger discourse contexts. Another attractive characteristic of these studies for the teacher of reading is that they are based mostly on the written rather than the spoken language.

The injunction of linguistics for teachers of reading may be summed in a sentence: Use the findings of linguistics. There are several difficulties here. (1) On a number of major issues linguists give separate instructions about what the teacher of reading should do. (2) On a number of other major issues the linguist himself is not sure what the teacher of reading should do. (3) On most of the major issues the linguist is still operating more on theory than on evidence. Perhaps worst of all, (4) some aspects of linguistic theory appear untestable in principle, e.g., the ideal of "deep structure."

In spite of the difficulties, the linguist is talking about things which the teacher of reading needs to know. The task is to keep up with the conversation and watch for the evidence.

REFERENCES

1. Devine, Thomas G. "Linguistic Research and the Teaching of Reading," *Journal of Reading,* IX (March, 1966), 273–277.

2. Chomsky, Noam. *Syntactic Structures* ('s Gravenhage: Mouton, 1957).

3. Wardhaugh, Ronald. "Current Linguistic Research and Its Implications for the Teaching of Reading," Paper read at IRA Convention, Seattle, 1967.

4. Fries, Charles C. *Linguistics and Reading* (New York: Holt, Rinehart & Winston, 1963).

5. Lefevre, Carl A. *Linguistics and the Teaching of Reading* (New York: McGraw-Hill, 1964).

6. Goodman, Kenneth. "Word Perception: Linguistic Basis," *Education* (May, 1967), 1–5.

7. Fries, Charles C. *The Structure of English* (New York: Harcourt, Brace, 1952).

8. Briggs, F. Allen. "Implications of Structure in Language for the Teaching of Reading," Paper read at the National Reading Conference Convention, St. Petersburg, 1966.

9. Brown, Roger and Ursula Bellugi. "Three Processes in the Child's Acquisition of Syntax, *Harvard Educational Review,* 34 (Spring, 1964), 133–152.

10. Jenkins, James J., Donald J. Ross, and Joseph H. Greenberg. "Phonological Distinctive Features as Cues in Learning," Paper read at American Psychological Association Convention, New York, 1966.

11. Epstein, William. "Temporal Schemata in Syntactically Structured Material," *The Journal of General Psychology,* 68 (1963), 157–164.

12. O'Connell, Daniel C., Elizabeth A. Turner, and Linda A. Onuska. "Intonation, Grammatical Structure, and Contextual Association in Immediate Recall," *Journal of Verbal Learning and Verbal Behavior* (in press).

13. Weaver, Wendell W. "The Word as the Unit of Language," *Journal of Reading,* X (January, 1967), 262–268.

14. Coleman, E. B. "Responses to a Scale of Grammaticalness," *Journal of Verbal Learning and Verbal Behavior,* 4 (December, 1965), 521–527.

15. Coleman, E. B. "Learning of Prose Written in Four Grammatical Transformations," *Journal of Applied Psychology,* 49, No. 5 (1965), 332–341.

16. Schlesinger, I. M. *The Influence of Sentence Structure on the Reading Process,* Technical Report No. 24, U.S. Office of Naval Research, Information Systems Branch, Jerusalem, Israel, October, 1966.

17. Odom, Penelope B. and Neal F. Johnson. "Phrase Learning in Deaf and Hearing Subject," Paper read at Midwestern Psychological Association Meeting, Chicago, 1966.

18. Wales, Roger. Unpublished Study. University of Edinburgh.

19. Segal, Edwin M. and Duane R. Martin. "The Influence of Transformational History on the Importance of Words in Sentences," Paper read at Psychonomic Society Meeting, October, 1966.

20. Martin, Edwin and Kelyn H. Roberts. "Grammatical Factors in Sentence Retention," *Journal of Verbal Learning and Verbal Behavior,* 5 (June, 1966), 211–218.

21. Roberts, Kelyn. "The Interaction of Normative Associations and Grammatical Factors in Sentence Retention," Paper read at the Midwestern Psychological Association Convention, Chicago, 1966.

22. Pike, Kenneth L. "Discourse Analysis and Tagmeme Matrices," *Oceanic Linguistics,* 3 (1964), 5–25.

23. Becker, Aleon L. "A Tagmemic Approach to Paragraph Analysis," *College Composition and Communication,* 16 (December, 1965), 237–242.

Questioning in Content Reading

Even though educational technology has made great progress in the last few decades, there is as yet no substitute in sight for the textbook. Textbooks have been produced in about the same manner since their history began and the very conservative tradition which has accompanied this development has tended to keep them the way they are. The text is divided into chapters, and at the end of the chapters there are questions. As many generations of students have chorused, the questions seem often to have little to do with the text. Many questions not only ask for an induction which goes far beyond the text material but require additional knowledge not presented in the text. When the questions sample the range of materials contained in the chapter, they often take on the characteristics of rather poorly constructed achievement tests. There is a growing body of research literature which suggests that questions related to textual material should not be taken so lightly and deserve better than to be turned over to the rather bored ministrations of the author's graduate students, as they are in many cases.

It has been known for some time that certain testlike operations facilitate learning. McKeachie [1] says in a brief review of these studies, "After dismal recitals of nonsignificant differences between differing teaching methods, it is refreshing to find positive results from variations in testing procedures" (p. 1154). These studies indicate that questioning of one kind or another facilitated learning when presented after lectures [2], films [3], and study [4]. The authors of these studies concluded that knowledge of results was the factor leading to the increment in learning. Hershberger [5, 6] and Hershberger and Terry [7], in studies more directly related to reading, have shown that subjects learn more if they are tested periodically on material which they are reading.

Some authors of study guides and reading improvement texts have noted the research accumulating in this area. In *Effective Study*, Robinson [8] reviews studies of the effects of questions. Holmes [9] found that administering a list of 20 questions before reading material was presented increased comprehension on those same questions presented at the end of the reading session. It did not increase comprehension on

(Co-authored with Albert J. Kingston.) Published originally in the *Journal of Reading*, 1967, 11, 140–143 and 150. Reprinted with the permission of the International Reading Association.

new questions, although it did not inhibit it either. In another study Washburne (10) introduced questions before, during, and after reading. Results of the study were obscured by the methodology since the test given at the end of the 25-minute study period contained the same questions already asked previously as well as new questions. Under these presentation conditions the most effective treatments were presenting all the questions together at the beginning and placing relevant questions for a particular section at the beginning of that section. It should be noted here that these modes of questioning accounted for facilitation of learning of specific portions of the reading passage—namely, those portions covered by the content of the questions.

Most authors of reading improvement books and study guides, while not referencing these findings directly, seem generally to take them into account. Most reading improvement texts present questions at the end of some (usually all) selections to be read. Furthermore, these questions are intended to be used for the improvement of the reading of the particular selection involved (11, 12, 13, 14, 15, 16). The problem presented, however, is that this technique must be transferred to textbook reading (where such careful questioning is the exception) if it is to be effective. The typical solution is to instruct the student to ask his own questions of the textbook material. There is no research evidence on the efficacy of this procedure.

Rothkopf (17, 18, 19, 20, 21) has performed a number of studies related to problems of learning from reading materials by variations of questioning procedures. In one study (22) Rothkopf made a distinction between the testing of reading which has a specific facilitative effect on learning, and testing which has a more general facilitative effect. He hypothesized that the general facilitative effect was connected with a class of behaviors he called inspection behaviors and found that questions administered *after* reading the materials on which the questions were based were more facilitative. Learning was facilitated whether or not the correct answer was supplied to the question by the subject; and there was no significant difference, whether or not the question was answered for the subjects. Specific facilitative effects of questions (as opposed to the general facilitative effects) were present regardless of the location of the questions in the instructive sequence. Specific facilitation was significantly increased by supplying correct answers for the questions.

General facilitative effects on learning were obtained also by giving directions about how to read the passage before the passage began. The instructions which were facilitative stated that the passages contained much detailed information and should be read slowly and with care. Although subjects under this condition performed like subjects who were asked the experimental questions, results showed that the experimental questions were instructive in themselves and were even more instructive when correct answers were provided.

Further evidence of the facilitating effect of questions presented shortly after the appropriate text segment is read is given by Rothkopf's (23) study of the reading by high school students of a 9,000-word passage from Rachel Carson's *The Sea Around Us.* Questions presented shortly before the relevant reading passage did not produce a facilitating effect. Nevertheless, there were indications that as the subjects proceeded through the text, exposure to further experimental questions in the shortly-after treatments increasingly facilitated learning. This was not due to the prior guiding effect of the question, however, for under the shortly-after condition the questions always followed the text to which they were relevant.

Under certain conditions—e.g., immediate repetition of the instructional sentence followed by overt responding to a test item—questions embedded within a text do not facilitate learning. For this reason, the conclusion should not be drawn that the effects of testing are always desirable.

It should be pointed out that Rothkopf's "questions" are of the fill-in-the-blank variety. Content words removed from intact sentences are used as "questions." With materials designed in this fashion, however, Rothkopf has shown that learning, as measured by independent achievement tests, is facilitated and that attentive reading behavior can be maintained over long periods of time. Others have had similar results with different methods. Hoffman (24) has shown that subjects reading continuous passages for four hours, without questions interposed, exhibited a deteriorating pattern of eye movements after only 30 minutes. Carmichael and Dearborn (25) interposed short series of questions throughout their reading passages and showed that the subjects maintained their efficiency over a six-hour period. No knowledge of results was given the subjects concerning the correctness of their answers.

Teachers are so well acquainted with asking questions and with seeing them in print that it is difficult to consider various aspects of questioning as selectively effective. The research indicates that questions for specific content answer are most effective when responses are required and when knowledge of results is given. On the other hand, another class of questions is not effective when presented before materials are read, but facilitates learning when presented after materials are read. Such questions seem to maintain efficient inspection behaviors over long periods of time, and knowledge of results is not necessary to obtain the facilitation of learning which results.

Rather than depending upon methods which allow little exertion of control—e.g., instructing the student to generate his own questions—teachers might well ask for manuals for reading improvement which attempt to ask questions at appropriate points within textual material in order to obtain general facilitation, without, of course, eliminating other questioning in order to obtain specific facilitating effects.

Reading improvement texts should be easily moved toward formats indicated by newer research. To move textbooks in this direction will be a much more formidable task.

REFERENCES

1. McKeachie, W. J. "Research on Teaching at the College and University Level," *Handbook of Research on Teaching,* edited by N. L. Gage (Chicago: Rand McNally, 1963), pp. 1118–1172.

2. Jones, H. D. "Experimental Studies of College Teaching," *Archives of Psychology,* 10, No. 68 (1923), 5–70.

3. May, M. A. and A. A. Lumsdaine. *Learning from Films* (New Haven: Yale University Press, 1958).

4. McKeachie, W. J. and W. Hiler. "The Problem Oriented Course to Teaching Psychology," *Journal of Educational Psychology,* 45 (July, 1954), 224–232.

5. Hershberger, W. A. *Learning via Programmed Reading and Cue versus Response in Programmed Reading* (American Institute for Research: July, 1963). Technical Report AIR-C28-7/63-TR.

6. ———. "Self-Evaluational Responding and Typological Cueing: Techniques for Programing Self-Instructional Reading Materials," *Journal of Educational Psychology,* 55 (October, 1964), 288–296.

7. ——— and D. F. Terry. *Delay of Self-Testing in Three Types of Programmed Test* (American Institute for Research: May, 1964). Technical Report AIR-C28-564-TR.

8. Robinson, F. P. *Effective Study* (New York: Harper & Brothers, 1941, 1946).

9. Holmes, E. "Reading Guided by Questions versus Careful Reading and Rereading without Questions," *School Review,* 39 (March, 1931), 361–371.

10. Washburne, J. N. "The Use of Questions in Social Science Material," *Journal of Educational Psychology,* 20 (October, 1929), 321–359.

11. Heilman, Arthur W. *Improve Your Reading Ability* (Columbus, Ohio: Charles E. Merrill, 1962).

12. Hill, W. and W. Eller. *Power in Reading Skills.* (Belmont, California: Wadsworth, 1964).

13. Gilbert, D. W. *Power and Speed in Reading* (Englewood Cliffs, N.J.: Prentice-Hall, 1956).

14. Leedy, Paul D. *Read with Speed and Precision* (New York: McGraw-Hill, 1963).

15. Shaw, P. B. and A. Townsend. *College Reading Manual* (New York: Thomas Y. Crowell, 1959).

16. Spache, G. D. and P. C. Berg. *The Art of Efficient Reading* (N.Y.: MacMillan, 1966).

17. Rothkopf, E. Z. "Learning from Written Sentences: Effects of Order of Presentation on Retention," *Psychological Reports* (June, 1962), 667–674.

18. ———. "Some Conjectures about Inspection Behavior in Learning for Written Sentences and the Response Mode Problem in Programed Self-Instruction," *Journal of Programed Instruction,* 2, No. 4, (October, 1963), 31–45.

19. ——— and E. U. Coke. "Repetition Interval and Rehearsal Method in Learning Equivalences from Written Sentences," *Journal of Verbal Learning and Behavior,* 2 (December, 1963), 406–416.

20. ———. "Learning from Written Sentences: Within-Sentence Order in the Acquisition of Name-Clause Equivalences," *Journal of Verbal Learning and Verbal Behavior,* 2 Nos. 5 and 6 (December, 1963), 470–475.

21. ———. "Some Theoretical and Experimental Approaches to Problems in Written Instruction," *Learning and the Educational Process,* edited by J. D. Krumboltz (Chicago: Rand McNally, 1965), pp. 193–221.

22. ———. "Learning from Written Instructive Material: I. An Exploration of the Control of Inspection Behavior by Test-Like Events," *American Educational Research Journal,* 3 (1966), 241–249.

23. ——— and E. E. Bisbicos. "Selective Facilitative Effects of Interspersed Questions on Learning from Written Materials," *Journal of Educational Psychology,* 58, No. 1 (March, 1967), 56–61.

24. Hoffman, A. C. "Eye Movements during Prolonged Reading," *Journal of Experimental Psychology,* 36 (April, 1946), 95–118.

25. Carmichael, L. and W. F. Dearborn. *Reading and Visual Fatigue* (Boston: Houghton Mifflin, 1947).

The Contribution of Research to Reading Theory

This paper involves a discussion of the intricacies of the relationship of theory to research. It begins with a description of the classical, natural science approach to theory. The question of the conceptual limits of a theory is considered next, under the section entitled "The Size of the Domain of a Theory." The discussion of the domain of a theory is continued by considering the psychological forces within individuals and sociological tendencies within several disciplines which tend to separate theory from research.

At this point, an analysis of theories of reading is begun with a consideration of the approaches of operationalism and introspectionism as methodologies for solution of the problems of reading theory. Measurement problems which limit research potential, and thereby limit theory testing, are discussed. Finally, specific research examples and their implications for theory are considered.

CLASSICAL THEORY–RESEARCH RELATIONSHIPS

The experimental ideal of the relationship of research to theory has been expounded often. One begins with a theory, or at least a set of more or less organized constructs. Alternative hypotheses are devised which are related to that theory. A crucial experiment with alternative possibilities that will exclude one or more of the hypotheses is devised. After carrying out the experiment the experimenter recycles the procedure, constantly reducing untested portions of the theory and revising the theory and alternative hypotheses in view of the experimental findings. Platt (1964), from whom the above list is derived in the main, calls this procedure, "strong inference."

Obviously, reading research and theory formation have not been blessed with large applications of strong inference. It is doubtful whether such an elegant methodological-theoretical relation has ever predominated in any science over its long-term development, but the body of reading research has not produced theoretical structures which would give us any confidence that any sort of research-theory interchange is

Published originally in the *Journal of Reading Behavior,* 1969, 2 (Spring), 3–18. Reprinted with the permission of the National Reading Conference.

going on. This criticism cannot be applied to the viable sciences, yet it is typical of all of educational and much of psychological research.

The last few decades have seen an enormous amount of finance and energy expended on producing and disseminating reading research. This research activity has not produced theory development. Actually, research is often as confusing to theory development as it is helpful, although no one should take this statement as implying that research is not necessary. Research not only eliminates alternatives, it generates further alternatives, often alternatives more complicated and difficult to test than the original ones.

THE SIZE OF THE DOMAIN OF A THEORY

One of the difficulties in developing a theory of reading is that the theoretician must decide on what level the theory is to operate. In the present state of the evidence concerning reading, there is a large amount of arbitrariness in this choice. If there is to be a general theory of reading that describes all elements of the reading process, few would disagree that this theory must rest on a theory of language and thought. To attempt such a theory in our present state of ignorance would quickly lead to a morass of the wildest sort of speculation, and, at least to the empirically minded, ultimately to the slough of despond. On the other hand, if one takes the path which stimulus-response psychologists traveled in the thirties and forties, one describes ever more elegantly smaller and smaller segments of the area of interest, and connections between segments become difficult to make, due directly to this over-specificity. One of the tasks of developing a theory of reading, then, is to delimit the domain of discourse so that it might cover a significant segment of process while maintaining a firm connection with the tested and the testable.

THE SEPARATION OF RESEARCH AND THEORY

Although a science is never possible without both empirical investigation and theoretical constructs, the individual researcher in his active testing of hypotheses may divorce research and theory. Research has controls other than systematic scientific theory. A very strong control is the contemporary scientific cynosure. Very few psychologists nowadays are Watsonian behaviorists. Any reading problems which might be amenable exclusively to the techniques of research arising from this point of view will not be solved. Models of behavior based on computer analogies are popular. Reading problems amenable to this kind of attack will be studied exhaustively. From the whole range of reading behaviors, researchers choose very small samples for examination. It is one task of theory to fill in the gaps with a logical structure, consistent with empirical findings, while waiting for experimental confirmations or denials of particular points of the theory.

There is seemingly an infinity of possible research studies, as the voluminous reading research literature testifies, but scientific knowledge is not a helter-skelter of data collection. The reading research literature is disappointing just because it lacks systematic theoretical structuring. One reason the literature is in this state is that, until the last few years, reading research has come, primarily, from reading instructors attempting to justify or clarify some point directly related to practice. While there is nothing inherently wrong with this kind of research as research, there is much wrong with it when one desires to develop scientific knowledge about reading. The research is expedient, non-theoretical and therefore, non-accumulative in its impact, i.e., it is not mapped into a body of tested principles. If research is to provide us with evidence, theory must tell us what evidence we need.

Some types of "theories" separate research from theory. B. F. Skinner and his followers have been very vocal advocates of an ostensibly atheoretical point of view for psychology.

Raygor (1967), though qualifying the position somewhat, advocates a similar position for a psychology of reading. Generally, the argument runs, the accumulation of data is necessary before pattern can be discerned. The task of a young science is simply to accumulate data without theoretical organization. This data is not to be collected haphazardly, however, but essentially the criteria for collection is the conditioning model. Actually, data are always collected from some extrinsic or intrinsic model superordinate to the data. The Skinnerian is operating on a very rigid theoretical base. The fact that he calls it methodology, or behavior analysis, or operant conditioning, is irrelevant.

If there is anything more useless than ad-lib speculation, it must be unorganized masses of data. Data rarely speaks for itself, and when it does, it speaks with a forked tongue. It is true, of course, that theory constrains the range of experimentation, and might even direct experimentation down dead-ends. This, however, is one of the prices one must pay for structure. As Robert Oppenheimer said of perceiving in his first William James Lecture at Harvard in 1957, "the price of perceiving anything at all is that not everything is perceived that can potentially be perceived." Analogously, the price of organizing any body of information, e.g., concerning reading, is to ignore certain aspects of that information.

Platt says that scientists should major in strong inference; scientists should also major in strong theory. The operant conditioner is successful research-wise just because he follows a consistent theoretical orientation. Operant theory is not even a good theory. It is naive, simple-minded, pedestrian, and explains very little without the most torturous mental gymnastics; even then, its explanations are unconvincing. It has the advantage of having devoted proponents who generate study after study which are related to one another.

An eclectic theory is rarely helpful scientifically, though mutually contradictory theories (e.g., the wave and particle theories of light propagation) can exist profitably apart. Research cannot supply evidence for "just any old theory." Most research is specific to a particular theory. This is one reason that, ultimately, choices between theories are rationally, not empirically, determined. The scientific community chooses one theory for acclaim and discards another because *in view of the problems it sees as important* one theory seems to subsume more of the evidence. Theories are "invented" categorical systems of rationality, not "discovered" universal ideas.

This leads to another way in which theory is separated from research. The philosophical premises concerning the nature of evidence can be formulated in such a manner that research is irrelevant to theory; theory becomes self-validating. The controversy between transformational grammarians, such as Chomsky, Katz, and Fodor (that is, the MIT linguistic school generally) and empirical psychologists, such as Osgood and Suppes, is centered in a conflict of positions on the nature of evidence. The transformational grammarian insists on a distinction between theories of competence and theories of performance. Empirical psychologists argue that to ignore empirical evidence as a basis for theory and to depend upon classical philosophical arguments for support of a position is "inappropriate and insufficient when a subject is inherently scientific and empirical in character" (Crothers and Suppes, 1967).

Competence is used by the linguist to mean the theory of the language itself apart from how it is acquired and used by speakers of the language. Performance is the actual language behavior of the speakers of the language. It seems obvious that theories of competency are always developed from the performance of individual sophisticates of a discipline. (Chomsky admits this but qualifies the admission in such a manner that the admission is rendered impotent. "Obviously one can find out about competence only by studying performance but this study must be carried out in devious and clever ways if any serious result is to be attained" [Billings and Brown, 1964, p. 36].) In this sense competency theories use the data of performance for their elaboration. Not only is the claim made that competence theories are not limited by their basis in performance, however; there is also a great indifference to the presentation and systematic analysis of any empirical data (Crothers and Suppes, 1967). The transformational linguist relies on classical philosophical arguments to support his theory, and uses a contentious patronizing tone which admits of no exceptions to his arguments, except the exceptions which he deigns to make.

Actually, to encompass a theory of language, a theory of competency, or any other theory, should include at least a theory of syntax, a theory of semantics, and a theory of phonology. Lefevre (personal communication) has remarked that one great weakness of Chomsky's linguistics has been the absence of a phonology theory integrated with syntax; this weakness is particularly evident in the neglect of English intonation at the syntactical level, and in ignoring the marked differences between American and British intonation. Phonology has been secondarily relegated to articles and not included in "the theory"; *The Sound Pattern of English* (1968) extends the dichotomy and essentially ignores intonation. A semantic theory has been attempted by Katz and Fodor (1963) but, for psychologists, a major restriction has been the separation of linguistic behavior from its situational context in this theory. Because much of oral language is incomprehensible or ambiguous when unrelated to a situational context, the proposition seems reasonable that even a theory of competence should have a theory of language situational embeddedness. Such a theory of competence moves much closer to a theory of performance. Be that as it may, transformational grammarians have made a theory of syntax the basis of all linguistics. Sentences such as, "They are cooking apples," are proffered as evidence that there are levels of analyses, "deep structures," below the "surface structure," even though, as Osgood (1965) has pointed out, sentences of this type are not, typically, ambiguous in a situational context, or even in a language context when pronoun reference is not indeterminate. Sentences such as, "Close the door," are used to argue that there must be an underlying deep structure when, performance wise, Skinner (1957) has a much more convincing explanation of these strings (he calls them "mands") as instances of straightforward operant conditioning.

Transformational theory has many of the abstract characteristics of Freudian theory—it simply operates on different data. The transformationalists purport to synthesize and explain large bodies of detail; they made universal claims for primacy of their theories; they have non-rational ultimate predications which are to be precisely inferred from surface behavior, but which subsume and determine surface behavior (the constructs "deep structure" and "the unconscious" are examples of these predications); perhaps irrelevantly, they proselyte for "true-believers" who irritate non-believers no end.

In psychological studies of language at least, theories of competence have proven to be excess baggage. Crothers and Suppes (1967) find no place for such constructs in their studies of second-language learning. Schlesinger (1966), an advocate of Chomskian theory, finds no logically necessary place for it in his empirical studies of structural effects on "readability." Miller (1962) discusses Chomskian theory, but his studies are related to the performance of individuals, not to some abstraction.

There can be no scientific theory of competence just because competence theories are untestable. They stand or fall on their rational formulation. They must be logically necessary and sufficient to explain all they purport to explain, otherwise they are useless. With some mathematical theories of competence, this is possible. There is nothing in transformational linguistics theories of competence which compels anyone to accept their logical necessity. They have had some success because (1) some would like to escape the rigors and the slow accruing of principles, which empiricism enforces, (2) competence theories have led to (loose) analogous principles in performance theories, portions of which have been empirically verified. The general effect of the competence theory of syntax has been to separate theory from research.

OPERATIONALISM AND INTROSPECTIONISM

Why can't one simply start at the beginning of the reading act and trace what the human organism does? Operationally, reading goes something like this. A person, seated or standing or lying, holding a book in his hands and facing it, is looking at the book (at least his eyes are trained in the general vicinity of the book). Observing the eyes of the individual (by having him hold a mirror slightly out of his line of sight with the observer looking in the mirror over his shoulder), they can be seen to be moving in short jumps from left to right (when the text is English). At times the eyes regress from right to left, and periodically there is a large swing from right to left. From time to time (which tends to be irregular if measured in seconds) the person looking at the book turns a page. That's reading. It is obvious that by using operational criteria one hasn't gone far toward analyzing the reading process or toward developing a theory about how it is done.

The reason a reader is able to make the statement above, i.e., "one hasn't gone far, etc." is that as readers, introspectively we "know" there is more to reading than looking at the book and having our eyes jump around the page. However, an extensive examination of a reader's introspections does not lead us very far. Agreements may be obtained on such items as, "What the book is about," or paraphrases of particular sections may be obtained; that is, a number of indications that the reader "comprehends" may be obtained by another sophisticated reader. Introspection tells one little about how he comprehends. The German introspectionists discovered years ago, while studying association intensively, that subjects simply do not know how they do what they do. This should not be so surprising. One may get all sorts of programmed behavior out of a functioning computer without getting any report of its circuitry, that is, how it does what it does. It is easy to forget that human mental operations depend ultimately on the physics and chemistry of physiological functioning, just as do all organic processes. On the other hand, there must be several levels of functional processing occurring in language production and interpretation before this molecular stratum is reached. It is these intermediate levels of functioning which hold hope for amenability to analysis in order to increase understanding of language as manifest in the output of the human organism. It is fairly clear, however, that operational definitions at molar levels, i.e., the level of complex behavioral phenomena, and introspection of the subject's conscious interpretations of what he is doing, hold little promise for clarifying the reading process.

MEASUREMENT AND INDUCTION
FROM MEASUREMENT

Words are not incorporated into the nervous system in the form in which they are structured spatially in the written language display. The nervous system uses an electrochemical, nerve-tract conducted code; the reading display is presented to the eye as patterns of more and less light energy traveling multidimensionally through space. One result of this disjuncture is that one cannot be sure, (1) where the reader is looking, i.e., where he is focusing his attention in the passage, (2) how much of the reading display he sees, and (3) which part or parts of the reading display he is processing. Foveal vision is required for reading, but reduced peripheral vision is inhibiting to speed and accuracy of comprehension. There are great technological difficulties in measuring eye fixations and eye-movements accurately, but this is not the crux of the problem. As John Jacob Geyer (personal communication) notes, "this type of error (the location of focus of the eye during reading) is bound up in the *theoretical position* (italics mine). I do not believe that what the eye sees can be adequately described through optics. I do not believe that input always occurs during the first instant of fixation nor that the word being attended to is always the word in the center of fixation. I think the function of the saccadic movement is to keep the eye generally pointed at the point of regard but that this is a flexible process, not a rigid optical function."

The point for theory is that Geyer's propositions outlined above are unthinkable in certain theoretical contexts. The classical behaviorist finds such statements unacceptable because they imply introspection—a dirty word for the behaviorist. Today's deterministic psychologists accept them much more readily, for the search now is for information exchange processes occurring within the central nervous system of the organism. The hard-nosed psychologist can live with terms such as sign, and symbol, and referent as long as they end in ultimate physical locales or temporal relations between energy sources, i.e., as long as their operations are assumed, at a final level of analysis, to be physical in nature.

The scientist, having had his orientation to the physical clarified by theory, can now search for measurement correlates of such constructs as information, control, concept, thinking, and problem-solving. The only scientific dialogue is between research and theory. Geyer (quoted above) went on to note that Hering and Helmholtz had made exactly the theoretical assumptions as he is making. The difference in the two situations is that research support was lacking in the larger scientific community when Hering and Helmholtz made the assumptions. There is much more likelihood today that the assumptions will be researched because theory and measurement possibilities are contiguous in time.

READING THEORY AND RESEARCH AT PRESENT

As noted before, there has been little dialogue between research and theory in the reading literature of the present. There are dangers that this situation may be continued due to popular linguistic rational theories which do not depend upon research for their verification, and to the shortage of researchers interested in reading (as contrasted with a large reading establishment interested in instruction). There has been some attempt, however, to relate research and theory in reading. Carroll, an empirical linguist and psychologist, has made several attempts at theorizing about reading. One of his statements is as follows: "If reading as a subject matter has a 'content,' that content is the relation between the structure of spoken messages and the system of marks or symbols used to represent these messages." (Carroll, 1964).

Leaving aside the question of whether or not this is an adequate description of the content of reading as a subject matter, let us consider the implications of this characterization as a delimiter of a reading theory. The question becomes, what is in the reading research literature already, and what studies should be performed in order to bring specific evidence to bear on the operation of this hypothesized process? It would seem necessary to know, (1) something about the structure of spoken messages,

(2) something about the processes involved in internalizing graphic information, i.e., inputting the marks or symbols used to represent the spoken messages, and (3) something about the internal process of converting the input graphic sequence into the form the message would have exhibited had it been spoken. Practically all elements of this process are covert, but so is the process of fission in atomic studies. The difficulty for examining the reading process is that the accurate instrumentation, i.e., the measurements, which is available to atomic research is not available to the reading researcher. Theory, however, in proposing that which one needs to know to structure a body of data, encourages the development of proper measurements.

The structure of the spoken message has been a major concern of the linguist. He considers that all language processes are built upon it. The spoken message has certain characteristics which are crucial; for example, it is temporal. It occurs in time, in particular rhythms (Lefevre, 1969). These rhythms are a part of the language structure, and are basic to the learning of the language. Evidence is accumulating that the child perceives stressed elements in the language (beginning at the word level and extending to larger units) as information carriers (see Brown, 1965). One phenomenon which has generated theory and research is the intricate hierarchy which seems to be present among units of language. The word has lost its place, if it ever had the place, as *the* unit of language (Weaver, 1967). Fodor and Bever (1965), and Garrett, Bever, and Fodor (1966), basing their work on a demonstration by Ladefoged (1959), superimposed clicks on taped sentences. The clicks were entered at points of the sentence within immediate constituents. Subjects were instructed to indicate the exact position on an accompanying script, i.e., at which word or letter within a word, where they heard the click. Fodor, et al., hypothesized that the clicks would be heard at the major grammatical breaks of the sentences. They concluded that this indicated the constituent itself is the unit of speech perception. If this were true, reading passages would need to be fitted to this constituent structure also.

Further evidence on this point is provided by Johnson (1964) who used numbers and sentences in a paired-associates learning situation to attempt to demonstrate the unitizing occurring in language. He would give his subject a number which the subject had previously related to a particular sentence. The subject's task was to recall the sentence in its normal order and repeat it exactly. Johnson found that the probability of an error of recall was much greater for parts of immediate constituents than for the entire constituent. He interpreted this to mean that the subject was processing in units of immediate constituent size.

Studies of this type are very helpful in directing one's attention to theoretical possibilities. The studies themselves, however, must be judged on more than the general impression given by the evidence; the theoretician should also look closely at the details of the manner in which the evidence is obtained. These findings indicate that *under the experimental conditions* imposed, decoding of messages (in the first case, non-language information was also involved) appeared to proceed in units larger than words. The term "appeared" is used here not to hedge, but rather, advisedly, to indicate that in Fodor's experiment certain subjects indicated they heard the click at the word within the constituent at the exact place it objectively occurred, and in Johnson's study certain subjects on certain sentences had higher error rates at the major grammatical break than within the constituents. There is scarcely a legitimate experiment which, internally, does not exhibit such contradictory results. Even in more precise scientific endeavor this is typically the case. No real gas obeys precisely the gas laws, elegant though their abstract statement is. Experimental error is not ultimately a removable fault in the experiment or the experimenter. Some variation of the particular in relation to the general is a characteristic of the real world. In this sense, data is ever tenuous, and theories based on the data share this tenuousness.

It cannot be determined from the Fodor and Johnson studies that the immediate constituent is the only unit of spoken language. Other research, which we cannot review here, indicates there are smaller units. Another body of research indicates there are larger units. Still other research indicates the units are hierarchically organized. Furthermore, there are other possible explanations of the Fodor-Johnson results, and in some ways the Fodor results are contradictory to Johnson's results. In the long run the test of the worth of these two studies is: Do they fit into the schema of a larger subsuming theory which itself is holding up under empirical testing of its various parts? In general, this is the relevance of all research for theory: Does a logically consistent theory maintain its consistency after the inclusion of the results from a particular data analysis? If the theory does encompass the data, the procedure is obvious—accept both. If the theory is inconsistent with the data, and there is no competing data of equal evidential validity, the theory should be modified until it will encompass the data. If the theory is inconsistent with the data, but the data is suspect, further experimentation is called for from the same theoretical bases. If two theories are contradictory and one body of data supports one theory, while another body of data supports the other theory, keep both theories, research both, and search for a general theoretical position which will ultimately reveal one theory as a special case of the other, or which will subsume both theories in a higher consistency.

These "rules" for scientific behavior seem so obvious as to be trite, yet the wildly disorganized state of reading research studies in relation to theoretical constructs indicates that the active researcher and theoretician either do not know the rules, or they reject them.

From the graphic language display the sensors and the nervous system must construct a single line, with left to right sequential ordering (for English), and with proper temporal segmentation (if it is correct to assume that reading requires an oral language transduction in the nervous system). This theoretical position leads to a particular kind of search. If the problem is posed in a different manner, the evidence for it tends to shift. Vernon (1960), in asking the same question about input, looks to Gestalt theory for formulating the problem. The answer to the problem of input is that the child perceives a general form or contour with certain dominating letters or parts of letters arising out of it. Ascending letters seem to play an important part, and the alternation of vertical and curved letters may also help in structuring the form. The implicit assumption here is that of some sort of spatial elaboration of graphic forms which are analyzed as wholes. The description is compatible with Gestalt assumptions that the organizing processes for perception are already available in the organism. The problems of the mechanics of this recognition process are ignored; they are simply dismissed as given in the organism's repertoire of behaviors.

The Carroll statement of reading content implies only indirectly that input in reading is a basic part of the process. The present-day trend of research and theory is toward analyzing information processing operations. If Carroll's statement were expanded in this direction, the nature of the input process becomes crucial for what happens during the operation. If the nervous system constructs an oral language passage from print, one might expect that alternating the form of the graphic input in various ways while studying the effect upon the semantic interpretation of the graphic input would lead to the sort of evidence which would support our theory. One might perform experiments such as those of Kolers and his associates (Kolers, Boyer, and Rosenthal, 1965). They demonstrate that applying rotation, reflection, inversion, and reversal of letter transformations to various reading texts leads first to disorganization of reading ability. With further practice, however, the subjects began reading the material directly. There are variations of difficulty among the transformations, but subjects "read" them all finally and obtain meaning from the text. Kolers notes that the program-like character of reading the transformed text is demonstrated by the fact that subjects are usually unable to read normally oriented English text after practicing with transformed text. When they identify the text for what it is, however, they proceed to read it without difficulty. From this experiment, Kolers concludes, "Recognizing static forms may be part of a temporally organized sequence in which processing an array is one of the acts which the observer performs."

Note that the Gestaltist could also give a theoretical framework for this sort of experiment. The various transformations could involve various "reorganizations" of the perceptual field. On the other hand, the Gestaltist could not logically argue that the figural perceptual process and the interpretation were the same functional system, for one has been varied— the graphic—and the other—comprehension—remained essentially invariate.

Empirical evidence for the conversion of the graphic reading display into spoken language is difficult to come by. The entire process is covert. Lefevre (1969) notes that not only does intonation play "a systematic role in the overall sound and rhythm of English speech and oral reading," but also, that "in successful silent reading, echoes and rhythms of intonation accompany and reinforce perception of meaning-bearing language patterns." It is not enough to convert graphemes to phonemes and phonemes into syllables, etc., if that is the course of the process. Rather, the reader must order the graphemes into a proper temporal segmentation. It is the task of a reading theory to relate the proper segmentation of the graphic language input. The task of research is to investigate the segmentation empirically, to seek actual measures of the relations involved, and to correct and illuminate theory.

REFERENCES

Brown, Roger. "Language: The System and Its Acquisition," Chapter 6, *Social Psychology*. New York: The Free Press, 1965.

Bellugi, Ursula, and Brown, R. W. (eds.) *The Acquisition of Language: Monograph of the Society for Research in Child Development,* 1964, 29, No. 1 (Whole No. 92).

Carroll, John. "The Analysis of Reading Instruction: Perspectives from Psychology and Linguistics." *Theories of Learning and Instruction—Sixty-third Yearbook of the National Society for the Study of Education.* (Edited by Ernest R. Hilgard.) Chicago: University of Chicago Press, 1964, pp. 336–353.

Crothers, Edward, and Suppes, Patrick. *Experiments in Second-Language Learning.* New York: Academic Press, 1967.

Fodor, J. A., and Bever, T. G. "The Psychological Reality of Linguistic Segments." *Journal of Verbal Learning and Verbal Behavior,* 4:414–20, 1965.

Garrett, M., Bever, T., and Fodor, J. "The Active Use of Grammar in Speech Perception." *Perception and Psychophysics,* 1:30–32, 1966.

Johnson, Neal F. "A Model of Sentence Generation." Paper presented at a symposium on Psychological Aspects of Language Structure, American Psychological Association, Los Angeles, 1964.

Katz, J., and Fodor, J. "The Structure of a Semantic Theory." *Language,* 39:170–210, 1963.

Kolers, P. A., Boyer, Ann C., and Rosenthal, Kathryn F. "Protracted Practice on Decoding Spacial Transformed Text." *Quarterly Research Reports,* 78:229–31, July 15, 1965. MIT, Research Laboratory of Electronics.

Ladefoged, P. *The Perception of Speech in the Mechanization of Thought.* London: H. M. Stationery Office, 1959.

Lefevre, Carl A. "American English Intonation," Chapter 10, *Linguistics, English, and the Language Arts.* Boston: Allyn and Bacon, 1969.

Osgood, Charles E. "From Models of L to Models of U." Paper presented to American Psychological Association, 1965.

Raygor, Alton A. "Progress Toward a Psychology of Reading." *Junior College and Adult Reading Programs—Expanding Fields.* (Edited by G. B. Schick and M. M. May.) Milwaukee: National Reading Conference, 1967, pp. 171–177.

Weaver, Wendell W. "The Word As the Unit of Language." *Journal of Reading* 10:262–268, January 1967.

Linguistic Assumptions and Reading Instruction

I want to comment on a few linguistic assumptions of my own choosing, assumptions which seem to me to be accepted dogma by some linguists and by many reading specialists. The term "linguists" as used here does not really exist as one sociological or intellectual entity; I am really using the term for the "Zeitgeist"—the "linguistic atmosphere" pervading the reading field brought about by the belated discovery that there is a philosophy and science dealing with language and that these philosophers and scientists of language seem to have something to say about reading.

Following are the assumptions which to some degree most linguists accept and which often appear in communications to reading specialists as natural law:

1. Speech is the only possible primary language coding modality.
2. Reading is nothing but interpreting written speech.
3. There is no difference in producing language and in interpreting it.
4. Language is a system organized apart from its referential function.
5. There are no such linguistic units as "words."

LANGUAGE AS SPEECH ALONE

If there is one thing about which all linguists are agreed it is that speech is primary among potential language modalities. To most linguists, language is speech and there is little more to be said—except about speech. On the other hand, people learn to read a foreign language without speaking it; the deaf and dumb learn language; and there are even cases of the deaf and dumb and blind learning language. There are several arguments presented to explain these performances, but the point is that while it would be foolish to argue against the primacy of speech as language has been performed by man (historically), it is little less than speculation to argue that language is impossible, for individual or community, without speech. This is not an academic question for the reading specialist for at least two reasons. First, the emphasis of linguists

Published originally in *The Psychology of Reading Behavior,* G. B. Schick and M. M. May, eds. The Eighteenth Yearbook of the National Reading Conference, 1969. Reprinted with the permission of the National Reading Conference.

on the primacy of speech has led to a condescending treatment of other language modalities, if other modalities are even mentioned. Recently, when linguists have been giving some attention to reading, the most common view is that reading involves a one-to-one transduction of graphic signs to verbal signs. This transduction is commonly considered to operate at the perceptual level with the underlying cognitive organization only entered with the verbal sign. The process, then, is from graphic sign to verbal sign to cognitive interpretation, and the contemporary linguistic thinker seems to view this sequence as immutable. This is in spite of the fact that oral productive language operations interfere with interpretive cognitive operations (Weaver & Holmes, 6). From this, it would seem that if verbal signs give entry to cognitive process while graphic signs do not, oral production of the signs should lead to greater comprehension. The other possibility is that oral production of verbal signs interferes with an internal processing of verbal signs within the organism. This assumes that oral production of verbal signs and "inner speech" production of verbal signs are in some way different processes. If they are different processes then speech is something different from inner speech and the primacy of speech for language again has competition.

Second, a common injunction to the reading specialist is to use the oral language of the child as an instructional basis for teaching reading. Since this injunction has been followed in the past in only the loosest way and many individuals have, nevertheless, learned to read, the doubt arises that such a technique is a necessary component of instruction. The efficacy of such techniques, then, needs testing in order to determine the contribution to instruction. Speculation should not be accepted as established principles for instructional use.

THE LINGUISTIC IDENTITY
OF PRODUCTION AND INTERPRETATION

Another assumption made by a number of linguists is that the processes of speech production are the same as the processes of speech interpretation. I take it, that by analogy, writing processes are the same as reading processes, though there is little commentary on this. Perhaps because it is not heard as much, the latter statement sounds more ridiculous than the former. This is probably an artifact; however, the statements are equally ridiculous. Linguists argue that the linguistics are the same but this sameness is concealed by the propensity of investigators to examine performance rather than competence. Performance includes many non-linguistic variables which account for the lack of observable congruencies. When one looks at competence, the argument goes, differences even among different languages vanish and certainly production-interpretation differences do so. The problem with this argument is that one comes to know competence only through performance. Some extra-empirical technique must then be applied in order to decide which elements of performance represent the immutability of competence and which are transient effects of individual psychology.

The psychologist finds great differences between language production and interpretation. Encoding involves a heavier information load for the organism. Speaking has a difficulty gradient which appears as pauses in speech (Goldman-Eisler, 3). Listening, one can afford no such hesitation. An individual reading aloud a difficult passage has no difficulties with the phonological contours of speech production, that is to say, he does not exhibit the hesitation behavior of extemporaneous speech production. Encoding involves recall-like operations: decoding mainly employs recognition. For an accomplished reader the cognitive load, in Bruner's (1) sense of the term, is light. Encoding involves a one-to-one relation between the source and the message; decoding involves a many-to-one relation between the message and the destination.

INTERACTION OF PRODUCTIVE AND INTERPRETIVE INFORMATION-FLOW AND MODALITIES

There are differences between speech and writing and between listening and reading. Few would claim that these processes are independent, but the psychologist should not accept pronouncements of linguists that observed differences are not language differences *because* they are psychological. There is no such thing as language without human psychological organization.

Most differences between listening and reading which are fairly open to observation involve storage and retrieval differences. A reading display is available over time; a listening sequence is only available for intervals not controlled by the subject. A reading display allows a focused search of static materials; the listener must store all he searches. A reading display allows the reader to postpone or "put out of mind" irrelevant parts of the display; the listener must decide on irrelevancy immediately or risk interference of one part of the sequence with another. Differences in speech and writing are, in part, an effect of the same processes. Speaking in conversational situations allows a convergence procedure for decoding since the listener can ask for repeats and clarifications. The listener, nevertheless, must put together the message segment by segment and depend upon internal retrieval processes to scan any portions of a message which is to be compared with other parts of the message.

Furthermore, if the listener is doing his editing while the speaker is producing, a heavier load is placed upon the memory of the speaker, for he has not only to produce elements of his own verbal organization, but he must remember how he has modified previously for the benefit of the listener. The writer has no such problem. He can consider the entire display of the message as many times as he wishes to repeat his perusal. The reader also can search at his leisure for the organization of the writer without great strain to his memory and retrieval processes. It is not trivial, then, for an understanding of language that these information handling processes are different. As the Chinese proverb puts it, "The palest ink is clearer than the best memory" (Webb et al., 7). Though the discussion here is concerned with psychological process direct relationship to linguistics can be demonstrated. For example, the fact that writing tends to be more formal than speech may be expressed as syntactical and lexical differences in the choice of language units in speech and writing which in turn may be ascribed to differing organismic requirements for information processing under the different conditions.

LANGUAGE AND REFERENCE

The syntactic component of a linguistic description is a set of rules that generates an infinite class of abstract formal structures, each of which describes the syntactic organization of a sentence. It is the source of the inputs to both the phonological and semantic components. The phonological component operates on such formal objects to determine their phonetic shape, while the semantic component operates on them to determine their meaning. Both the phonological and semantic components are, therefore, purely interpretive: they relate the abstract formal structures underlying sentences to a scheme for pronunciation, on the one hand, and to a representation of conceptualization on the other (Katz. 4, p. 111).

The implication of this statement is that language is not organized from experiences of the organism with the "real" world; language (and primarily the syntactic domain) organizes the real world. This is not the place to argue the philosophical merits of such a statement, but it is of great interest to reading specialists that learning from reading, assuming this statement to be true, is no longer interpretable in terms of the psychological learning formulations of the past seventy-five years or so. Since most reading specialists have not paid a great deal of attention to this tradition anyway, perhaps this will not be a loss of great impact. However, there are a number of characteristics of this point-of-view that place discourse at this level far away from propositions which might be helpful to the reading teacher. This statement is made, not of a particular language, but of all languages. According to this view, language is a species specific characteristic of man and in its elements (as defined by the linguists) it is universal. Notice, input is to phonological and semantic components; therefore, speech is a necessary (in a strict sense) language dimension; other coding modalities are only secondarily possible. The semantic component of this system is not meaningful in its own right; it interprets a separate "representation of conceptualization." That is, non-linguistic entities are in a separate functional system which is not analyzed because it is not linguistic. In effect, from this point linguistic investigation may proceed apart from the confounding effects of what the language refers to.

There is little firm evidence one way or another for or against this particular formulation; certainly, there are alternative formulations that have as much persuasive power. The difficulty with this statement for a psychologist is that the theory is not stated in testable terms. The theory will probably never be so stated, for contemporary linguists who have formulated the theory have abrogated empirical tests as the court of final appeal.

WORDS AND THE LINGUISTS

Even before contemporary theoretical formulations linguists have abhorred words as language units. Analytically, the word is obviously not an elementary unit, but then neither are morphemes or phonemes. These constructs have assumed an elemental status because linguists have been able to define them in precise ways, although the precision is less than perfect. There are a number of objections to the word as a basic unit, but this is true of more linguistically acceptable units also. Chomsky (2) is now finding many objections to the phoneme as a unit. Among teachers and psychologists words have proven to be useful entities. All beginning reading programs end up with certain word criteria for instructional effectiveness, and many programs begin with words as units. There may be a better way, but it remains to be shown. Wherever children learn to read all of the difficulties of those who do not learn cannot be attributed to the method. Generative analyses of the constituents of sentences typically end with words. There is better evidence for the word as a psychological unit than any other unit the linguists have proposed. I take it that much of the vehemence of the linguists who are in contact with reading instruction against the word as a unit is a reaction to the mistaken assumption of teachers and researchers that the word is the only unit of language, and to the mistaken notion that if words are learned nothing else is necessary for accomplished language behavior. If the reading specialist asks what is to be substituted in an instructional procedure that does not use the word as a unit of language the linguist has little to offer. Individuals knowledgeable in linguistics and concerned with reading instruction who offer help to reading teachers do not ignore words as language components but, rather, seek to place the word in proper perspective for the teacher.

The linguist, generally, begins with the assumption that language may be analyzed separately from "meaning," and he rejects the concept of the word as unit. He, thus, is able to develop an elegant, that is, internally consistent, model of language. Nevertheless, there is much more "pragmatic" evidence that the approach of the reading teacher leads to improvement in language and conceptualization in students. There are few applications of linguistic findings to the teaching of language to a native speaker or writer, and even fewer to the teaching of listening and reading (Weaver, 5).

CONCLUSION

The present impact of linguistics upon instruction is very much like the impact of psychological research in the 40's and 50's. We do not quite understand what's going on, but it sounds good. Under these conditions the most dramatic ideas tend to be the ones which are introduced and which, though often grossly misunderstood, gain favor. The problem is that poor scholarship interpreting ideas from basic studies magnifies the effects of that poor scholarship. Teachers become confused and frustrated and suspicious of the value of all scholarship. Instruction can only be informed in part by basic studies. The ratio of what we do not know to what we do know is so great that instruction must proceed on its day-to-day course largely by traditional and expedient methodologies. Philosophical systems whether psychological or linguistic cannot function as instructional models because they are filled with error and the greater the detail (with which instruction is concerned) forced from the system the more the error. Linguists have some things to tell the reading instructor which he can use and some other things to tell him which he can't use but which are relevant to his understanding of his task; but the linguist communicates chiefly with his own kind and this communication, given the present state of the discourse, the reading instructor, in his role of instructor, would do better to ignore.

REFERENCES

1. Bruner, Jerome S., J. J. Goodnow, and G. A. Austin. *A Study of Thinking.* New York: John Wiley, 1956.

2. Chomsky, Noam. *Aspects of the Theory of Syntax.* Cambridge: The M. I. T. Press, 1965.

3. Goldman-Eisler, Frieda. "Hesitation and Information in Speech," in *Information Theory, Fourth London Symposium.* London: Butterworths, 1961.

4. Katz, Jerrold J. *The Philosophy of Language.* New York: Harper and Row, 1966.

5. Weaver, Wendell W. "The Word as the Unit of Language," *Journal of Reading,* January, 1967, 10, 262–268.

6. Weaver, Wendell W. & C. Curtis Holmes. "The Effect of Reading Modality, Punctuation Condition, and Content Difficulty on Latency and Comprehension of Close Deletions." Paper read at the American Psychological Association Convention. Los Angeles, 1968.

7. Webb, Eugene J., D. T. Campbell, R. D. Schwartz, and L. Sechrest, *Unobtrusive Measures: Nonreactive Research in the Social Sciences.* Chicago: Rand McNally, 1966.

Oral and Oral-Written Language Measures
with First Grade Pupils

The extent to which success in learning to read is dependent upon oral language abilities long has intrigued researchers and teachers. Many reading specialists and first grade instructors believe that a child's success in learning to read actually is dependent upon his possession of "adequate" oral language. One illustration should suffice. "Proficiency in oral communication, therefore is the foundation upon which competency in reading is built." [Lord, Van Deman, and Miles, 1965, p. 5]. Such proponents argue that the normal process by which language should be mastered is by following a sequence of listening, speaking, reading, and finally writing. Reading thus is regarded as a direct extension of oral language and one important measure of the child's readiness to read is his ability to listen and to speak. Beliefs of this sort apparently are behind recent efforts to teach English as a second language to culturally disadvantaged children and members of ethnic groups.

Despite such contentions little empirical evidence has been proffered to support these widely held beliefs. Exactly what adequate language is has not been delineated, nor have reliable and valid tests been developed. Furthermore little evidence is available to indicate that language is mastered more efficiently or that reading is learned more effectively in a hierarchical fashion, viz.: listening, speaking, reading, and writing. The fact that most present day adults who have studied foreign languages tend to be able to read the second language somewhat better than they can understand it aurally or speak it tends to contradict the belief that this sequence is either necessary or even desirable. In fact, it seems unlikely that even when learning one's native language this sequential pattern is followed. The fact that language ability is correlated positively with mental ability, socio-economic status, sex, and similar attributes which help a child to succeed in school, may have led teachers to overgeneralize its importance to beginning reading.

Recent interest in the opinions of linguists and in the scientific study of language also has raised questions about the relationships between oral and written language. Bloomfield (1942), one of the earliest linguists to

(Co-authored with Albert J. Kingston.) Published originally in *Reading: The Right to Participate,* F. P. Greene, ed. The Twentieth Yearbook of the National Reading Conference, 1971. Reprinted with the permission of the National Reading Conference.

discuss reading, stressed that the reading act consists of transforming written symbols into sounds. Soffietti (1955), Fries (1963), Lefevre (1964), and Carroll (1964) also have presented the linguist's view that reading requires the decoding of printed symbols and transforming them to subvocal speech sounds. Fries (1963) even states that "the process of learning to read in one's native language is *the process of transfer* from auditory signs for language signals which the child has already learned to the new visual signs for the same signals [p. 119]."

When an adult looks back and tries to recall how he learned his oral-written language, the impression that both oral and written were identical processes seems to be overwhelming. However careful analysis of the learning tasks faced by children reveals considerable differences in the conditions imposed by oral and written language. In learning natural language of the oral type the child functions in a real life situation. Language learning is a must. A child's speech emissions are reinforced spontaneously. His models speak and he speaks. He does not learn rules; he behaves according to rules (i.e., predictable patterns). He learns continuously over many years in a myriad of circumstances. His lessons are not intensive and compressed as they are in learning to read.

Language also is related to cognitive development. Piaget (1969) and Vygotsky (1962) seem to feel that although language is necessary for high level reasoning, language and conceptualization are not identical, but rather represent separate functional systems. It seems likely that some types of concepts are developed without language playing an essential role. Similarly there do not seem to be compelling reasons to assume that children need well developed oral language in order to conceptualize certain verbal units. It seems more probable that for the beginning reader the transfer of meaning from oral to graphic representation of language is less simple and direct than commonly assumed. Certainly at higher age levels for more skillful readers the transformation between oral and written and written to oral language is not simple and straight forward. A major difficulty in studying the relationship between oral and written language proficiency lies in the lack of reliable psychometric instruments. What are the criteria to be employed in judging language capabilities? How do we weigh structure, vocabulary, intonation, pitch, stress, pronunciation, etc.? Should language be stimulated by the use of specific stimuli or should language be comparatively free and unprovoked? The lack of common agreement concerning performance criteria is one reason for a dearth of reliable and valid measure. Reading specialists however often suggest that such abilities as auditory perception of sounds, ability to pronounce words, extent of vocabulary, and sentence structure and length of sentences spoken be observed and noted in assessing the child's "readiness" for reading instruction. Standardized readiness tests however fail to appraise the child's oral language abilities, but rather concentrate on more restricted tasks such as discrimination, memory, etc.

The measurement of the language of naive readers (1st Graders) further is complicated by the pupils' lack of maturity, inconsistent behavior, and by unfamiliarity with testing procedures. Unless considerable time is spent establishing rapport, providing warm-up sessions, assuring that the nature of the tasks to be performed is understood, encouraging the unsure and monitoring the disinterested, the results attained are likely to be highly unreliable and invalid. Most researchers who have interviewed and examined children of kindergarten and first grade age have numerous stories to relate concerning pupils whom they badly misjudged, or misunderstood.

For several years the authors have been studying the problem of obtaining adequate language measures from beginning readers. Our underlying assumption has been that oral language dimensions are analyzable into discriminable parts—that grammar or syntax for example, is in measurable ways different from vocabulary. The same assumption was made about reading, namely, that the reading act or reading behavior is analyzable into a set of discriminable components. Following the hypothesis of many linguists it is further assumed that oral language and reading language share major components, so that oral language grammar is highly related to reading language grammar and oral language vocabulary is highly related to reading language vocabulary.

From a number of initial attempts at measurement, four types of instruments were decided upon for further study. The first was an oral cloze measure developed to measure the child's knowledge of standard English language structure. Written cloze measures have been widely used in reading and psycholinguistic research. Cloze results have been shown to correlate positively with reading ability, language capability and intelligence. Kingston and Weaver (1970) have demonstrated that it is feasible to employ cloze techniques with culturally disadvantaged beginning readers. A second cloze test also was designed to test the child's knowledge and use of lexical as contrasted to structural words. Each of these tests consisted of presenting sentences to the children first intact, and then with one or more words of a particular type deleted. The structural and lexical dichotomy was adopted from Fries (1957) who spoke of structural and lexical meanings in English. According to Fries structural meaning is carried chiefly by function words, i.e., words which are not nouns, main verbs, adjectives, or adverbs. Other linguists sometimes use the terms grammatical meaning and syntactical meaning.

In contrast is structural meanings. Fries employed the term lexical meaning to describe meanings carried mainly by nouns, adjectives, main verbs, and adverbs. Other linguists have used the terms semantic meaning, content word meaning, or non-grammatical meaning for this construct. In both tests children were requested to supply the proper word for the missing one. Extreme care was taken to assure that each child understood the nature of the task presented and certain warm-up or practice sentences were provided. Sample items from the lexical cloze measure follow:

1. My sister has a *diamond* ring.
2. A *microscope* makes little things look big.
3. The *hero* caught the bank robber.

Sample items from the structural cloze measures are:

1. The girl lost *a* glove.
2. It *is* cold today.
3. John *and* Joe are at school.

A third test was designed to assess a characteristic often described by child psychologists and elementary teachers: the child's ability to reason intelligently on an abstract-concrete continuum. Piaget, Vygotsky, and others often have postulated that children's thinking tends to move from concrete to abstract as the child matures. Psychiatrists also have observed that certain types of brain damage and psychopathology seems to cause regressive patterns in adults from abstract to more concrete patterns of thought. Coleman (1966) experimenting with college students had employed the concept, abstract, in a more precise manner. To Coleman, a concrete word was one with a perceivable referent. (Coleman seems to have ignored the fact that a class referent in itself is abstract. Thus, for Coleman, boy is concrete, so is mother. Home and play are abstract.) In developing this test it was planned originally to follow Coleman's definition as nearly as possible. Experience, however, showed that deleting abstract terms in cloze measures required more context than was feasible for the first grader to handle. As analogies have been successfully employed for more than fifty years, to measure reasoning ability, it was decided to modify such tasks by making them cloze measures. That is, analogic pairs taken from the WIPPSC (Wechsler, 1967) were placed in the context of sentences with one member of the pair deleted so as to form a cloze task. Typical sentences were:

1. Brother is a boy; sister is a *girl.*
2. A bird flies; a fish *swims.*
3. Fire is hot; ice is *cold.*

All three measures were administered orally in individual, private sessions to 102 first graders in a North Georgia rural elementary school. All tests were administered within a three week period during the first month of the child's enrollment in first grade. These measures represent Method One (Oral Method) in a Campbell-Fiske (1959) Construct Discriminant Validity Model. These data will be presented elsewhere.

Instruments developed for Method Two, the Oral-Written Method, were designed to parallel the tests developed for Method One. Test one was a structural cloze test, test two, a lexical cloze test, and test three, an analogies task. The major differences between these measures and those employed in Method One was that the children listened to sentences on a tape recorder while reading the sentences. The child's task was to circle the word that went in the blank.

The analogies test was similar to that used in Method One except that the examiner read the statement while the child read the statement silently and selected the proper word from three presented. Examples are:

1. A man is big; a child is _____.
   large
   long
   small
2. Women are mothers; men are _____.
   fathers
   sisters
   aunts

These three types of measures were administered in February and March to groups consisting of four or five children each.

Method Three consisted of a standardized reading test, a test of grammar, and a multiple-choice analogies test. Subtest VI titled Phonetic Analysis and Subtest VII, Structural Analysis of the Basal Reader Test were used as the structural measures and five subtests, I Sentence Meaning, II Sensory Images, III Emotional Reactions, IV Perceiving Relationships, and V Scrutiny-Control were combined and employed as a lexical measure. A specially developed multiple-choice test of analogies was employed as the measure of abstraction. Typical of the items are the following:

1. Boys grow up to be men and girls to be _____.
   sisters
   women
2. Schools have books; garages have _____.
   cars
   movies

These tests were administered in May just prior to the end of the school year.

There was very little evidence, using the Campbell-Fiske criteria, of discriminable constructs. The major separation was between the oral method of test presentation and the two presentations of the low reliability of the oral tests.

Our experiences have shown that certain procedures in obtaining measures on young children should be adhered to if satisfactory results are to be obtained.

1. Children should know the examiner well in non-test situations.
2. Testing at any one session should be short—10-15 items, 15 to 20 minutes total testing time.
3. Children who show test anxiety should be released immediately and tried again another day.
4. Test length for adequate reliability should be obtained by summing over two or more short testing sessions.
5. Instructions for the test should be in the form of examples of the task to be performed. Several examples should be given.
6. Immediate reinforcement is not essential, but a small reward given at the end of a testing session provided eagerness to return for more.
7. Difficulty on cloze tests should be increased first by increasing context, e.g., two sentences, 1 word deletion. The next difficult step is increasing number of deletions.
8. First graders, in general, are not able to complete nth word cloze tasks.

Few research reports devote sufficient time to a discussion of the trials and errors of working with children in a school situation. Schools of course are organized for instruction, not research. Research teams are required to demonstrate the diplomatic skill of senior ambassadors if they are to succeed in collecting data without outliving their welcome. This means that researchers must be flexible in their schedules, willing to be displaced from their assigned places, and able to take on additional duties when requested by teachers and the principal. Teachers often have only meager or perhaps even erroneous information concerning the activities of a university team. If they are insecure or suspicious, they may have a negative effect on the responses made by pupils. They can even discourage children in a number of subtle or even unsubtle ways. In our study teachers were informed at all steps of the nature of the project. A teacher appreciation day was held the last month of school in which cookies, coffee, ice cream, and cokes were furnished by the research team. The teachers were thanked properly for their assistance and cooperation. In the beginning of the school year all first grade teachers met with the research team to agree on rules of the game or procedure. Close co-operative relations were maintained throughout the year and teachers were made to feel they were an important part of the project. Continuous liaison is necessary, however, in order to collect reliable and valid data. In the study reported it had been decided that pupils who mastered the tasks would be reinforced with plastic tokens. Our psychometrists however could not stand the pain and disappointment of those who failed the tests. After a rapid consultation it was decided to reinforce all children. This was a good decision because each child became highly motivated and eager to master the presented tests. The difference in motivation may be a major factor in the success our subjects had in mastering complex tasks. All our subjects were actually involved in the tasks presented to them. Similarly the close rapport developed by expert psychometrists insured maximum pupil involvement. One can only wonder how many studies of first grade children are invalid because the teachers and pupils were given tests without really knowing who is administering them or why they are being administered, or what's in it for everyone. In our opinion, it is necessary for researchers to be able to show that their subjects were eagerly and actively involved. Our research team also discovered that children must be carefully monitored if optimal results are to be obtained. Individual measures were employed for all oral tests. The written measures involved only three to five children. All subjects were given sufficient training so that they understood thoroughly the nature of the tasks they were given. Rest periods were provided whenever a child seemed to tire or lag in interest. Finally, although the women's liberation movement may take exception, we thought the fact that our research team consisted of males was an advantage. All our psychometrists were vigorous young masculine types. In our elementary school where all primary grade teachers were female, the boys seemed to welcome the chance of working with men. Perhaps they did not see these able young men as teachers and hence were more able to enter into the "game-like" activities.

Our experiences have convinced us that first graders are able to perform successfully with oral and written cloze measures. Care must be taken to ensure that the children actively become involved in the tasks. The research activities, furthermore, must be conducted in an environment where the research team is present so often that children and teachers regard the research activity as a normal part of the school function.

REFERENCES

Bloomfield, L. Linguistics in reading. *Elementary English Review,* 1942, 19, 125–130.

Campbell, D. T., and Fisk, D. W. Convergent and discriminate validation by the multitrait-multimethod matrix. *Psychological Bulletin,* 1959, 56, 81–105.

Carroll, J. The analysis of reading instruction: Perspectives from psychology and linguistics. In E. R. Hilgard (ed.), *Theories of learning and instruction.* National Society for Study of Education, 63, (1), 1964.

Coleman, E. B. Developing a technology of written instruction: Some determiners of the complexity of prose. Paper presented at Symposium on Verbal Learning and Written Instruction. New York: Columbia University, March, 1966.

Fries, C. C. Linguistics and reading. New York: Holt, Rinehart and Winston, 1957.

Kingston, A. J., and Weaver, W. W. Feasibility of cloze techniques for teaching and evaluating culturally disadvantaged beginning readers. *Journal of Social Psychology,* 1970, 82, 205–214.

Lefevre, C. A. *Linguistics and the teaching of reading.* New York: McGraw-Hill, 1964.

Lord, E. M., Van Deman, D. D. D., and Miles, L. E. *Basic learning in the language arts.* Chicago: Scott Foresman, 1965.

Piaget, J., and Inhelder, B. *The psychology of the child.* Paris: Presser, 1969.

Soffietti, J. P. Why children fail to read: A linguistic analysis. *Harvard Educational Review,* 1955, 25, 63–84.

Vygotsky, L. S. *Thought and language.* Cambridge: Massachusetts Institute of Technology Press, 1962.

Wechsler, D. *Manual for the Wechsler Preschool and Primary Scale of Intelligence.* New York: Psychology Corporation, 1967.

Modeling the Effects of Oral Language upon Reading Literature

INFORMATION AND CONTROL

American experimental psychology through its short history has derived most of its method and a large amount of its philosophy from the more exact sciences. This is true of that ubiquitous set of constructs, stimulus and response. Another assumption was made about stimulus and response; namely, energy exchange of one kind or another was viewed as the physical entity which was the concern of the psychological organism. Behavior is an act, the overt functioning of a muscle or gland (see Weaver, 1966). As interest in cognitive processes began to expand in the '50's and '60's, the analysis of exchanges of energy for such phenomena was inappropriate. While it is possible to estimate the energy output of the brain, the energy involved is low and does not directly affect information and control functions performed by the brain as long as it has a minimum necessary level.

Actually, this kind of problem was not unknown to the physical sciences. Physicists had long puzzled over Clerk Maxwell's demon (see Shannon & Weaver, 1961), a perpetual motion heat machine constructed with a rigid container. The container was divided into two compartments and in the dividing wall was an opening, closed by a small gate. A homunculus stood by the gate, and when he observed a particle moving faster than the average velocity of all particles approaching the gate, he would open the gate, letting the particle into compartment B. When he observed a particle moving slower than the average of all the particles, he would keep the gate closed, retaining the slow moving particles in compartment A. When the two compartments were connected to a heat engine, a perpetual motion machine was obtained. Norbert Wiener's (1948) analysis of the Maxwell demon is that the demon must receive information and act on it in order for the system to work. Therefore, though the demon reduces the entropy of the system, the information he must receive and the acting he must do adds the entropy back to the system. Due to these relationships, the system cannot maintain perpetual

(Co-authored with Albert J. Kingston.) Originally published in *The Literature of Research in Reading with Emphasis on Models,* F. B. Davis, ed. New Brunswick Graduate School of Education, Rutgers University, 1971. Reprinted in the *Reading Research Quarterly,* 1972, 7, 613–627. Reprinted with the permission of the editor and the National Reading Association.

motion. The interesting point for those of us interested in cognitive processes, however, is that information, when it is defined in probabilistic terms, can be demonstrated to have a physical effect which to the individual with scientific predispositions is the only "real" effect. It should also be observed that the demon, to a degree, exhibits *sign behavior*. In studying cognitive process, we are primarily interested in sign behavior, which though it operates at a low level of energy exchange, controls other, more powerful, energies within the system.

SIGN BEHAVIOR

Stimuli and Significants

The types of operations which are humanized by Maxwell's demon have been considered extensively by philosophers under the rubric symbiotics. The American pragmatist, Charles Pierce, did extensive analyses of sign behavior (see Morris, 1938). Psychologically, sign behavior is difficult to approach with our analytic tools because its major processes are covert. Only the effects of sign behavior are represented in overt behaviors. A number of psychologists and educators interested in reading have obviously felt the importance of dealing with this kind of behavior, though it is rarely mentioned specifically. Goodman (1969), for example, in dealing with miscues in the oral reading of early readers, proposes a kind of information-flow model to explain the ways in which early readers miscue. The final result is a kind of information-flow chart with the flow model resembling the various squares, rectangles, triangles, and various odd figures of the IBM flow chart, but actually representing different sorts of channel processing and exchanges which are hypothesized to occur within the organism. This model is begun by hypothesizing that the miscues are random processes which are assignable to the fact that visual input of graphic materials is sampled. At times, then, there are gaps or blanks in the sampling, and, in oral reading, these gaps or blanks sometimes come out as what appear to be misreadings.

There is a great deal of evidence for sampling processes in visual input. Studies of the behavior of subjects on rotor pursuit tasks indicate that this sampling is indeed a time-limited kind of behavior (Stroud, 1949). Geyer (1966) shows that time sampling of visual input occurs in eye movements in reading and hypothesizes that the sampling is constant. The fact that visual thresholds are highly raised during eye movements, whether the movements be large saccades or micro-movements, is another indication of a sampling characteristic. Nevertheless, in any information model based upon the characteristics of the stimulus input and upon certain observable coding phenomena occurring at the periphery of the perceptual process, there is little light thrown on the processes by which physical graphic representations are elevated to the level of signs for the organism.

The perceptual theory of reading proposed by Eleanor Gibson (1970a, 1970b) is also confronted with this problem. No matter how precisely one traces the processes by which words or parts of words, immediate constituents, or sentences, or whatever linguistic unit one might study, one cannot explain the transmutation of the direct physical information into sign operations within the organism. As Osgood, Suci, and Tannenbaum (1961) note, the pattern of stimulation which is the sign is never identical with the pattern of stimulation which is the significant. The linguistic "bed" is not the bed one sleeps in. This last statement does not appear to be true for the child, however, or, perhaps, for the primitive. Developmentally, the sign seems to begin as an attribute of the thing (Brown, 1958). As mature conceptualization occurs, the sign becomes an entity apart. Signs may be manipulated, juxtaposed with other signs in order to explain, or describe, or solve a problem—all without any direct reference to the thing.

Brown (1958, p. 52) notes, "What the comprehension effect may be it is difficult to tell for this effect is hidden away inside the organism." This kind of statement is of little aid to the psychologist, however, especially for psychologists who are interested in model building. Models of the ephemeral which are themselves ephemeral are useless.

Oral Signs and Written Signs

There are, then, a number of assumptions which linguists tend to equate with tested hypotheses, and which end up as having characteristics of "natural law." Chief of these is that oral language is the only possible language modality. It is, therefore, primary and all other forms secondary—well, let's face it—really, nonlanguage. On the other hand, with all the struggling of graduate students to meet the Ph.D. requirements in foreign language, there must have been one who learned to read the language without speaking it. In this case, one is enough. Most congenitally deaf people learn language; even deaf and blind people have learned language. Historically, it would be foolish to argue that oral language is not overwhelmingly prepreponderant, but it is just as counter to the evidence to argue that language without hearing and speech is impossible as it is to demonstrate psychologically that there are differences between oral and written language. The impact of language is in terms of information as well as in mode of presentation, and which has more power is a moot question.

This is not an academic question for reading models, for the high status of this attitude has led to a condescending treatment of other language modalities—especially the visual. Recently, when more and more psychologists have been adopting linguistic propositions as psychological models of language, this had led to the common view documented above. Specifically, reading is nothing but a transduction of graphic forms into the oral language. "This transduction is commonly considered to operate at the perceptual level with the underlying cognitive level only entered with the verbal sign. The process, then, is from graphic sign to verbal sign to cognitive interpretation, and the contemporary linguistic thinker seems to view this sequence as immutable" (Weaver, 1969, pp. 107–108). There are studies, however, which indicate that oral-productive language operations interfere with interpretive cognitive operations (Johnson, 1970; Weaver, Holmes, & Reynolds, 1970). Furthermore, it is well known that high school and college reading teachers have long tried to suppress vocalization in readers because of the interference vocalization causes with understanding.

Linguists argue that there is a simple one-to-one relationship between language production and interpretation. This is not at all apparent observationally. The child carries out verbal instructions before he speaks and he speaks words indicating interpretive relations, e.g., "because," before he understands the relation (Vygotsky, 1962). The argument goes that if one looks at "competence," performance differences disappear. The difficulty with this argument, to the empirical scientist anyway, is that competence is only known through performance.

The psychologists find great differences between language (speech or writing) and language interpretation. Encoding has a heavier information load as shown by Goldman-Eisler's (1961) investigations of pauses in speech. Pauses in reading aloud are short, related only to breathing and phrasing. Encoding involves "recall-like" operations; decoding seems to proceed as a rapid recognition.

The importance for a reading model is that analyses of speech acts do not account for writing and certainly not for auding and reading. The linguist draws evidence (as Suppes [in debate with Jerry Fodor at APA Convention, Washington, D.C., 1968] says, "largely anecdotal") from a speech or writing corpus and is unsure whether he means to be psychological or not (Chomsky, 1968). However he resolves this issue, he excludes such psychologically important considerations as the nature of the memory store—a store reviewable depending upon the memory of the speaker (in a conversation), and not reviewable in the case of a formal speech such as this one.

There are other psychological considerations just as important as those mentioned above which are ignored by linguistic models of reading. Perhaps the most important of these are the relationships among language, concepts, and referential entities and relations in the physical world. Linguists have reduced language analysis to an abstract, rational system. The goal seems to be to move even further until linguistic models approach abstract mathematical models. This appears to be an inappropriate goal for psychologists. Language is learned by people to be used; it is learned because it is useful. It is learned as a part of a world which the organism accepts as real. A word means some thing or some action. Another word means relationships between things and actions. Reading is for use, also, and writing is not necessarily a secondary language form. In a completely deaf culture, writing and reading could occur. It is highly speculative to assume that reading is necessarily dependent upon oral language, or that if oral language is a mediator in learning to read, it remains so for the accomplished reader.

Categories and Information

One way to make sign behavior less ephemeral is to conceptualize it as some kind of information processing; that is, some process which takes the sensory data from an aural or a graphic representation and through some logical neural net relates the data to schemas already existing within the organism. Again, some substance seems lent to a model when categories of certain kinds are the organizational elements of the schemas. It does not appear likely that these categories exist in something like a word-to-thing. For one reason, this seems enormously inefficient, even for the very inefficient nervous system. Furthermore, the word as we know it externally does not exist until the coordination of the vocal musculature forms a unitary sound. Sign behavior seems to require the positing of hierarchically organized kinds of categorical arrangements. As Brown (1958) points out, it is also important to have an empty category. One hears a word for the first time and it is not understood. What is understood is that the substance of the category is to be filled in with further experience with that word in its many contexts. Jenkins (1965) considers concepts to be categories, i.e., a system of relationships defined by rules. Language, then (oral and reading language), operates by a set of categories—syntactical, semantical, phonological, morphological, and probably many others. It should be emphasized that these categories, as are all our scientific categories, are inventions. In this case, then, they may or may not be psychological. The demonstration of the psychological reality of these categories in oral and reading language constitutes a great part of our research tasks.

ORAL LANGUAGE AND BEGINNING READING

An adult examining oral and written language becomes highly impressed by the characteristics they share. He finds the evidence so overwhelming that he tends to view written and oral language as identical in nature. This is especially true if oral-language samples are transposed to written form and these compared linguistically to other written production. Typically such a procedure tends to divorce the language from its psychological reality. It is doubtful, however, that the naive learner of a written language, i.e., a naive reader, is aware of this apparent relationship. In fact, an advantage claimed by adherents to the "Language Experience Approach" to beginning reading instruction is that the system helps the child to see the relationship of his oral language to written language. Even such a common appearing concept as "word" may not be in the concept storage of young children (see Meltzer & Herse, 1969).

One can argue that even if the commonalities of features of written and oral language seem to impress an adult, it does not necessarily follow that the six-year-old child will note the same common elements. As many researchers have discovered, children do not function linguistically or intellectually in the same manner as adults.

A number of readily apparent differences in learning oral natural language and in learning to read one's language can be noted. First, the young child and infant learns his natural language in the "real" environment of which he is a part. Much of his oral language is learned in relationship to his needs, which are expressed by significant others and himself. At an early age his attempts at discriminating the speech of others or attempting to express his own needs are reinforced positively and with compounding consistency. Typically, the more responses he makes and the more actively he engages in language learning, the more positive are the schedules of reinforcement that ensue. In the schoolroom, reinforcement for learning to read language is neither so regularly nor so positively reinforced. Again, in learning one's language orally, it should be noted that the period for learning extends over a period of many years. The average child can discriminate certain aspects of oral language at approximately six months of age. Six months later, at one year of age, the child can produce words (McCarthy, 1954). By 18 months of age, the typical child can communicate many of his needs, although he may use gestures extensively. From that period until school entrance, all aspects of language develop constantly. By contrast, the acquisition of much reading language is telescoped over a period of three years of the primary grades. Although some reading specialists believe reading skills require a lifetime to develop, most persons regard the primary grades as the essential or critical years for "learning to read." Certainly the fourth-grade child who has not mastered fundamental reading skills is doomed to a school life of considerable difficulty. It also should be noted, however, that for any child—regardless of his socioeconomic position, familial position, or other status—failure to develop oral communication skills represents a severe hardship in learning, socialization, or the mastery of any developmental task composed by the major or his own particular subculture. Hence, he functions under considerable stress or need to master oral language skills. In contrast, many children either fail to recognize the need to acquire reading language or are not sufficiently motivated to achieve the desired goals.

In learning oral language, it should be noted, the young child does not learn "rules." Rather, he behaves and is reinforced accordingly. He learns how to act, not how he acts. His models speak, he speaks. He can say some things before he "knows" what he is saying and he can do other things before he can say what he is doing (Vygotsky, 1962). Language is intimately related to intelligence and thought. Piaget and Inhelder (1969) argue, however, that while language is necessary for the highest levels of conceptual thinking, language and conceptualization are separate functional systems and many elemental as well as certain elaborate concepts are developed without language playing an essential role.

Finally it should be noted that many linguists feel that any time a language is transposed from an oral to a written form, some damage or alteration ensues. They argue that such important characteristics as phonology, intonation, pauses, etc., are lost. It should be noted, however, that some language learners (usually mature) can move successfully in language learning from written forms to oral forms (Durkin, 1966). This is noticeable in the language achievements of the deaf and hard of hearing as well as certain learners of second languages.

Apparently the transfer of "meaning" from spoken to graphic representation may not be the direct, simple operation commonly assumed. Nor does it follow that the ability to demonstrate language facility is a necessary antecedent condition to learning reading behavior. Even if the linguist is correct in hypothesizing that reading is merely a transduction of verbal symbols, the process by which the human performs this process is by no means simple.

Those who teach children to read have no doubt that oral language is crucial in learning to read. Furthermore, the feeling is, usually, the better the oral language accomplishment, the better the reading accomplishment. Robinson (1955) says that the extent to which the child uses the language with which he reads is basic to reading success. In a more formal research discussion, Calfee and Venezky (1968) examined the factors reported in the literature as being involved in beginning reading. There was little evidence given here for maintaining the concept, "component skills of reading." Calfee and Venezky concluded that in all the measurements of these skills there tended to be only two general factors which were adequately separated: (1) the ability to follow instructions and (2) a general verbal factor. This general verbal factor seems the kind of correlation that bridges oral language and reading language. It is a far cry, however, from a hypothesized general ability factor which appears in practically all measurement studies involving language (generally identified by a high loading on a vocabulary component) to a specific oral language ability which harbingers success in reading. Tests attempting to show a variety of language components such as the Illinois Test of Psycholinguistic Abilities do not show side separation of supposedly different subtests when subjected to correlational analysis. Quereshi (1967) found a developmental factor in the subtest of the ITPA with correlations at later ages focusing at .45. It is very questionable, however, that the ITPA, if subjected to a rigorous procedure such as the Campbell-Fiske analysis, would separate distinct factorial components. In short, while no one would argue that reading behavior develops in the child with the basis in oral language, specifics of that dependency upon oral language have not been identified.

In the light of this sort of information about the operation of oral language in reading, it is difficult to see how such injunctions as "the syntactic ability of the child ought to be improved because the concentration at the present is upon his vocabulary" can be maintained (see Fleming, 1968). If the effect of oral language in general is not understood, certainly the effect of syntax is even more obscure. Another palliative for the difficulty of children in learning to read is proposed by John Downing (1970). Downing thinks that cognitive confusion and lack of system in beginning reading is a basic characteristic of reading disability. He finds that because children have vague ideas about how people read and have special difficulty in understanding the purposes of written language, they have difficulty reading. This same concern is indicated by such papers as that of Meltzer and Herse (1969) where it is found generally that first graders are unable to discriminate boundaries of the word and thus have reading difficulties.

Another sort of approach to the problem of the effect of oral language on reading is in proposals put forth by Marquardt (1964). Marquardt speculates that the spoken word may be analyzed into at least two distinct styles of behavior: (a) conversation, and (b) spoken prose, which consists of monologue and reading aloud. Marquardt hypothesizes that reading is much more like spoken prose than like conversation. He goes further to speculate that an appropriate educational sequence might be to move from conversation to spoken prose and then to reading.

If oral-language dimensions can be shown to maintain their characteristics when reading dimensions are substituted, these variables can be considered to be the same across modalities. Reading specialists (and most linguists) have assumed that a child's success in learning to read is dependent upon an "adequate" oral language. This has seemed so obvious that few definitions of "adequate" have been forthcoming. Fries (1952, p. 119) states, "The process of learning to read in one's native language is the *process of transfer* from auditory sign for language signals which the child has already learned to the new visual signs for the same signals [italics are Fries']." Bloomfield (1946), one of the earliest linguists to discuss reading, stressed that the reading act consists of transforming written symbols into sounds; Ilg and Ames (1950), Soffietti (1955), Lefevre (1964), and Carroll (1964) have, in essence, supported this view.

Weaver and Kingston were thinking of these rather overwhelming opinions when they began a set of studies to attempt to separate certain language constructs (e.g., structure and abstraction) into verified entities. In the first year, the Campbell-Fiske construct—discriminant validity analysis—was applied to several oral and written language dimensions (Campbell & Fiske, 1959). When the data were in, the separation was not among the constructs but between the oral measurement tasks and the written measurement tasks (Weaver & Kingston, 1971).

All the measures used during the first year were revised, a number of new measures were selected, and during the second year another attempt was made to validate the constructs. Again the constructs hypothesized did not separate, while the method of testing, oral or written, was the main source of variation. This year, oral-language variables which are reflected in reading success are still being sought, but the Campbell-Fiske analysis has been abandoned as too costly for this purpose.

Any observant analysis of the learning tasks faced by the child shows considerable differences in the learning conditions imposed by oral and written language. In learning oral language, the child functions in his life situation. Language learning is a "must." The child's speech emissions are usually reinforced immediately; his understanding of messages to him obtains immediate reward. He learns hour by hour over years in situations where language, referents, and meanings are in one system. His lessons are not intensive, compressed, and divorced from life, as "learning-to-read" situations tend to be. If a child in learning to read leans heavily on the oral language, this does not at all imply that oral language and reading language share the same psychological operations when the child has made the step to reading proficiency. In fact, if the child's reading ability does not soon grow beyond his oral-language capacity in terms of speed and processing, and volume and accuracy of information, his learning facility is questioned.

ON AN ECLECTIC MODEL OF READING

Building an eclectic model of reading presents problems because many of the most important component parts are missing. We do not know, for example, how an electrochemical impulse becomes "meaning." As one looks at the results of this literature search, he finds that much is known about a few things and little is known about a lot of things. Unfortunately, the little that is known includes some of the most necessary variables. Our assignment was to conjure up a model, but we are not sure of its value because of the paucity of information necessary to build a model. Although we located syntax-to-meaning models, we found no referent-to-meaning models. Such a potential model is easily conceived in verbal terms. Consider the following set of propositions:

1. Language is first learned by relating perceptual entities to verbal signs; i.e., words—oral, visual, or tactile.

2. At the beginning, the verbal sign is an attribute of the perceptual entity.

3. Abstract and figurative language develops as analogies, similes, etc., are constructed from perceptual entities and their verbal signs, and are assigned new verbal signs.

4. The morpheme is the unit of meaning.

5. Free morphemes and bound morphemes develop in different functional systems.

6. Bound morphemes and functors (words forming exhaustive categories; e.g., prepositions) are in the same functional system.

7. Speech and listening involve some different processes, as do writing and reading.

8. Oral language and written language are interrelated in that they use the same concept "storage."

9. Reading process and oral-language process diverge as the reader becomes more adept.

10. Access to concept storage becomes directly available for the graphic sign as reading skill increases.

11. Morphemes can be concatenated to form new units of meaning; e.g., house means something, white house means something else, large white house means something else again.

12. Morphemes and concatenations of morphemes can be related by drawing items from a learned set of relational classes.

       Example: a. white house
                  b. river road
                  c. the
                  d. on
                  e. The white house on the river road.

13. Syntactical rules are built from the relationship of entities and phenomena in the physical word.

14. Concatenation of morphemes and relations among classes are juxtaposed by the organism's conceptions of what the verbal signs mean in the physical world. Syntax as the linguists abstract that construct, then, is an artifact of the organism's information processing, not the cause of it.

There is some evidence in the literature for each of the propositions listed above. There is contradictory evidence in the literature for each of the propositions listed above. Our conclusion is that the time is not propitious for model building if the model is to arise from tested theory. There are too many contradictory findings which require empirical resolution in order that a consistent set of theoretical propositions might be drawn. Elaborate models cut out of whole cloth are of dubious value to science (see Kingston, 1971).

REFERENCES

Bloomfield, L. *Language.* New York: Holt, Rinehart, & Winston, 1946.

Brown, R. *Words and things.* New York: Free Press, 1958.

Calfee, R. C., & Venezky, R. L. Component skills in beginning reading. In K. S. Goodman & J. T. Fleming (Eds.), *Psycholinguistics and the teaching of reading.* Newark, Del.: International Reading Association, 1968.

Campbell, D. T., & Fiske, D. W. Convergent and discriminant validation by the multitrait-multimethod matrix. *Psychological Bulletin,* 1959, 56, 81–105.

Carroll, J. B. The analysis of reading instruction: Perspectives from psychology and linguistics. In E. R. Hilgard (Ed.), *Theories of learning and instruction.* Chicago: National Society for the Study of Education, 1964.

Chomsky, N. *Language and mind.* New York: Harcourt, Brace & World, 1968.

Downing, J. The development of linguistic concepts in children's thinking. *Research in the Teaching of Reading,* 1970, 4, 5–19.

Durkin, D. *Children who read early: Two longitudinal studies.* New York: Teachers College Press, 1966.

Fleming, J. T. A pilot study of children's perception of different speech forms. Paper read at the American Educational Research Association annual convention, Chicago, 1968.

Fries, C. C. *The structure of English.* New York: Harcourt, Brace & World, 1952.

Geyer, J. Perceptual systems in reading: A temporal eye-voice span constant. Unpublished doctoral dissertation, University of California, Berkeley, 1966.

Gibson, E. J. Perceptual learning and the theory of word perception. Paper read at the American Psychological Association annual convention, Miami, 1970. (a)

Gibson, E. J. A working paper summarizing theory-based research on reading and its implications for instruction. (Mimeographed) 1970. (b)

Goldman-Eisler, F. Hesitation and information in speech. *In Symposium on information theory.* London: Butterworths, 1961.

Goodman, K. S. A study of oral reading miscues that result in grammatical retransformations. Final Report, Project No. 7-E-219, U.S.O.E., June·1969.

Ilg, F. L., & Ames, L. B. Developmental needs in reading behavior. *Journal of Genetic Psychology,* 1950, 76, 291–312.

Jenkins, J. J. Meaningfulness and concepts: Concepts and meaningfulness. In H. J. Klausmeier & C. W. Harris (Eds.), *Analysis of concept learning.* New York: Academic Press, 1965:

Johnson, D. C. The effects of reading and punctuation variations upon reading comprehension. Unpublished master's thesis, University of Georgia, 1970.

Kingston, A. J. Ephemeral models and disjunctive categories. Paper read at the International Reading Association annual convention, Atlantic City, 1971.

Lefevre, C. A. *Linguistics and the teaching of reading.* New York: McGraw-Hill, 1964.

McCarthy, D. Language development in children. In L. Carmichael (Ed.), *Manual of child psychology.* New York: Wiley, 1954.

Marquardt, W. F. Language interference in reading. *The Reading Teacher,* 1964, 18, 214–218.

Meltzer, N. S., & Herse, R. The boundaries of written words as seen by first graders. *Journal of Reading Behavior.* 1969, 1, 3–13.

Morris, C. Foundations of the theory of signs. *International Encyclopedia of Unified Science* (Chicago), 1938, 2, 3–4.

Osgood, C. E., Suci, G., & Tannenbaum, P. The logic of semantic differentiation. In S. Saporta (Ed.), *Psycholinguistics.* New York: Holt, Rinehart, & Winston, 1961.

Piaget, J., & Inhelder, B. *The psychology of the child.* New York: Basic Books, 1969.

Quereshi, M. Y. Patterns of psycholinguistic development during early and middle childhood. *Educational and Psychological Measurement,* 1967, 27, 353–365.

Robinson, H. M. Factors which effect success in reading. *Elementary School Journal,* 1955, 55, 263–269.

Shannon, C. L., & Weaver, W. The mathematical theory of communication. In S. Saporta (Ed.), *Psycholinguistics.* New York: Holt, Rinehart, & Winston, 1961.

Soffietti, J. P. Why children fail to read: Linguistic analysis. *Harvard Educational Review,* 1955, 25, 63–84.

Stroud, J. Cybernetics. In H. Von Foerster (Ed.), *Transactions of the society.* New York: Macy, 1949.

Vygotsky, L. S. *Thought and language.* Cambridge, Mass.: M.I.T. Press, 1962.

Weaver, W. W. Units of measurement and units of language. Paper presented at symposium on the technology of written instruction. U.S. Office of Naval Research, Columbia University, New York, 1966.

Weaver, W. W. Linguistic assumptions and reading implications. In G. B. Schick & M. May (Eds.), *Eighteenth Yearbook of the National Reading Conference.* Milwaukee, Wis.: Marquette University Press, 1969. Pp. 107–112.

Weaver, W. W., Holmes, C. C., & Reynolds, R. R. The effect of reading variation and punctuation condition. *Journal of Reading Behavior,* 1970, 2, 75–84.

Weaver, W. W., & Kingston, A. J. Assessment of oral-written language behaviors with the Campbell-Fiske analysis procedure. Paper read at a symposium on the Information-Flow Theory of Learning to Read and the Reading Process at the American Educational Research Association annual convention, New York, 1971.

Wiener, N. *Cybernetics*. New York: Wiley, 1948.

II

EMPIRICAL STUDIES

OF READING AND LANGUAGE

While a graduate student Weaver read Rankin's 1965 paper on the cloze.[1] The implications for using the technique for the study of language intrigued him immediately. His dissertation, "An Examination of Some Differences in Oral and Written Language Using the Cloze Procedure," was his first effort to employ the technique.

Weaver was particularly interested in Rankin's efforts to measure separately lexical and structural (or functional) words. During much of his career he used these constructs to probe language and reading

1. E. F. Rankin, Jr., "The Cloze Procedure—Its Validity and Utility," in O. S. Causey and W. Eller, *Starting and Improving College Reading Programs,* Eighth Yearbook of the National Reading Conference (Ft. Worth: Texas Christian University Press, 1959), 131–44.

comprehension. A short abstract of his thesis is the first paper in this section. In his doctoral research Weaver investigated the relationship of cloze deletions to structural and lexical meanings. He followed up this study subsequently in the second paper titled "Structural-Lexical Predictability of Materials Which Predictor Has Previously Produced or Read."

The third paper, "A Factor Analysis of the Cloze Procedure and Other Measures of Reading and Language Ability" represents one of the earliest attempts to study the factor loadings of the cloze. This study subsequently has been widely discussed by other researchers, some of whom have found similar factors while others have not. Weaver apparently felt that subsequent factor analyses were of limited value, for he failed to follow up this study. Instead he intensified his search for discovering how readers achieve meaning. "The Effect of Direction of Context on Word Predictability" was presented at the National Reading Conference in December 1962.

The fifth paper in this section, "An Empirical Examination of Cloze Scores Derived from 'Natural' and 'Mutilated' Language Segments," might easily have been placed in Section I. It represents a serious attempt to describe the functions of the cloze procedure. "The Coding of Phrases" reports a series of experiments designed to study the effects of "chunking" on prepositional phrases. The seventh paper included in this section, "Some Differences in Encoding and Decoding Messages," is a follow-up of the one titled "Structural-Lexical Predictability of Materials Which Predictor Has Previously Produced or Read." This paper was presented at the American Educational Research Association Convention in New York, February 1967, and later was published in the *Journal of the Reading Specialist.*

Weaver's interest in the cloze, chunking, and similar techniques designed to study language was due in part to his belief that reading tests were inadequate for probing the psychological dimensions of the reading. The eighth and ninth papers included in Section II represent two of his efforts to probe those inadequacies more precisely. "Sources of Information for Responses to Reading Test Items" demonstrated empirically that reading test results are partly dependent on factors other than reading. This paper has been widely cited and discussed. "A Cross-Validation Study of the Relationship of Reading Test Items to Their Relevant Paragraphs" represents an extension and slight modification of the earlier investigation. The next article titled "The Effect of Reading Variation and Punctuation Conditions upon Reading Comprehension" reports the effect that varying the methods of reading (i.e., reading silently, reading silently but stating the last word in each sentence aloud, and reading aloud) and varying punctuation conditions have on reading comprehension.

In the paper "Affective Correlates of Reading Comprehension," Weaver makes what is for him a rare attempt to explore the relationship of personality to reading comprehension. Generally Weaver preferred to employ cognitive or linguistic constructs in his research. The discussion found in "Information-Flow Difficulty in Relation to Reading Comprehension" is more typical of his approach. This work examines the relationship between reading, cloze, rote learning, and personality variables yet it discusses the subject in terms of information processing.

The study reported in "Vertical and Horizontal Constraints in the Context Reading of Sentences" represents an attempt to modify the cloze procedure so that the constraints of the sentence as well as those of previous responses could be systematically studied. Tuinman, in assessing Weaver's contributions, believes Weaver's concepts of horizontal and vertical constraints are a major contribution to research.

The final two papers in this section are included to illustrate the interest Weaver developed during the latter years of his life in the beginning stages of reading. As mentioned in the introduction to section 1, Weaver became interested in trying to establish a base for assessing the oral language of first-grade children and then in utilizing the same units and methods for assessing the acquisition of reading skills of the identical subjects. He often decried the lack of common measures for this purpose. Heretofore in his work he had employed mature readers. Unfortunately death intervened and prevented him from fully exploiting his interest in the acquisition of reading by naive first-grade pupils.

An Examination of Some Differences in Oral and Written Language Using the Cloze Procedure

The research problem was to determine if differences existed in the ability of subjects to predict words systematically deleted from language passages presented orally and in writing. Such tests have been named "cloze" tasks.

Two groups of 80 subjects each (juniors and seniors enrolled at the University of Georgia) were employed in the study. The subjects were assigned to one of 16 sections (10 subjects per section) and administered eight cloze tests in various sequences. In each instance the last test administered was the experimental test. The cloze measures employed were constructed by deleting every tenth word and by deleting every tenth noun or main verbs in other language passages. Passages were administered both by aural and written presentation.

One group of subjects received cloze reading tests and cloze aural tests in a multiple-pass situation, i.e., the groups were allowed as many repetitions of the aural materials as desired. The other group received the cloze reading and aural tests in a single-pass situation, i.e., they were allowed to hear the aural materials once.

A $2 \times 2 \times 4$ analysis of variance design was used for the statistical analysis of the data. The multiple-pass and single-pass situations were analyzed separately.

The results indicated that although the multiple-pass aural tasks increased the predictability of the missing words, the relationships within the same situations were essentially the same. The central finding is that structural meaning, as shown by the predictability of "any-word" cloze, is conveyed significantly better by silent reading, while lexical meaning, as shown by the predictability of nouns and main verbs, is conveyed equally well by either listening or by silent reading. Whatever advantage allowed the greater predictability of structural meaning in the silent reading situation is in some manner lost in the listening situation. This loss may be due to the relatively small context necessary for supplying predictive information in the lexical case in most situations compared to the relatively larger context required to supply all of the structural meaning

An abstract of Wendell Weaver's unpublished doctoral dissertation. University of Georgia, Athens, Georgia, 1961.

available in a passage. The fact that large context trial elements can be analyzed only with difficulty in a listening situation may force the organism to use a strategy of depending on a smaller context in both structural and lexical situations. Thereby the subject loses the structural meanings which depend upon the large context.

The Effect of Direction of Context
on Word Predictability

The year 1948 was the advent of Norbert Wiener's *Cybernetics* and C. E. Shannon's *A Mathematical Theory of Communication*. Ideas put forth here and related ideas have proven a catalyst to the study of the statistical characteristics of language. One of the important concepts of Shannon was the concept of redundancy. Redundancy is the degree to which language is recodable or, from a more usable psychological standpoint, the degree to which language is predictable when only parts of it are known.

Somewhat the opposite of redundancy is uncertainty. The more uncertain a language unit, the more unpredictable it is. Uncertainty of language is greatly reduced when one has a particular language unit available for decoding. On the other hand, uncertainty is not entirely reduced for practically all language units are affected to a greater or less degree by the context of the language unit. That is, after a particular word in a sentence is known its meaning in many instances depends on other sentence elements in addition to the particular known word.

A word may have many relationships to its context. These relationships may be situational. In the statement "The man sat on the board" the interpretation of the word "board" would be different depending on whether the situation concerned sitting on wooden objects, or participation in an organizational hierarchy. In written language the interpretation of this relationship may depend entirely on words that follow the word "board." If the statement went on to read, "The man sat on the board whittling," our interpretation would be different than if the statement read, "The man sat on the board of directors."

It appears in this instance that we can say the word "board" is constrained in meaning by the words that follow it. If one were predicting words that follow the word "board" from the preceding context alone he would be more uncertain than if he had the context following the word to add information. With the context as follows, "The man sat on the

Published originally in *New Developments in Programs and Procedures in College-Adult Reading,* R. C. Staiger and C. Y. Melton, eds. The Thirteenth Yearbook of the National Reading Conference, 1963. Reprinted with the permission of the National Reading Conference.

board _____," one designates the context as unilateral. When the context takes the form "The man sat on the board _____ directors of the ABC Company," one designates the context as bilateral.

Not only is the predictability of words according to the direction of context an interesting problem of language structure; it has direct practical implications. Investigators of the possibilities of the mechanical translation of languages have found that the context following a target word has important uses for interpreting the target word. Reifler says, "When the first matching action has resulted in the supply of multiple alternative semantic information, it is necessary to delay the final matching and translation of an input form until the first matching of another coherent input form has yielded supplementary informa-tion"(3:153). In other words, to achieve predictability in this instance a bilateral context is needed.

That bilateral context allows better prediction has not been definitely shown however. In fact Garner (2:265) using the data of a study by Shepard (4) and another study by Carson (1) draws the opposite conclusion. Both of the latter studies were based on the uncertainty of letters within words rather than uncertainties of the words measured directly. Shepard measured word uncertainty in a bilateral setting (five words on either side of the deletion); Carson used a unilateral arrangement (five words preceding the deletion).

Garner concludes, "The fact that these two experimental conditions give word uncertainty so nearly the same suggests that with words the bilateral context is not particularly advantageous compared to the unilateral context" (2:266).

In the light of these latter two studies one might make the further observation that the unilateral context which allows predictability is the context *preceding* an omission. This would seem to have implications for the nature of language processing in the central nervous system, for if predictability is not increased, or uncertainty is not reduced, by context following a word then listening and reading should be similar communi-cation processes as far as the strategy of decoding is concerned. It would not be advantageous for a listener to lag behind a speaker's words as he seeks to interpret what is said, just as it would be of little avail for the reader to have knowledge of words on both sides of a target word. It is also difficult to see how the problem of the mechanical translator as outlined previously, arises at all.

The effect of laterality on context, then, is an important problem, not only theoretically, but practically. It has far reaching implications for knowledge of how the human organism communicates.

HYPOTHESIS

It is hypothesized that there is no significant difference in the ability of subjects to predict words in a bilateral context as opposed to the ability of subjects to predict words in a unilateral context. The five per cent level is taken as the criterion of the rejection of the hypothesis.

SUBJECTS

The subjects were 112 sophomores and juniors enrolled in psychology and education courses at Campbell College. They were divided into eight groups of fourteen subjects each in such a manner that the mean of each group on the comprehension section of the Cooperative Reading Test was not significantly different from the means of the other groups. This was assumed to be a control of reading ability.

PROCEDURE

Reading tests designated by their publishers for the fourth, seventh, tenth, and college grade levels were collected and a random selection made of one test at each grade level. Stimulus material was selected randomly from the expository paragraphs of each test selected. Each item of stimulus material consisted of ten context words and a standard size blank to be filled in. Four of the samples, one for each difficulty level, were arranged with the blank following the ten context words. This is the unilateral condition. The same items were then rearranged with five context words preceding and five context words following the blank. This was the bilateral condition.

The score for each subject was the number of blanks filled in with the exact word which was removed originally. There was no time limit and all subjects completed all blanks.

Variances were computed and Hartley's "largest F ratio test" was used to determine homogeneity of variance. The ratio of maximum variance to minimum variance was 5.32. Using Hartley's table, the 95 percentile value of F maximum in a set of eight mean squares each based on thirteen degrees of freedom was 6.01 (6). The variances were assumed therefore to come from the same population. No test of normality was attempted.

RESULTS

The data were analyzed using a randomized block design. The analysis of variance is presented in Table 1. The interaction mean square was analysed in terms of the "within subclasses" mean square. This proved significant. Thus the row and column analyses were carried out in terms of the interaction mean square.

Table 1. The analysis of variance

Variance	Degrees of freedom	Sum of squares	Mean square	F ratio
Between directionalities	1	270.60	270.60	13.81*
Among reading difficulty	3	96.00	32.00	1.63
Interaction	3	58.73	19.60	3.98*
Among subclasses	7	425.33	60.76	19.09*
Within subclasses	104	326.26	3.13	
Total	111	751.59		

*Significant at 5% level or greater. The interaction mean square is the denominator for the analysis of directionalities and reading difficulty.

The test of the hypothesis, then, is the ratio of the mean square of directionalities (rows) to the interaction mean square. This ratio is significant at the five per cent level of confidence and the null hypothesis is thus rejected. In this study the difference between the predictability of words in a unilateral context and in a bilateral context is considered a real difference.

DISCUSSION

The results of this study indicate that a context is most restrictive when a word is embedded within it. Bilateral context seems to improve the precision of language. This could be one difference between reading and listening. The listener may be at a disadvantage not only because he must use an internal memory operation to relate the parts of the language, but also because at any point in time the next word has high uncertainty. Using a bilateral context the reader can use following context as he needs it for precise interpretations.

One could make a good case for viewing listening and reading as more fundamentally different processes than is ordinarily assumed, especially different processes in the sense of requiring different strategies for successful completion.

The listener appears to be more of a "unilateral observer" than the reader. In many cases he cannot "look back" to "see" what has gone on before. In terms of this paper, he cannot reduce his uncertainty bilaterally to the same degree as may the reader. Listening is ordered on a time scale, and the redundancy of repetition is not always available. Reading is ordered spacially. While relatively short spans are surveyed at any particular time the eyes move rapidly (5), and it is usually feasible to regress to points of high uncertainty and use the surrounding context to reduce that uncertainty.

It should be noted however that in the reading situation bilaterality may be advantageous only for analyzing operations. It would seem that the reader proceeding rapidly gains little from bilateral context. It would appear that pauses long enough to permit bilateral scanning and the analyses carried out during that pause would be the strategy to which the values of bilaterality accrue.

SUMMARY

In this report it was hypothesized that direction of context, bilateral or unilateral, had no effect on the ability of subjects to predict words which were omitted from that context. This hypothesis was rejected.

Generally, the unilateral situation seems to increase the uncertainty of the context. Bilateral context seems to increase precision. The possibility that this result could be used to explore relationships between reading and listening was raised.

REFERENCES

1. Carson, D. H., "Letter Constraints Within Words in Printed English," *Kybernetik*, 1961, 1, 46–54. In Wendell R. Garner. *Uncertainty and Structure as Psychological Concepts.* New York: John Wiley, 1962.

2. Garner, Wendell R., *Uncertainty and Structure as Psychological Concepts.* New York: John Wiley, 1962.

3. Reifler, Erwin, "The Mechanical Determination of Meaning," in William N. Locke and A. Donald Booth (eds.) *Machine Translation of Languages.* New York: MIT Press and John Wiley, 1955.

4. Shepard, R. N., "Production of Constrained Associates and the Informational Uncertainty of the Constraint," American Journal of Psychology, 1962 (in press). In Wendell R. Garner, *Uncertainty and Structure as Psychological Concepts.* New York: John Wiley, 1962.

5. Taylor, Stanford E., "An Evaluation of Forty-One Trainees Who Had Recently Completed the 'Reading Dynamics' Program," In Emery P. Bliesmer and Ralph C. Staiger (eds.) *Problems, Programs and Projects in College-Adult Reading, Eleventh Yearbook of the National Reading Conference.* Milwaukee: National Reading Conference, 1961.

6. Walker, Helen M. and Joseph Lev, *Statistical Inference.* New York: Henry Holt, 1953.

A Factor Analysis of the Cloze Procedure and Other Measures of Reading and Language Ability

Psychologists, reading specialists and linguists have become increasingly concerned with the nature of language abilities. The techniques of factor analysis have been employed to study the basic components of various measures presumed to reflect language capability. This study explores a number of measures of language ability and attempts to isolate a set of fundamental components.

Taylor developed a number of tests by deleting words from a series of language passages. He hypothesized that the replacement of deleted words by a subject was analogous to the process of closure in Gestalt psychology and called the technique the "cloze procedure."[1] Although the similarity between Taylor's hypothesis and the classical Gestalt experiments has not been confirmed, a number of studies employing the procedure have been made. Taylor found the measure to be related to individual aptitudes,[2] Rankin found the procedure to be related to reading ability[3] and Osgood[4] and Jenkins[5] used it to measure stereotypy of verbal production.

Except for stereotype studies, the use of the cloze procedure appears to duplicate the results obtained by seemingly more pertinent and usable instruments. As a measure of aptitude, the cloze procedure has only its ease of construction to recommend it and, because the exact relationship of the word deleted to the kind of material deleted is not known, this ease may be illusory. When nouns and main verbs (lexical deletions) are the only words deleted, there appears to be a high correlation between the subject's scores on the cloze tests and on objective reading tests covering similar materials.[6] As the cloze procedure represents an awkward type of measurement, correlates highly with other types of measurements and appears to have a low "face validity,"[7] it seems more important to investigate the degree to which it varies from other more traditional and better standardized instruments. Unless the cloze procedure can be shown to elicit variance from some source other than those of more commonly used reading and language objective tests, its use is likely to remain more of an interesting curiosity than a valuable research and measurement tool.

(Co-authored with Albert J. Kingston.) Published originally in the *Journal of Communications*, 1963, 13, 252–261. Reprinted with permission of the *Journal of Communications*.

Two types of cloze deletions have been widely used: structural, in which every nth word in a passage is deleted and lexical, in which every nth noun or main verb (and rarely, adjective) is deleted. Structural deletions correlate significantly more highly with vocabulary and reading comprehension sections of the Diagnostic Reading Test than do lexical deletions; lexical deletions correlate significantly more highly with the story comprehension section of the DRT than do structural deletions.[8] Structural deletions have been shown to be easier to complete when presented for reading than when presented for listening, while lexical deletions are of equal difficulty whether read or listened to.[9]

This study explores performance on both reading cloze tests and listening cloze tests, and is designed to determine the proportions of variance which can be assigned to factors basic to more commonly employed tests of vocabulary, language aptitude and reading ability.

METHOD

Subjects

The subjects were 160 members of the junior class of the University of Georgia. The group was evenly distributed over the fall, winter and spring quarters.

Procedure

Eight cloze tests were presented in random order to small groups of eight to twelve subjects. Each test contained 40 cloze units for the subjects to complete. In each test the exact word removed had to be supplied by the subjects, and the total score was the sum of the number of correctly replaced words. Each cloze test, whether read or listened to, had a 30-minute time limit. The cloze reading tests were mimeographed and the cloze listening tests were taped.

When the subject was taking a listening test, he was allowed to hear the tape completely through. He was then allowed to ask for repetition of the context of any cloze unit by asking for the cloze unit number. The entire sentence context of the cloze unit which was requested was then reread by the examiners. In all readings by the examiners and by tape, four-second pauses were used to indicate deletions. All requests for repetitions were granted. At the end of the session of repeated readings the tape was rerun in its entirety.

The other tests used in this analysis were administered using the instructions for administration in the pertinent test manuals. All tests used in the factor analysis and the numbers which are used to designate them throughout the study are listed and described below.

1. *The Davis Reading Test.* This is a test of reading comprehension. It is normally scored to yield a "speed of reading" and a "level of reading" score.[10] In this analysis the total raw score was used exclusively.

2. *The MLAT Number Learning Subtest.* This is a subtest of the Modern Language Aptitude Test, as are tests 3, 4, 5 and 6 to be described below. These tests were chosen as samples of various symbolizing abilities involved in language aptitude. This particular subtest has a large memory component.[11]

3. *The MLAT Phonetic Script Subtest.* This subtest is a measure of sound-symbol associative ability.[12]

4. *The MLAT Spelling Clues Subtest.* The authors remark that this subtest depends on English vocabulary knowledge.[13]

5. *The MLAT Words in Sentences Subtest.* This subtest has to do with the sensitivity to grammatical structure, although it does not require a recall of grammatical rules.[14]

6. *The MLAT Paired Associates Subtest.* This is a test of rote memory.

7. *STEP Listening Test.* This is a test in the Sequential Tests of Educational Progress battery. It is the easiest of the tests in this series and correlates highly with the School and College Ability Test, verbal section.[15] It is designed as a test of listening comprehension. The raw score, rather than the standard score conversion, was used in this analysis.

8. *The Ohio State Psychological Examination—Vocabulary.* This subtest is a test of same-opposite relationships.[16]

9. *The Ohio State Psychological Examination—Word Relations.* This subtest is an analogies test.

10. *The Ohio State Psychological Examination—Reading Comprehension.* This subtest is a reading comprehension test which is designed to sample sophisticated comprehension skills.

11. *Cloze I—A Structural Deletion of Essay Material.* The subject reads the material silently.

12. *Cloze II—A Lexical Deletion of Essay Material.* The subject reads the material silently.

13. *Cloze III—A Structural Deletion of a Speech.* The subject reads the material silently.

14. *Cloze IV—A Lexical Deletion of a Speech.* The subject reads the material silently.

15. *Cloze V—A Structural Deletion of Essay Material.* The subject listens to the material read aloud.

16. *Cloze VI—A Lexical Deletion of Essay Material.* The subject listens to the material read aloud.

17. *Cloze VII—A Structural Deletion of a Speech.* The subject listens to the material read aloud.

18. *Cloze VIII—A Lexical Deletion of a Speech.* The subject listens to the material read aloud.

Test scores of all subjects were recorded on IBM work sheets, and IBM 709 Program FAR 1 was used to compute a Varimax (orthogonal) factor analysis and rotation.[17]

The rotation was an iterative procedure. A case of the program was chosen in which "the number of factors to be rotated are equal to the number of eigenvalues of the correlation matrix (with ones in the diagonals) which are greater than unity."[18]

RESULTS

The means, standard deviations and possible scores on each test are given in Table 1.

Correlation coefficients are given in Table 2.

Table 3 is the rotated factor matrix.

As may be seen, the common variance is subsumed under three factors.

Table 1. Means, standard deviations, and possible scores
of tests used in the factor analysis

Test	Mean	Standard deviation	Possible score
1. Davis reading	36.8	13.4	80
2. Number Learning, MLAT	26.4	8.7	43
3. Phonetic Script, MLAT	21.4	4.7	30
4. Spelling Clues, MLAT	14.2	8.1	50
5. Words in Sentences, MLAT	25.5	8.7	45
6. Paired Associates, MLAT	16.7	5.4	24
7. Listening, STEP	20.3	7.3	72
8. Vocabulary, Ohio State Psy	16.2	6.0	30
9. Word Relations, Ohio State Psy	32.5	12.8	60
10. Reading Comprehension, Ohio State Psy	33.9	11.2	60
11. Cloze I	21.4	4.5	40
12. Cloze II	16.1	4.1	40
13. Cloze III	18.1	4.6	40
14. Cloze IV	12.9	4.1	40
15. Cloze V	15.3	4.6	40
16. Cloze VI	12.7	4.4	40
17. Cloze VII	15.2	5.2	40
18. Cloze VIII	15.4	4.6	40

Table 2. Correlation coefficients

	2	3	4	5	6	7	8	9	10	11	12	13	14	15	16	17	18
1.	.38	.46	.58	.50	.39	.77	.69	.61	.75	.25	.36	.51	.21	.49	.50	.56	.60
2.		.47	.30	.51	.49	.35	.42	.49	.43	.27	.29	.34	.22	.22	.30	.44	.39
3.			.53	.52	.40	.49	.50	.55	.51	.27	.28	.46	.14	.36	.31	.46	.44
4.				.37	.37	.50	.54	.53	.48	.31	.26	.46	.16	.40	.41	.49	.50
5.					.52	.43	.46	.63	.56	.23	.28	.44	.19	.38	.31	.46	.41
6.						.38	.36	.45	.42	.21	.21	.32	.11	.16	.24	.32	.37
7.							.58	.57	.69	.31	.39	.51	.16	.48	.45	.50	.54
8.								.81	.73	.31	.40	.54	.20	.42	.50	.57	.57
9.									.76	.32	.43	.56	.28	.47	.42	.55	.46
10.										.33	.45	.61	.29	.52	.53	.61	.58
11.											.49	.50	.27	.43	.41	.41	.40
12.												.61	.47	.49	.47	.60	.44
13.													.47	.57	.53	.69	.58
14.														.45	.44	.45	.33
15.															.57	.60	.55
16.																.64	.54
17.																	.69

Factor II is clearly defined, with no ambiguities. Factor I is only slightly less well defined, some ambiguity being introduced by Cloze III. Factor III, though less clearly defined, appears interpretable.

DISCUSSION

Factor I has its heaviest loadings on the reading comprehension, listening and vocabulary tests. This is apparently the verbal comprehension factor which one would expect from tests of this kind. The high loading of the vocabulary test on this factor and its relatively low loading on the other two factors help establish the verbal comprehension factor.[19]

The fact that the listening test had a high loading on this factor and negligible loading on the other two factors indicates the heavy involvement of the test with the elements of reading comprehension. The fact that parts of the listening test require reading may have some bearing on this loading.

Tests made up of cloze blanks which are filled in by reading have low loading on this factor. Test 13, a structural deletion of material intended to be spoken, is the only exception to this. It seems to group with the cloze

Table 3. Rotated factor matrix

| | Factors | | | |
Tests	I	II	III	Communalities
1. Davis Reading	.84	.19	.22	.80
2. Number Learning, MLAT	.14	.23	.79	.69
3. Phonetic Script, MLAT	.47	.14	.55	.54
4. Spelling Clues, MLAT	.66	.17	.24	.53
5. Words in Sentences, MLAT	.35	.17	.70	.65
6. Paired Associates, MLAT	.22	.06	.75	.62
7. Listening, STEP	.78	.20	.20	.69
8. Vocabulary, Ohio State Psy	.75	.24	.31	.71
9. Word Relations, Ohio State Psy	.63	.26	.50	.71
10. Reading Comprehension, Ohio State Psy	.73	.32	.34	.75
11. Cloze I	.13	.63	.17	.44
12. Cloze II	.19	.76	.16	.64
13. Cloze III	.42	.67	.25	.69
14. Cloze IV	−.03	.76	.09	.59
15. Cloze V	.47	.65	.01	.64
16. Cloze VI	.45	.63	.05	.60
17. Cloze VII	.47	.66	.27	.72
18. Cloze VIII	.56	.49	.22	.60
Σ^2	4.83	3.93	2.84	

tests completed by listening. Cloze tests completed by listening show a moderate loading on the verbal comprehension factor.

Factor II is a cloze factor. All the cloze tests load moderately to high on this factor, whether they are structural or lexical deletions, or presented by speech or print. Taylor has shown a correlation of −0.87 between this ability to supply the proper words to fill cloze units and "entropy" measures.[20] That is, the more possible choices (choices which fit the situation according to the structure of the language), the greater the difficulty of filling the cloze unit with the exact word of the original text. The fact that the correct word can be supplied many times is an indication of the predictability which is supplied by the context of the cloze unit. If language is some 50 to 75% redundant, as most estimates assert, cloze units should be completed about this proportion of the time. As indicated by Table 1, this level of predictability is attained only on test 11 (Cloze I). Most redundancy estimates are arrived at, however, by guessing letters rather than by guessing words. The expectation that words would be less redundant than letters (and thus less predictable) seems justified. The underlying ability here seems to be the recognition of redundancy characteristics of language. This factor is called therefore "redundancy utilization."

Factor III is loaded on all subtests of the Modern Language Aptitude Test except the "Spelling Clues" subtest. The highest loadings are "Number Learning" and "Paired Associates," both having high memory components. The "Words in Sentences" subtest of the MLAT loads moderately on this factor, as does the Ohio State Word Relations subtest. All of these tests seem related to symbol manipulation by retention and retrieval processes, and this could be the common element.

This factor apparently goes beyond what we ordinarily call "rote memory." It is difficult to see how an "analogies" loading on this factor can be assigned to "rote memory" as it is usually conceived. The "Words in Sentences" subtest does not seem directly connected to "rote memory." Even in the "Number Learning" subtest, the memory task is more variable than that usually ascribed to "rote memory." It seems proper to make a distinction here. The distinction is indicated by labeling the factor "rote memory, flexible retrieval": the "flexible" being intended to point out that a wider range of retrieval processes seem to be operating than those which accompany the factor commonly designated "rote memory." There is little loading of cloze tests on this factor.

CONCLUSION

This analysis was carried out to examine the relationship of cloze tests to standard tests of reading, listening and language-symbolizing ability. The relationships of the cloze tests used to the standard tests used are from little relationship to moderate relationship. The cloze tests are related only moderately to the verbal comprehension factor. This is unexpected, since the literature of the subject to date has emphasized the close relationship of structural deletions to standard intelligence tests and of lexical deletions to objective reading tests. Yet three of these reading cloze tests have insignificant loadings on the verbal comprehension factor. There is a moderate connection between the cloze tests presented by speaking and the verbal comprehension factor. This connection is apparently in the mode or channel of communication, since it is absent in the reading channel condition.

Factor II clearly delineates the cloze tests. As the second major source of common variance it indicates that an aptitude, distinct from verbal

Table 4. Communalities and Flanagan split-half reliabilities
of cloze tests used in the factor analysis

Tests	Communalities	Reliabilities
11. Cloze I	.44	.90
12. Cloze II	.64	.86
13. Cloze III	.69	.84
14. Cloze IV	.59	.58
15. Cloze V	.64	.78
16. Cloze VI	.60	.76
17. Cloze VII	.72	.74
18. Cloze VIII	.60	.80

comprehension, underlies at least the cloze tests presented by reading. In
Table 4 the communalities of the cloze tests are compared to split-half
reliabilities computed by Flanagan's formula.[21]

The cloze tests, excepting 14 and 17, have communalities short of their
reliability coefficients, indicating a considerable amount of specific variance not explained in this analysis. Only further analyses which include
factors not found in this battery of tests can account for this variance.

The MLAT was included in this analysis as a group of subtests which
seemed to tap a variety of abilities connected with the symbolizing
processes of language. It was felt that some of these abilities would also be
related to those abilities used to complete cloze deletions. There is little
indication from this analysis that this is true. Factor III contains most of
the variance supplied by the MLAT and little else.

The central implication of this analysis is that cloze tests of varied kinds
are more related to each other than to the other two factors isolated by
this analysis, verbal comprehension and "rote memory, flexible retrieval."
It is also important to note that there is much specific variance connected
with the cloze procedure which is unexplained by this analysis. Further
attempts to relate this specific variance to other variances seem to offer
interesting possibilities.

SUMMARY

By means of an orthogonal factor analysis, three factors were extracted
from 18 tests of reading, listening, language symbol manipulation and
mutilated language completions. These factors were identified as verbal

comprehension, redundancy utilization and (much more tentatively) "rote memory, flexible retrieval." Cloze tests are most closely related to redundancy utilization.

REFERENCES

1. W. L. Taylor, "Application of 'Cloze' and Entropy Measures to the Study of Contextual Constraints in Continuous Prose" (unpublished Ph.D. dissertation, University of Illinois, Urbana, 1954), p. 8.

2. W. L. Taylor, "Cloze Readability Scores as Indices of Individual Differences in Comprehension and Aptitude," *Journal of Applied Psychology*, 41 (1957), 12–26.

3. E. F. Rankin, "An Evaluation of the Cloze Procedure as a Technique for Measuring Reading Comprehension" (unpublished Ph.D. dissertation, University of Michigan, Ann Arbor, 1957), p. 57.

4. Charles E. Osgood, "Some Effects of Motivation on Style of Encoding," *Style in Language,* ed. Thomas A. Sebeok, Massachusetts Institute of Technology and John Wiley & Sons, (New York, 1960), 293–306.

5. James J. Jenkins, "Communality of Associations as an Indicator of More General Patterns of Verbal Behavior," *Style,* ed. Sebeok, 307–329.

6. E. F. Rankin, Jr., "The Cloze Procedure—Its Validity and Utility," *Starting and Improving College Reading Programs,* ed. Oscar S. Causey and William Eller, Eighth Yearbook of the National Reading Conference, Texas Christian University Press (Fort Worth, 1959), 131–138.

7. Ibid., p. 135.

8. Rankin, "The Cloze Procedure," p. 134.

9. W. W. Weaver, "An Examination of Some Differences in Oral and Written Language Using the Cloze Procedure" (unpublished Ed.D. dissertation, University of Georgia, Athens, 1961), p. 93.

10. Frederick B. Davis and Charlotte Croon Davis, *Davis Reading Test Manual,* The Psychological Corporation (New York, 1957), p. 4.

11. John B. Carroll and Stanley M. Sapon. *Modern Language Aptitude Test Manual,* The Psychological Corporation (New York, 1957), p. 4.

12. Ibid.

13. Ibid.

14. Ibid.

15. Althea Berry et al., *Sequential Tests of Educational Progress—Technical Report,* Educational Testing Service (Princeton, 1957), p. 12.

16. Herbert A. Toops, *The Ohio State University Psychological Test,* Science Research Associates (Chicago, 1941), p. 1.

17. The authors wish to thank the computing center of Florida State University for the use of their computer for this analysis.

18. This program originated as BIMD 17, from the Division of Biostatistics, Department of Preventive Medicine and Public Health, U.C.L.A. The quotation is from the mimeographed write-up of this program.

19. Benjamin Fructer, *Introduction to Factor Analysis,* D. Van Nostrand Company (Princeton, 1954), p. 150.

20. Taylor, "Application of 'Cloze,' " p. 94.

21. J. P. Gulford, *Psychometric Methods,* McGraw-Hill Book Company (New York, 1954), p. 379.

The Coding of Phrases: An Experimental Study

The central purpose of this paper is to report a series of experiments which examines the effects of sequence on the "chunking," i.e., coding, of the prepositional phrase.

Quastler and Wulff had typists type sequences of 100 symbols each, chosen randomly from sets of 4, 8, 16, or 32 alternatives. The informational transmission rate increased steadily with the number of alternatives (15). The same essential linearity has been demonstrated for "disjunctive reaction time minus simple reaction time" by Hick and Hyman (5, 6); for continuous information transmission with subjects responding to patterns of lights by Klemmer and Muller (9); and again by Quastler and Wulff using the transmissions of expert pianists (15).

On the other hand, in the measurement of recall from short-term memory, the number of items recalled tend to be unrelated to the size of the set of items from which the recalled items are drawn. The channel capacity of immediate memory is apparently small in view of the transmission tasks it must perform. George Miller's idea is that this lack of capacity is bridged by a process called "chunking," and that the operation of this process is responsible for the lack of invariance under information (11).

A common illustration of this process involves the immediate memory span for digits. This span is about seven digits. By recoding sets of three digits and representing these three digits by a new symbol, immediate memory may be expanded to handle from 21 to 24 digits (12). There is some interference from the more complex process of coding itself, but the immediate memory is expanded by the coding device so that some three times the amount of information is handled with the same channel capacity. Chunking, then, implies that multiple units are recoded into one unit in some fashion so as to conserve space or time or both.

A similar lack of invariance under information has been demonstrated for the rate of transmission of verbal information. Sumby and Pollack acquainted subjects with a restricted vocabulary of from 2 to 256 words (16). The informational content therefore varied from 1 to 8 bits. The increase in average transmission time for the lower information content was very slight. Attneave suggests that similar principles may apply to

(Co-authored with Nelson Garrison.) Published originally in the *Journal of Communications*, 1966, 16, 192–198. Reprinted with the permission of the *Journal of Communications*.

both rate of transmission and to immediate memory, because both transmission and immediate memory require the storage of information for brief intervals (1). Certain memory operations are required even for operations such as speech, reading, tracking, discriminating, in fact, for most psychological processes. Both recall studies and rate of transmission studies should give information about storage and retrieval processes.

Even though recall and rate of transmission are not invariate under information, the human organism operates as a communications channel which does not have a constant rate of transmission (except possibly for the articulation parameter) and which must have a limiting rate of transmission. When information is processed through a human channel, the highest rates of processing which have been demonstrated to occur are associated with oral reading (10). Thus measured, human processing capacity is about 40–50 bits/second. A study by Pierce and Karlin was designed "to provide an evaluation of and understanding of the limitations on the information rate of the human channel" (14). It was concluded that the important determinants of words were familiarity, as measured by the frequency in printed materials, and the length of the words in number of syllables.

Pierce and Karlin used as stimulus materials lists of single words in a vertical row of 12 groups of 5 words each, a total of 60 words per page. This technique would apparently eliminate most sequential dependency between individual words. Their study makes no comment, therefore, on the effect of sequence on rate of transmission. It does provide a method for studying information transmission and, through the relationship of transmission to storage, a method for studying storage and retrieval characteristics of the human organism.

A study of Fodor and Bever indicates that linguistic segments which are related in a constituent analysis of sentences have psychological reality (2). They demonstrate that clicks sounded within segments marked by formal constituent structure analysis are heard at the nearest major syntactic boundary. Johnson also demonstrates the psychological reality of immediate constituents by showing sharp spikes in the "transitional error probability" at sentence element transitions which also represent transitions between functional behavioral units (7). He uses a paired-associates learning task with digits serving as the stimulus member and sentences as the response member. "Transitional error probability" is calculated from recall errors. This paper examines the psychological reality of language segments by choosing a particular segment, the prepositional phrase, and hypothesizing that latency of coding will occur when the elements of the phrase are out of sequence.

The experiment began with the simple observation that one piece of evidence for a "chunking" operation would be a demonstration that latency of the "chunks" is decreased in relation to the latency of the individual verbal units, or, what would amount to the same thing, that units in a verbal sequence in one direction are not handled at the same transmission rate as a rearrangement of the sequence. A previous study by Miller demonstrates a deterioration in intelligibility of listening in reversed grammatical sequences (13). The present study was designed to examine the effect of reversed sequences of prepositional phrases on the latency of reading those phrases.

The prepositional phrase is a very familiar grammatical unit in the English language. Jones, Goodman, and Wepman, classifying a speech sample of 34 thousand words from 12 adults, found 31 prepositions accounting for 11% of all the occurrences of words (8). In most cases the preposition is followed by its object so this is the approximate percentage of prepositional phrases.

The prepositional phrase in the sentence, "The majority of the men were married," is in a typical context. As in this sentence, it is quite common in English for the prepositional phrases to be preceded by a noun which in another context might well serve as the object of the preposition. In the sentence above "majority of" is such a case; in fact, to take the first part of the sample sentence, "the majority of," is to choose the *elements* of a prepositional phrase lacking only the attribute of order. Conversely, the prepositional phrase itself, "of the men," often appears in a rearranged order in sentences beginning, "the men of." Although correlated frequencies may be shown, one does not think of phrases of the form, "the majority of," as entities. Pauses in reading, for example, would be rare after "of" in "the majority of."

It is not that the "of" in this example has no semantic function. The speaker of English has no difficulty discriminating "the majority of," "the majority to," "the majority from," etc. There is, of course, the sense of incompleteness, but there is no obvious reason this should produce more incompleteness and greater latency than that of "of the majority," "to the majority," "from the majority," etc.

These characteristics of the natural language were used in this study as follows. Prepositional phrases and phrases ending with a preposition were selected randomly from four "levels of difficulty"—a sixth grade basal reader, a sixth grade science text, a novel by Steinbeck, and several issues of *Science*. Phrases of the type "of the dog" appearing in the source material were selected alternately with phrases of the type "the dog of." Eight lists of 60 phrases each were constructed from these materials and arranged for presentation according to the reading pattern of the Pierce and Karlin study mentioned earlier. Four of the lists, one for each level of difficulty, were phrases arranged with the preposition first—"of the dog, on the mountain," etc. The other four lists were phrases with the same constituent words but with the preposition occurring last—"the dog of, the mountain on," etc. Information content of the two types of lists was estimated by the Shannon guessing procedure and by diagram and trigram counts. In no case were the computations more than a tenth bit apart. These lists, in random order, were given to forty subjects with instructions to read the list aloud as rapidly as possible.

Three lists of 60 monosyllabic English words were interspersed after the second, fourth, and sixth experimental lists read by the subjects in order to ascertain whether or not fatigue effects seemed to be affecting results. These lists were always presented in the same order.

Separate analysis of variance for correlated measures were run on the experimental lists and on the monosyllabic words. The difference in reading time for the three lists of monosyllabic words was not significant.

A three-way analysis of variance was computed on the experimental lists—prepositional position by difficulties by subjects (see Table 1). There was a statistically significant difference between the speed of reading the lists of phrases when the preposition is first and when the preposition is last; a statistically significant difference in reading speed for the difficulty levels; and a statistically significant difference in reading speed among subjects. All interactions were non-significant.

The increased latency involved in reading lists of phrases with the preposition last is apparently an effect of the sequence alone. It is not related to the difficulty of the materials or to the processing speed of the subject.

On the completion of this experiment it was noted that the experimental lists with the preposition first often had a vowel as the first articulatory

Table 1. Analysis of variance of prepositional phrases
and their reversals

Variance	Degrees of freedom	Sum of squares	Mean square	F ratio
Preposition "position"	1	968.11	968.11	62.06*
Difficulties	3	6,284.58	2,094.86	134.29*
Subjects	39	19,100.80	489.76	31.39*
Preposition "position" × difficulty	3	29.01	9.67	0.62
Preposition "position" × subjects	39	722.39	18.52	1.19
Difficulty × subjects	117	1,370.43	11.71	0.75
Difficulty × subjects × preposition "position"	117	2,182.48	18.90	1.21

*Statistically significant at the 5% level of confidence.

element while the lists with the preposition last rarely had this attribute. Two lists were then made using the same prepositions ("by" and "for") at the beginning of each phrase. Each prepositional phrase and its reversal then began with a consonant. The difference in reading time remained significant.

Sixteen different lists were then constructed and presented to subjects in random order except for the lists fifteen and sixteen, prepositions first and last respectively. The difference in reading speed was still present for lists fifteen and sixteen. The effect disappears rapidly, however, with the rereading of the same lists. Using two of the original lists, by the fourth reading there were no significant differences. The same subjects then read the sixteen different lists the next day, and there was a significant difference on lists fifteen and sixteen.

Some attempts have been made to locate more specifically the position within the phrases or between the phrases where longer pauses are occurring. Considering the experiments of the English linguist Goldman-Eisler, longer pauses occurring before lexical items were expected, and since in the reversed phrases the lexical items came first, these pauses were expected to be longer than usual (3, 4). In other words, the pauses in speech which Goldman-Eisler has shown to be related to the amount of information at a particular locus in a passage were expected to have a sequential component. Therefore, an interaction between sequence and difficulty was expected which did not appear. Apparently the subjects attempt to read the lists as continuous prose, and thus over the entire set of phrases they make about the same length of pause before the lexical item no matter the position of the item.

The measurement of articulation time within the phrases was attempted also. Some of these times are less than 1/10th second and "home-made" equipment was used, but even so, a very interesting general pattern seems to be emerging. When the phrase "of the flag" is articulated by one particular subject for example, the word "of" consumes approximately one and a half times the articulation time of "the flag." On the other hand, for the same subject speaking "the flag of," "of" consumes only 1/10 the articulation time of "the flag." This effect in different proportions occurs in phrase after phrase. It is as if elements which "lead" in the sequence consume more time, but they also allow a reduction in time for elements which follow. Thus, when "the flag" is first, the latency of "of" is decreased over the latency of "of" when it occurs first. When the preposition "leads," however, there is a greater proportionate reduction of latency for elements which follow than is the case when another grammatical category "leads."

An important question that still has no adequate answer in language studies is, "What are the small, frequent words in the language for?" The findings of this study support the idea—one should not presume to use the word "theory" as yet—that these highly redundant elements perform a "programming" or planning function which has to do with the retrieval and storage of lexical elements.

REFERENCES

1. Attneave, Fred. Applications of Information Theory to Psychology, New York: Henry Holt and Co., 1959, p. 78.

2. Fodor, J. A., and F. G. Bever. "The Psychological reality of linguistic segments," Journal of Learning and Verbal Behavior, Vol. 4, No. 5, October, 1965.

3. Goldman-Eisler, Freida. "The Predictability of Words," Language and Speech, September, 1958, 226–231.

4. Goldman-Eisler, Freida. "Speech Production and the Predictability of Words in Context," Quarterly Journal of Experimental Psychology. Vol. X, Pt. 2, May, 1958.

5. Hick, W. E. "On the rate gain of information," Quarterly Journal of Experimental Psychology, 1952, 4, 11–26.

6. Hyman, R. "Stimulus information as a determinant of reaction time," Journal of Experimental Psychology, 1953, 45, 188–196.

7. Johnson, Neal F. "A model of sentence generation," Paper presented at symposium on Psychological Aspects of Language Structure APA, Los Angeles, 1964.

8. Jones, Lyle V., Morris F. Goodman, and Joseph M. Wepman. "The Classification of parts of speech for the characterization of Aphasia," Language and Speech, Vol. 6, Pt. 2, April–June, 1963, 94–107.

9. Klemmer, E. T., and P. F. Muller. "The rate of handling information: Key pressing response to light patterns," HFORL MEMO Report, No. 34, March, 1953.

10. Licklider, J. C. R., K. N. Stevens, and J. R. M. Hayes. "Studies in Speech, Hearing and Communication, Technical Report, Acoustics Laboratory," MIT, September 30, 1954.

11. Miller, G. A. "The Magical Number Seven, Plus or Minus Two," Psychological Review, 1956, 63, 81–97.

12. Miller, G. A. Psychology: The Science of Mental Life, New York: Harper and Row, 1962.

13. Miller, G. A. "Some Psychological Studies of Grammar," American Psychologist, 1962, 17, 748–762.

14. Pierce, J. R., and J. E. Karlin. "Reading Rates and the Information Rate of a Human Channel," The Bell System Technical Journal, March, 1957.

15. Quastler, H. and V. J. Wulff. "Human Performance in information transmission, Part One: simple sequential routinized tasks." Manuscript.

16. Sumby, W. H. and I. Pollack. "Short-time processing of information." HFORL Report, Tr-54-6, January, 1954.

The Retrieval of Learning Sets
by the External Display of Reading Materials

One gets the impression that teachers of reading, more often than not, have thought of reading as a display of materials from which the reader extracts some *quality* called "meaning." Of course reading teachers, by the nature of their task, are well aware that there is another level of analysis of the materials relative to the letters and words of the language. This analysis is the discrimination of the particular sign from the set of other signs, as distinct from the sign's function or its referent. Some teachers add another process when the reader has the intention to learn material he is reading.

In general, eye-movement variations may be noted for each of these reading processes. When the reader is concentrating on perceiving letters and words there is a concentration of fixations at the particular locus of the letter or word. When the reader is retrieving parts of his previous learnings, fixations are regular and relatively short in time. There are few regressions. When the reader is learning, there are vertical and horizontal excursions to locate materials further afield than that on the line being read. There are regressions and concentrations on content words. Difficulties arise, however, when one attempts to quantify these impressions. In the first place, confoundings appear. Then too, about 40 percent of the words do not appear as directly focused upon. It is impossible to tell at any particular fixation the area of acuity which will allow recognition. Fixations appear between words. To complete the confusion, the reliability of the placement of the central focus which is the reference point for measurement is seldom available. Obviously, to date, eye-movement photography has raised many more questions than it has answered (4, 5, 6, 8, 9, 12, 14, 24).

If we consider the gross characteristics of eye-movement photographs, however, even the more reliable type which do not attempt to locate eye fixations relative to a specific part of a text (24), it is apparent that there are variations in the number and length of fixations when a particular individual reads. While this is not an astounding observation in itself, the

(Co-authored with A. C. Bickley.) Published originally in *Junior College and Adult Reading Programs–Expanded Fields*, G. B. Schick and M. M. May, eds. The Sixteenth Yearbook of the National Reading Conference, 1967. Reprinted with the permission of the National Reading Conference.

fact of variation raises a crucial question for the understanding of the reading process, namely, where is the locus of the control of the movements? If the movements are not all the same size (as they are not) i.e. if they do not cover the same number of significant units each time, some control must operate to determine what units to cover, when to regress, when inaccuracy of fixation has occurred, etc. It is apparent, from the rate with which these decisions have to be made, that conscious control of these parameters is impossible at typical reading speeds (15, 16).

There have been attempts to locate the control of eye-movements in the language display itself. The idea of "training" eye-movement is closely connected with the assumption that reading is controlled by information already present in appropriate units on the printed page. One might say then, language is read word by word and mean by this, that each printer's space marks out a separate language unit which must be processed directly from the display. Eye-movement photographs do not indicate fixations at every word; in fact, as we noted before, some 40 percent of the words are skipped. This apparent skipping might be an artifact, however, of the inability to determine how far from focus peripheral acuity is extending. The number of words skipped by central focus increases continuously and (using percentage of total words as the measure) linearly, from 5 percent of six-letter words skipped, to 75 percent of two-letter words skipped in some 300-lines of eye-movement photographs we examined. Nevertheless if the length of the acuity sufficient for perception were controlling one could count letter-space intervals between fixations and obtain a "near-constant." If one objects that this constant does not appear because parts of words are not meaningful units to process, and thus only a particular part of the "sufficient" acuity span is processed, this explanation itself assigns control to some locus other than the language text.

Taylor asserts that to read "with complete accuracy" one must "see" all the words he reads. The difficulty here is with the word "see." There is the "seeing" of proof-reading where an accurate job requires ignoring the implications of words in order to note the accuracy of their construction. There is the "seeing" of reading a "who-done-it" where the intent to comprehend a puzzling situation is paramount. Here, the situations and their verbal elaborations are ordinarily well known to the reader; it is the particular arrangement that counts and the details of the input of that information are not even thought of. There is the "seeing" of reading Whitehead and Russell's *Principia Mathematica* where practically every sentence, for many of us, is so laden with semantic information that a constant learning is required to keep up with the text.

Many psychologists would classify the above activities as complex processes with elaborate central nervous system controls. It is reasonable to argue, however, that all of reading cannot be a central nervous system operation. Lashley (15) observed that in a rapid sequential operation such as speech production, the discrete acts making up the production of long, rapid sequences have shorter latencies than the maximum transmission rate of fibers leading to and from the central nervous system. Licklider, Stevens and Haynes (16), Quastler and Wulff (22), and Pierce and Karlin (21) have independently, and using different techniques, calculated the information transmission rate of oral reading as 35 to 45 bits per second—the fastest information processing rates which have been demonstrated for any human act. We assume that silent reading is an even more rapid process. Since it is unimaginable, within the framework of a naturalistic science, to have action rates greater than nerve impulse rates, the favored assumption is that peripheral coding allows the triggering of integrated sequences as units. Luria (17) speaks of these sorts of rapid motor acts as the elaboration of "melodies"; Osgood (20) speaking specifically of language calls them "predictive integrations."

The idea of the retina as supplying only afferent information has long supported the proposition that the retina is a passive passageway to the processing capacities of the central nervous system. Investigations by Gershuni, Leont'ev, and Sokolov (17) indicate that the retina incorporates effector elements which tune the peripheral receptors to essential components of the signal being received. One example of this phenomenon is Granit's (11) demonstration that foveal flicker fusion points are raised by a steady light to the periphery and that peripheral sensitivity is enhanced by simultaneous macular stimulation. While these experiments are not concerned with patterns, there is at least the possibility that similar processes might enhance recognition or perhaps set up a more favorable situation for recognition of high-frequency language patterns. It is interesting in this regard to note that in fixation records of first-graders, fixations on the word "the" (in our materials the only word occurring frequently enough to examine in this manner) dropped off with the number of occurrences of the word in the material.

The indications of peripheral control of visual processes do not by any means offer complete explanation of all phenomena. In Tinker's (25) study of eye-movements in reading formulas, the fixations for the prose-part of the context was very similar in pattern to regular prose text. At the formulas themselves, both algebraic formulas and chemical formulas, there was an immediate decrease of eye-movement span and an increase in time of fixation. This seems to be a fairly clear indication that difficult or unfamiliar materials require the exertion of central nervous system control. This control is not directly connected with the external display of the materials in any regular way we could discover. In Frandsen's (9) study of eye-movements in reading objective examination questions, the same phenomenon of control by content is exhibited. Frandsen explains the photographs where fixations are clustered around a particular response, e.g., in a multiple-choice question with few or no fixations at the other choices, as an item where the subject knew the right answer. When the subjects get unfamiliar items there is an almost letter by letter searching of all the alternatives. Again these seem to be clear cases of the control of eye-movements by semantic requirements.

Goldman-Eisler (10) has shown that the length of pauses in conversational speech is related to the informational content of the language at that point. The technique was to construct cloze tests for long and short pauses and to demonstrate that the words removed after short pauses were much more accurately replaced than words following long pauses. Pauses less than ¼ second were considered phrase or punctuation pauses and were excluded. In oral reading by an accomplished reader, only phrase and punctuation pauses appear. Eye photographs of the silent reading of familiar material imply a similar situation. That is, reading, in these cases, takes place as if there were no differential information intake for various segments of the reading. This appears analogous to the findings in tachistoscopic studies that as exposure time is increased, an exposure time is reached where all words (whatever their frequency of occurrence in the language) are equally recognizable. Studies of words spoken in noise which show that frequency of occurrence is related to accurate perception of words only when a masking noise is present also seem relevant. The reading of familiar materials is also a well-practiced, habitual action which seldom goes beyond the recognition stage of mental processing. It is only when a task is imposed that interrupts the routine, that large variations occur in eye-movements.

There are a number of investigations which strongly imply that reading is not the continuous-input sort of operation as it is normally pictured, but rather, involves a sampling of the environment. One set of these studies concentrates on apparent periodicies in visual tasks resembling reading (1). Stroud and his colleagues (23) view their data from rotary pursuit studies as indicating sampling by the eyes. Barlow (2) describes perception as occurring early in the total activity of processing information. This chain of operations may be summarized as (a) an input which is partially sampled and selectively perceived, (b) other intervening central nervous system processes such as retrieval, storage, and (c) a feedback to the periphery to guide the next input or to trigger a motor act. These processes are conceived of as sequential, and thus perception occupies only approximately the first third of the cycle.

Such constructions as the one given above are important when we consider such questions as how one can know the next word until he "sees" it. If one answers, there is no way to know, he has made an implicit processing model which assumes a continuous visual input without feedback. To assume that a visual system does not have feedback makes the explanation of the many observations of the operation of constraints exceedingly tedious. It has become common in the last few years to demonstrate that language has sequential constraints—constraints involving at different times letters, words, and semantic content. In this regard, it is interesting to consider what happens when one attempts to have a computer "read" information in a printed form. One obvious approach is to have a "template" set up in the computer. When a matching form is put into the machine, that form is passed into further processing. There are capital letters and small letters. Words have different numbers of letters. Letter by letter identification is slow in computers as it is in people, etc. Most programmers have abandoned the template as a model.

Another approach is to analyze letters and words in relationship to specific shape and context paradigms which discriminate one sign from another. Only certain parts of letters and words are now used for recognition purposes. The judgments used are probabilistic and context becomes extremely important. David and Selfridge (7) say, "even knowing diagram letter of syllable frequencies can improve decisions about letters or phonemes." They also say that syntactical, grammatical, and even semantic information would improve recognition. The interesting point for this paper is that eventually the computer will not have to "see" every word. Some words in highly constrained positions do not have to be "seen" at all. Many other words are identified from the first few letters. The middle of the word is especially low in information. The first few and the last few letters reduce most of the uncertainty. Bruner (3) has also shown this result using human subjects.

When the organism is "reading," the intent, usually, is to derive significance from the graphic signs. Perception of what is being read at any particular point certainly has a sensory component, but it is not at all clear how much of this component is necessary for the perception to occur. There are some locales within the sentence which are so highly constrained that the sign is determined, for the sophisticated reader, before it appears. This is ordinarily true, however, only if bilateral context is available. For example the missing word in the sentence, "The boys _____ going," is much more constrained than the blank in the fragment, "The boys _____." There are instances, however, where the semantics of preceding context highly constrain language elements, occurring in a particular site of the passage. For example, note the following passages: "The Pythagorean theorem was the end product of long years of practical experience with triangles. In its abstract elaboration by Pythagoras, this _____." With a high proportion of successes, the element represented by this blank would be supplied by readers capable of understanding the passage, without viewing a physical representation of the word.

The probability seems high, however, that bilateral context is available to the reader. As the eyes fixate on a particular point of a reading passage, language elements to the right, as well as to the left, are within the viewing area of the reader. Several studies have shown that the major effect of constraint is from five words or less on each side of the constrained word. Evidence derived from photographs of the "reading" eye indicates that words a short distance away from a point of focus are blurred in vision and severe distortion is present when the eye is in motion. Nevertheless, fixations do occur at the rate of four or five a second. Even if only three or four words are "put in" at each fixation, the number of words which seem to introduce most of the constraint would be available in the organism within the maximum limit of one second and in many cases in less time. This input rate would represent a reading rate of some 720–1,200 words per minute. This rate so far exceeds normal reading operations that again the probability is brought to mind that not input but, rather, central processing operations impede reading speed.

Another empirical indication that following context is available for use by the organism is the eye-voice span. If the source of light a subject is reading by is suddenly extinguished, the subject continues to verbalize for some time after the event—he goes on for an average of about five words. These words must have been "put in" and continue in the process of decoding. Processing, then, by this indicator is lagging behind input. Thus, bilateral context would be available. Also, one may observe the phenomenon of regression. Even in good readers there is some regression. As reading materials become more difficult there is more regression. Regression is a rerun of a past input—a kind of redundancy. There is a great likelihood that the input, before the regression, was processed in part. Regression provides a situation which not only allows total redundancy but also supplies, in effect, a longer bilateral context.

Several studies have indicated that bilateral context, i.e., words on both sides of a target word, reduce more uncertainty about the target word than words preceding only or following only, i.e., unilateral context. This appears to evidence that processing of language data is *not* entirely in the sequential ordering of the input. There seems to be a basic difference, however, in the reading process and the sign deletion techniques by which the constraint of context is often measured. An unknown word in reading occurs at a particular sentence locus where a graphic representation is present, and there is usually no uncertainty about the sign. All the letters of the sign are known for example and, for the sophisticated reader, even if the sign is unfamiliar, he probably can group the letters into syllables and give a reasonably accurate pronunciation. Parts of the sign may give cues to possible decoding—the reader may recognize the root for example. On the other hand, if the sign itself is missing, as in a cloze deletion of words, the many cues connected with the perception of a particular word are not present. The subject must search for the most probable sign, usually among a number of signs with somewhat similar probabilities. Reading in this situation is no longer a many-cued, direct, recognition process, but now a more or less uncertain search problem is involved. The reader *may not* need to reduce his uncertainty about short range constraint at all. The decoding need in this process may be that of relating particular language units, e.g., a prepositional phrase as the subject, to the larger topic of the passage. If this be true, central processing in reading may only be difficult when (a) much of the material read is unfamiliar to the subject, i.e., it is not in storage; (b) the material is of such a nature that early parts of the passage are necessary for understanding later parts, i.e. the cognitive load on memory is excessive; (c) the subject lacks "rules" of the grammar (in the "immediate con-stituents" sense) so that his relating of various smaller language units is inappropriate or inefficient. The "total" impression of these tasks is that successful reading at most particular points in a passage is controlled by the "extensional, field-like" recognition matrix (whatever that means) which has preceded and which immediately follows, that point.

While there is an amount of observable evidence from which to draw inferences that internal control is operating, the specific processes at a molar or molecular level are much more obscure. What is needed is some sort of known variation of internal processes which may be used to in-dex the external dependencies of eye-movements on this internal process. We consider one possible candidate for this standardization of covert processes to be transformational variations of kernals. It has been shown by Miller (19), Jenkins (13) and others, that various transformations of sentence forms called kernals (usually, the declarative, active form of the sentence) into, for example, the passive or the passive-negative, result in an increase in reaction times to the sentence. While there are disputations about the actual ordering of the relative reaction times of the various transformations, gross relationships are the same in most studies, e.g., the passive-negative transformation is always slower than the nega-tive transformation alone. It would seem to be a test of whether eye-movements are controlled by these structural characteristics of the language to present various transformations and predict eye-movements changes connected with the supposedly greater informational load of the transformations.

The consistencies in eye-movement data to the present have been mainly noted in data across subjects. Average number of fixations per word decrease with age; fixations occur in reading languages elaborated left-right, up-down; good readers (by some cognitive criteria) have fewer fixations, i.e., longer spans, than poor readers; all these are examples of the state of our knowledge concerning fixations. There are few examples of what we need to know to understand what fixations are all about within the individual subject.

Actually, we should not expect eye-movements to tell us the whole story of what the person is taking in when he reads. For most reading situations, we feel, he is only taking in cues to "material" which is already present in the organism. Reading, typically, is a selecting of the parts of what we already know. The novelty is in a different arrangement of events from one we have used before and the substitution of material we have always used in one context into a different context. In this aspect it is an easy, enjoyable activity for the accomplished. When material foreign to our learning history is read, the task becomes quite different. More of the information must be gathered from outside the storage of the nervous system. Eye-movements seem to reflect this increase in difficulty.

REFERENCES

1. Auginstine, Leroy G. "Evidences of Periodicities in Human Task Performance," in *Information Theory in Psychology,* Henry Quatter ed., Glencoe, Illinois: The Free Press, 1955.

2. Barlow, J. S. "Evoked Responses in Relation to Visual Perception and Oculomotor Reaction Times in Man," *Annals of the New York Academy of Science,* 1964, 112: 432–467.

3. Bruner, Jerome S. and Donald O'Dowd. "A Note on the Informativeness of Parts of Words," *Language and Speech,* April-June 1958, part 2: 98–101.

4. Buswell, G. T. "An Experimental Study of the Eye-voice Span in Reading," *Supplementary Educational Monographs,* No. 7, 1920.

5. Buswell, Guy Thomas. "Fundamental Reading Habits: A Study of Their Development," *Supplementary Educational Monographs,* No. 21, Chicago: Univ. of Chicago Press, 1922.

6. Buswell, G. T. "How Adults Read," *Supplementary Educational Monographs,* No. 45, 1937.

7. David, E. E. Jr. and O. G. Selfridge. "Eyes and Ears for Computers," *Proceedings of the I.R.E.,* 1962, 50: 1093–1101.

8. Dearborn, W. F. "An Experimental Study of the Reading Pauses and

Movements of the Eye," *Archives of Philosophy, Psychology, and Scientific Methods,* No. 4, 1906.

9. Frandsen, A. "An Eye Movement Study of Objective Examination Question," *Genetic Psychology Monographs,* 1934, 16: 79–183.

10. Goldman-Eisler, Frieda. "The Predictability of Words in Context and the Length of Pauses in Speech," *Journal of Communication,* 1961, 11: 95–99.

11. Granit, Ragnar. *Receptors and Sensory Perception,* New Haven: Yale Univ. Press, 1955.

12. Gray, W. S. "Remedial Cases in Reading: Their Diagnosis and Treatment," *Supplementary Educational Monographs,* No. 22, 1922.

13. Jenkins, James J. "Syntactic and Semantic Factors in Generalization," Paper presented at APA meeting, Los Angeles, September, 1964.

14. Judd, C. H. and G. T. Buswell. "Silent Reading: a Study of the Various Types," *Supplementary Educational Monographs,* No. 45, 1937.

15. Lashley, Karl S. "The Problem of Serial Order in Behavior," in *Cerebral Mechanisms in Behavior,* (The Hixon Symposium) ed. L. A. Jeffress, New York: Wiley and Sons, 1951, pp. 121–132.

16. Licklider, J. C. R., Stevens, K. N., and Hayes, J. R. M. *Studies in Speech, Hearing, and Communication,* Technical Report, Acoustics Laboratory, MIT, September 31, 1954.

17. Luria, Aleksandr Romanovich. *Higher Cortical Functions in Man,* New York: Basic Books, 1966. Trans. from Russian: Basil Haigh.

18. MacGintie, Walter H. "Contextual Constraints in English Prose Paragraphs," *Journal of Psychology,* 1961; 51: 121–130.

19. Miller, George A. "Some Psychological Studies of Grammar," *American Psychologist,* 1962, 17: 748–762.

20. Osgood, Charles E. "A Behavioristic Analysis of Perception and Language as Cognitive Phenomena," in *Contemporary Approaches to Cognition,* Cambridge, Mass: Harvard Univ. Press, 1957, pp. 75–118.

21. Pierce, J. R. and Karlin, J. E. "Reading Rates and the Information Rate of a Human Channel," *The Bell System Technical Journal,* March, 1957.

22. Quastler, Henry *et al. Human Performance in Information Transmission,* Report No. R-62, Control Systems Laboratory, University of Illinois, March, 1955.

23. Stroud, John in *Cybernetics,* H. von Foerster, ed., 6th transactions of the Society, N.Y.: Macy and Co., 1949.

24. Taylor, Stanford E. "Eye-movements in Reading: Facts and Fallacies," *American Educational Research Journal,* November, 1965, 4: 187–202.

25. Tinker, Miles A. "A Photographic Study of Eye-movements in Reading Formulae," *Genetic Psychology Monographs,* 1928, 2: 65–182.

Some Differences in Encoding
and Decoding Messages

The purpose of this study is to determine the ability of subjects to predict the omissions from a natural language text which they had previously produced themselves, as contrasted with the ability of other subjects to predict omissions from these same texts which they had read at the time of production.

Relationships between language production and language interpretation are still largely undefined. One difficulty is that of establishing from the use of the natural language the degree of organization and flexibility under encoding and decoding. One of the most productive ways to think of organization is in terms of predictability. The more predictable an event, the more organized. Variability implies a degree of unpredictability, i.e., of disorganization. This holds true in the second law of thermodynamics as well as in the mathematical statements of the redundancy of a communication system. Language when viewed as the transmission of signals carrying a message through a communication channel might well be interpreted in terms of these "more or less predictable" paradigms also.

Considered in this manner it would seem that the individual organism would be more organized, that is, he would exhibit more predictable language behavior, if he were later decoding messages which he originated as source, than if he were decoding messages originated by other sources.

There are obvious symmetries between "encoding"—the process whereby a message (originating in a source) is transformed into signals that can be carried by a communications channel, and "decoding"—the process where a receiver transforms signals into messages for a destination. The physical form of particular signals are the same whether transmitted or received. For example, "dog" is sent and received in the same form. At the level of the sign-vehicle then, it seems appropriate to assume that in the neutral code "dog" has the same representation whether it is transmitted or received. Within the interpretive system there are asymmetries however, as when a wife says to a husband, "you sly dog," and the husband decodes this as, "I'm a clever man," but the wife as source is originating the message, "you dirty dog."

(Co-authored with A. C. Bickley.) Published originally in the *Journal of the Reading Specialist,* 1967, 7, 18–25. Reprinted with the permission of the College Reading Association.

Analysis of language as a communications model is complicated by the fact that one unit, i.e., the person, is both source, transmitter, receiver, and destination of messages. In his role as source the individual probably produces messages beyond his capacity to transduce into signals appropriate for communications. These incommunicable neurophysiological states, however, overlap with states of the organism which can be communicated, in such a manner that at many points difficulty arises within the organism in distinguishing those states which have been communicated from those which have not. It also would seem that as in all communications systems a matching of states, at the level of source and destination as well as at the level of transmitting and receiving, is necessary if communication is to occur. If this be true, messages of the transmitting organism will be lost on certain receivers because of them; part of the transmission is in the form of misinterpreted signals, i.e., noise.

One difficulty present in drawing analogies between human and electronic communications system is the differing effect of "noise" in the two systems. In an electronic system noise is introduced in the "channel" and there is a constant attempt to overcome its distorting effects. In the human communication system noise in the channel is likewise undesirable, but this is not the only noise present. There is noise introduced by the prior organization, i.e., the past learnings, of the destination of a message. This noise may take the form of "misreadings" or the form of "variant readings" to use I. A. Richards' (1960) terms. Because they ordinarily indicate deficient decoding skills, misreadings should be eliminated, but variant readings are quite another matter. Strictly speaking, communication only occurs when the intent of the author is interpreted precisely by the destination. One would guess however, that much of advancing knowledge is built on the use of one individual's verbal production to buttress conceptual structures quite foreign to the intention of that individual. Communication fails, but the intended communication has an effect, and perhaps a profound one, nevertheless. Noise, then, in a human communications system may have, socially, a facilitating effect. Also, within a single organism these problems of transduction and matching should be greatly attenuated.

In a communications system constructed by a communications engineer the function of the various parts of the system are readily separable and thus the characteristics of each element easily ascertained or designed. In animate matter, however, functional relationships of elements can only be inferred from confounded organismic output, either elicited or emitted.

Since the system most open to us is the signal system, the transmitting and receiving functions of human communication are more open to us. The great difficulty is that of going beyond the signal production and signal perception mechanisms to examine the source and the destination of messages. Here, apparently, lie most of the asymmetries in human communications systems; this is where most of the "noise" originates. Some of these asymmetries undoubtedly have genetic bases; others probably are of a chemical and physical nature relating to the specific structure and metabolism of the organism; others are related to the differential storage of information concerning the environment, i.e., learning. A message, then, having its source, transmission, reception, and destination in one organism would seem to be the most highly organized, i.e., the most predictable, message possible for that individual. One would expect the person to be able to reproduce his own language productions with higher accuracy than he would be able to reproduce the language productions of another.

In this paper the terms "source," "transmitter," "channel," "receiver," "destination," "message," and "noise" are used in the technical communication theory sense. The idea is that when a person writes he codes internal neurophysiological messages into a language display which permits its transmission through a communication channel; when a person reads he decodes incoming signals from a language display into internal neurophysiological messages.

METHOD

The experimental procedure involved requiring language production (encoding) of one group of subjects in response to TAT stimulus cards. Another group of subjects read these productions soon after they were finished. Later, all subjects (producers and readers) were tested for their ability to replace words which had been deleted from these productions.

Cloze tests are made by a language mutilation technique developed by Wilson Taylor in 1953. All cloze tests in this study were made by completely deleting every seventh word, beginning the count with the first word, in the TAT stories which were produced by one experimental group. This is generally called an "any-word" cloze deletion. The task of the subject is to try to supply the exact word which was removed from the passage.

The subjects were 64 sophomores randomly selected from 255 sophomores at Campbell College and assigned, again at random, to four conditions.

Two experimental and two control treatments were designed. One experimental group was assigned the task of producing written stories in response to two TAT cards (numbers 2 and 17GF). Two days later they were given cloze tests which were made by deleting every seventh word of their own stories. The second experimental group was assigned the task of reading the stories produced by the first experimental group above. Two days later they were given cloze tests covering the material they had read, and which, of course, was the same cloze test that the producer of the story had completed.

One control group was assigned the task of producing written stories in the same manner as the experimental group. They did not see these stories again. As soon as they had finished writing their stories they were given stories produced by the experimental group, above, to read. Two days later they were given cloze tests covering the material they had read. The other control group did not produce but were given randomly assigned TAT stories to read. Two days later these were given cloze tests produced by the experimental group but which they had not seen before. To summarize: the four treatments were *encoding* (i.e., producers), *decoding* (i.e., readers) and the two control groups, *irrelevant encoders–decoders,* and *naive decoders.*

The statistical analysis was by a planned comparison among means. Weights were assigned as in Table 1. The reasons for the orthogonal comparisons are as follows.

Table 1. Weights for orthogonal comparison of means

	Encoding	Decoding	Irrelevant encoding-decoding	Naive decoding
Comparisons	I	II	III	IV
1	1	−1	0	0
2	−1/2	−1/2	1	0
3	−1/3	−1/3	−1/3	1

1. The encoding group should have a significantly higher mean score than the decoding group. The encoding group having encoded a message which they subsequently re-encoded, in part, should score higher than the group who encoded, in part, a message which they had only decoded before.

2. The encoding and decoding group should have significantly higher mean score than the irrelevant encoding–decoding groups. The encoding–decoding group had previously encoded a message using the same stimuli as that of the decoding group. Their cloze scores however are based on material which they had previously decoded. They were thus encoding, in part, the specific message which they had only decoded

before and thus, should be more like the decoding group. A nonsignificant difference here would indicate a relationship between encoding and decoding related to prior encoding or messages on topics similar but not identical to the original topic.

3. The naive decoders should have a mean score significantly lower than the mean of all other groups. Numerous studies have noted differences between pre-cloze–cloze tests given with previous experience without the particular language passage, and post-cloze–cloze tests which are given after experience with particular language passage. This differential exists in this comparison.

RESULTS

The results of the planned comparisons are given in Table 2.

The level of confidence was set at .01 (one-tailed test) before statistical computations were carried out. The three comparisons were statistically significant in the predicted directions.

It is also important to note here that the results from two previous pilot studies confirmed the relationships exhibited here. In addition, both pilot studies varied the time, between the same treatments discussed here and the measurement by the cloze tests, for the fixed conditions of two and eight days. There was no significant difference between days or of interaction between days and treatments.

DISCUSSION

When the subject sees his production in the reading display, he receives his own message by his "language" cue system. If length of the message is beyond the span of his immediate memory he must use the same system to reduce uncertainty that he uses for messages which he did not produce. The message, however, a product of his nervous system, is more predictable in its *more variant aspects,* i.e., those parts which are most uncertain, because the structure of "markers" and lexical selection restrictions are more congruent with the form of the display, than they would be in a non-producer of the language.

The producer does not reproduce, exactly, his own prior production however. As *destination* of his own message he does not have identical internal states with those under which he produced the message. He has a degree of uncertainty, therefore, about what he has produced.

The fact that the producer does not reproduce his own production exactly indicates that the producer cannot communicate with himself precisely, at least not, when parts of his original encodings are destroyed.

Table 2. Planned comparisons—t's

Comparisons	Difference in means	Variance estimate	t
1. Encoding; decoding	3.625	.554	4.87*
2. Encoding + decoding; irrelevant encoding–decoding	1.563	.416	2.44*
3. Post-cloze; pre-cloze	3.1957	.369	5.26*
Variance	SS	df	Mean square
Within groups	266	60	4.433

*Significant at .01 level (one-tailed)

That is, supposedly, if a producer views substantial parts of his own language production and his productive and interpretive codings were one-to-one transductions, there is no obvious reason he (the producer) could not repeat his original production verbatim.

It is demonstrated here that predictability of missing elements in a language passage is increased when a subject is source of a message as well as destination. Predictability is not perfect however. Reconstruction of the original message is, on the average, 86 percent. In other words, at least, the signal system of the language maintains a degree of variability when transmission is entirely within the organism.

Predictability of missing elements in a language passage is increased when a subject is the destination of a message, parts of which he later attempts to encode, but there is less reconstruction as compared to the original encoder, reencoding. Here, after two days, reconstruction is down to 70 percent. The reconstruction of the "pre-cloze" tests was about 60 percent.

Memory differentials do not seem to be a factor in predictions covering the periods of time studies. Though in all three studies, subjects were instructed to remember, as they would be tested later, in both pilot studies, there was no difference in recall from two to eight days, nor was there interaction between treatments and recall. The low difficulty of the TAT stories might be a factor here. Nevertheless under these conditions no "memory" loss over time is exhibited.

If the difference between the encoders and the decoders is a true one, the prior structure of the communication system itself must determine the differential between encoders and decoders. In the encoder, it would seem, the hierarchy of language elements exhibit a more stationary characteristic over time. That is, identical context leads more probably to the same response as before. The decoder who is asked to encode parts of a previous encoding of another person does not have the same probabilities of supplying a particular signal in a particular language context which the original encoder would supply. The implication is that the characteristic which allows the encoder to reencode parts of his message more precisely than a decoder attempting the same reconstruction is the individual probabilities of response. On the other hand there is much more agreement than disagreement.

An interesting question here is, "what happens to 'meaning' under these circumstances." If two individuals respond to the same language signals in different manners this implies that psychologically the two individuals derive different messages, to some degree, from this particular signal. Communication under these conditions would be very different from an electronic system for every message would only convey an approximate meaning.

REFERENCE

Richards, I. A. "Poetic Process and Literary Analysis," *Style in Language*, T. Sebeok (ed.). N.Y.: Technological Press of MIT and John Wiley, 1960.

Sources of Information for
Responses to Reading Test Items

It is not uncommon to find in the reading literature the question, "What do reading tests really measure?" (Kingston, 1965). A cursory look at the task imposed by a reading comprehension test indicates that the person taking the test is to read the paragraph and then answer the multiple-choice questions which follow. The assumption is that the antecedent behavior of reading the paragraph is necessary (even if not sufficient) for answering the test items correctly. That a prior perusal of a graphic display is a requirement for reading to have occurred is indicated by the definition of reading in English and English (1958, p. 442). Reading is defined as "the perception of written, printed, or engraved symbols constituting a communication." One of the purposes of this study is to attempt to clarify empirically the source of semantic information as measured by reading comprehension tests.

Language has been divided into two categories by numerous linguists. Hockett (1963) has pointed out that a characteristic of languages which has been called a universal of language is the dichotomy between grammatical and nongrammatical meaning. Nongrammatical meaning is synonymous with the term "conceptual information." Rankin (1957) has shown that conceptual information is dependent upon the nouns and verbs in the reading passage more than is grammatical meaning and that grammatical meaning is more closely connected with function words than it is with nouns and verbs (often called "lexical" words). Another purpose of this study is to examine the relationship between grammatical and nongrammatical features of language with regard to their effects upon conceptual information as measured by the multiple-choice items on reading comprehension tests.

METHOD

The blackout technique was developed by Holland and Kemp (1965) for the study of programmed instruction. They were attempting to determine which frames were, and which frames were not, giving information which

(Co-authored with A. C. Bickley.) Published originally in the Proceedings of the Seventy-fifth Annual Convention of the American Psychological Association, 1967, 293–294. Reprinted with the permission of the American Psychological Association.

allowed the response frame to be completed correctly. It was found that many frames had cues to the correct answer that were unrelated to the topic which the programmers intended to teach. These experimenters chose words to black out that they judged to contain crucial information for answering the questions asked about the material.

It was hoped that this technique could be used to analyze reading comprehension tests. However, it soon became apparent that many reading test items were not dependent on specific locations or specific words in the reading display. Therefore, in this study percentages of content words were blacked out.

The materials were paragraphs sampled from reading tests listed in Buros' (1965) sixth yearbook. The paragraphs taken from the different tests were selected arbitrarily with length and number of questions pertaining to the paragraphs the only constraining criteria.

The subjects were 147 sophomores, randomly selected from 240 sophomores enrolled in courses in introductory psychology at Campbell College and randomly assigned to seven treatments, as follows:

1. All of the reading passage blacked out.
2. All nouns, verbs, and adjectives blacked out.
3. All function words blacked out.
4. None of the reading paragraph blacked out.
5. 10% of the nouns, verbs, and adjectives blacked out.
6. 50% of the nouns, verbs, and adjectives blacked out.
7. 90% of the nouns, verbs, and adjectives blacked out.

The questions pertaining to the reading passages were not altered in any way and the subjects were instructed to answer all the questions from whatever information was available to them in their particular reading passages.

RESULTS

Two types of orthogonal comparisons were planned (see Table 1). One set of comparisons was whether a significant difference was present between the means of Treatments 1 and 3 and between Treatments 3 and 4. For the former comparison, a nonsignificant difference would indicate that function words add nothing to conceptual meaning; for the latter, a difference would indicate the function words, on their own, add conceptual meaning.

The other set of comparisons was a trend analysis of the effect of blacking out increasing percentages of nouns, verbs, and adjectives. It was

Table 1. Weights of planned comparisons

Comparisons	Treatments						
	1	2	3	4	5	6	7
1	1	0	−1	0	0	0	0
2	0	1	0	−1	0	0	0
3	0	0	0	0	−1	0	1
4	0	0	0	0	1	−2	1

assumed that a deletion of 10 percent, 50 percent, and 90 percent of lexical items, while leaving the function words intact, would be related linearly to the number of multiple-choice items answered correctly.

Orthogonal planned comparisons of means and a trend analysis were computed. There was a significant difference in the number of correct answers to multiple-choice items on a passage when the paragraph on which the items (supposedly) depended was intact, as opposed to correct answers to the same items when function words were blacked out and only lexical words remained. There was no significant difference in multiple-choice item responses when function words alone were compared to a complete deletion of the paragraph from which the items were drawn (see Table 2).

There is a significant linear trend with a nonsignificant quadratic component. While not statistically appropriate in this analysis, adding the 100 percent deletion treatment and the 0 percent treatment to the series increases the F ratio.

DISCUSSION

The relationship of function words and lexical words to the completion of multiple-choice items on reading tests is a complex one. For this population, function words alone supplied no conceptual information. Lexical words alone supplied twice as much information as no paragraph at all (when the guessing score was subtracted). Function words in combination with lexical words (the normal language situation) have a large effect on the completion of the multiple-choice items, but by no means the unique effect ordinarily assumed by users of reading tests.

The effect of removing increasing proportions of lexical words with the rest of the context intact is linear (see Table 2). This implies that the conceptual information needed to reduce uncertainty about reading test

Table 2. Significance levels of orthogonal comparisons

Variation source	Mean difference	df	t	MS	F
Comparison 1	3.95[b]	126	4.76[a]		
Comparison 2	1.24[b]	126	1.49		
Comparison 3		1		247.	15.[a]
Deviations		1		7.	
Within groups		60		15.	

[a]Significant at .05 level.
[b]Standard error .83.

items is scattered widely throughout a passage. A reduction of nouns, verbs, and adjectives reduces available conceptual information proportionally.

The general impression of the results is that there are at least two relatively distinct sources of information for the completion of multiple-choice items in reading comprehension tests. One source is the conceptual information the subject brings to the testing situation about the topics which the test samples. The previously learned information apparently allows subjects to correctly respond to test items on the basis of greatly reduced cues in the reading passages, or in the absence of a reading passage, on the basis of cues in the test items alone. The subjects who had no reading passage to aid in answering the item, nevertheless, correctly completed 67 percent as many items as subjects with all the reading passage. Perhaps this was accomplished in one or more of the following ways:

1. The subjects knew the correct answer from past learning.
2. The subjects eliminated distractors which were not likely in any reading situation.
3. The subjects used information from preceding items to reduce uncertainty about succeeding items.

It was possible, using the data gathered in this study, to make an informed guess as to whether or not subjects used information from preceding items to reduce uncertainty about items which followed. There were five sets of three sequential items each, e.g., 21, 22, 23, for which there were high proportions of correct responses under the complete blackout treatment. Other than these five sets, only two single items had over 50 percent correct responses under the complete blackout treatment.

A modification of Guttman's scaling technique was used to analyze the responses. In all but one of the five sets proportionality was greater than .90—in that case it was .82. While nothing more than a highly suggestive relationship should be inferred from these "rough-and-ready" operations, indications are that a potential major source of cues to conceptual information on a paragraph reading test is the information derived from preceding items concerning a particular topic.

The results of this study indicate that reading comprehension tests are highly dependent on examinee characteristics which often have little to do with the reading task the examiner assumes he is presenting. Reading tests are measuring past learning, word association, irrelevance of distractors, and "item conceptual-information constraints," as well as the person's ability to answer multiple-choice items directly from cues in the reading display. The sources of variation are so confounded that two, or more, factors could be hidden here, and one would never know. Much of the confounding could be reduced by changes in methods of selecting items.

REFERENCES

Buros, O. K. (ed.) *The sixth mental measurements yearbook*. Highland Park, N. J.: The Gryphon Press, 1965.

English, H. B., & English, A. C. *A comprehensive dictionary of psychological and psychoanalytic terms*. N. Y.: David McKay Co., 1958.

Hockett, C. F. The problem of universals in language. In J. H. Greenberg (ed.), *Universals of language*. Cambridge: The Massachusetts Institute of Technology Press. 1963. Pp. 1–22. Reprinted in Hockett, *The View from Language: Selected Essays, 1948–1974*. Athens: The University of Georgia Press, 1977. Pp. 163–186.

Holland, J. G., & Kemp, F. C. A measure of programming in teaching-machine material. *Journal of Educational Psychology*, 1965, 56, 264–269.

Kingston, A. J. Is reading what the reading test tests? In E. L. Thurston & L. E. Hafner (eds.), *The philosophical and sociological basis of reading. 14th Yearbook National Reading Conference*, Milwaukee: Marquette University Reading Center, 1965. Pp. 106–109.

Rankin, E. F., Jr. An evaluation of the cloze procedure as a technique for measuring reading comprehension. Unpublished doctoral dissertation, University of Michigan, 1957.

An Empirical Examination of Cloze Scores Derived from "Natural" and "Mutilated" Language Segments

The cloze procedure is a language deletion technique devised by Wilson Taylor (1954). It is similar to other language deletion techniques such as the Minkus completion task of the Binet test, except that in its original form, Taylor conceived of mechanical deletions—that is, deleting every nth word (e.g., every fifth word, or every tenth) in a language passage of substantial size.

Taylor devised the technique to measure what he called "entropy." At any particular deletion point in a language text, the number of subjects who responded with the same word were used as the numerator of a fraction. The denominator was the total number of words produced. The "so-called" probabilities of a word occurring were then summed by the $-p$ log p formula, designated "entropy," and the resulting value for a particular context correlated with a score derived from the number of times the subjects supplied the exact word for the context. Taylor found a correlation of $-.87$ between these two scores. The deletions were then interpreted in terms of information theory. In this dissertation, Taylor also noted the superficial appearance of his task to visual closure measures and precipitately, and rather unfortunately for clearness of conceptualization, named his task the cloze procedure. Attempts to relate the cloze procedure to closure (as measured for example by Thurstone's tasks) have not been successful.

Taylor correlated cloze scores with a number of standard psychological tests. Correlations with intelligence scales, e.g., the AGCT, were in the seventies. Correlations were even higher with objectively-scored achievement tests constructed by Taylor to measure content learning in Air Force instruction manuals. A whole host of studies sprang up which deleted natural language materials in some form, had subjects complete the deleted materials, and then attempted to relate the scores to such constructs as reading comprehension, readability, commonality, social distance, prognosis in schizophrenia, and stereotypy of language as revealed in literary and actual suicide notes.

(Co-authored with A. C. Bickley.) Originally presented at the meeting of the Southeastern Psychological Association, Atlanta, Georgia, April, 1967. Reprinted with the permission of the Southeastern Psychological Association.

In most of these instances the language measure itself distributes close to normal (as well as closeness of fit may be deduced from plots on probability paper). Its validity in measuring such a variety of constructs is another question.

The reliability of the cloze procedure is quite varied. With any-word cloze (the standard form) if deletions are started with the first word, there will obviously be a different pattern of deletions than if the deletions are started with the second word, etc. The reliability of deletions begun from the first word may be substantially different from deletions counted from the second word. Split-half reliabilities of any-word cloze are typically in the 80s and 90s, with the 70s being low. Test-retest reliabilities are rarely under 70 for any-word deletions when there are 50 or more deletions. Nevertheless, after extensive reliability studies John Carroll (1959)

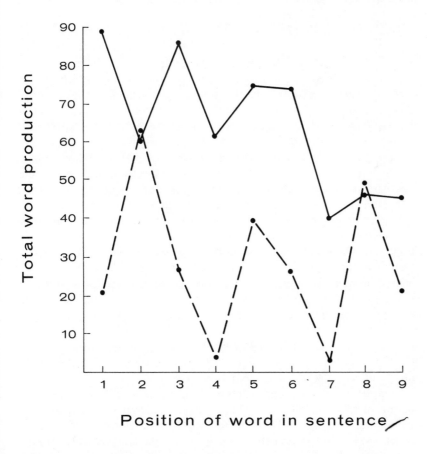

Figure 1. Constraint from the bilateral to the unilateral situation

decided that the measure was too unstable to use in the prediction of success in learning foreign languages.

While Taylor used the designation "cloze procedure" for the mechanical, any nth word deletion pattern, a number of deletion patterns have been widely used. Rankin (1957) used the terminology and concepts of the linguist C. C. Fries to define a "structural" and "lexical" cloze deletion. The "structural" deletion is any-word cloze as it is defined above. The "lexical" deletions are deletions of "content" or "lexical" words only, in Rankin's studies essentially the grammatical categories noun and main verb, but expanded by other investigators to include adjective and more rarely, adverb. First the lexical items are determined for a passage by the categorizations of the experimenter or of judges, and then an nth word deletion is carried out on those items. Rankin showed that the two deletion types correlated differentially with different subtests of the Diagnostic Reading Tests.

The lexical deletion has also had wide use. Some claim it to be a better predictor of achievement scores than the any-word deletion. It suffers from several faults: (1) A number of items in a lexical deletion may be impossible to predict, e.g., numbers, proper names, etc., which are not cued in scores derived from the text. This particular deletion often deviates from the normal, and reliabilities are much more dependent on the particular word entering the deletion pattern. Split-half reliabilities in the 40s and 50s are not uncommon, although test-retest reliabilities tend to be higher. Greene claims that the reliability of this deletion may be greatly improved by a perusal of the proposed deletions in order to judge members of infinite sets, e.g., numbers (and the categories mentioned before). Correlations in the 90s with standard achievement test and with instructor-made objective test are regularly reported using this deletion.

The cloze procedure holds a number of interesting facets for students of language. There have been a number of studies of the cloze procedure where the directionality of context has been the variable. If a word is deleted in the midst of other words so that context extends on both sides of the word, this is called bilateral context. If a word is deleted and the context is only on one side of the word (right or left in English) this is called unilateral context. A number of studies have demonstrated that though subjects feel it is more difficult to complete unilateral deletions when the context is on the right of the word, there is no difference in unilateral scores whether context is right or left.

Completion of unilateral deletions is much more difficult than completion of bilateral deletions. There is also a difference in the pattern of responding (see figure 1). Note in this figure that the bilateral cloze forms a sawtooth pattern that ends at about the level of completion of deletions at the end of the sentence as the level of completions at the beginning. This is a typical pattern. Sentences much longer than the ones illustrated here tend to present continuing repetition of this pattern, with the repetitions correlated with the clause structure of the sentence.

Notice in figure 1 that the unilateral completions (the curve at the top) reveal a downward trend, indicating that the completions become fewer toward the end of the sentence. This indicates less constraint at the end of the sentence than in the bilateral situation. This unilateral pattern also is repeated in longer sentences, again correlated with the clause structure of the sentence.

There seems to be potential here for study of stochastic models of language production. Unilateral deletions present a situation with the superficial appearance at least of a Markov Chain. Bilateral deletions imply types of language processing requiring more than (in English) a left to right sequential analysis of the language. Roger Shepard (1963) used deletions in another manner in order to obtain language measures. He deleted words in various size contexts and instructed subjects to fill in the deletion site with all the words which fitted that context. Subjects were allowed to continue for five minutes and the number of words produced per 30-second intervals were recorded. Shepard hypothesized that subjects would produce words at a decreasing rate as time proceeded, indicating that a category of words was being exhausted at a decreasing rate. Figure 2 is an examination of the relationship between the Shepard procedure and the cloze procedure. Twenty subjects were assigned to each procedure and a unilateral guessing procedure followed for each word of an eight-word sentence with forty words of preceding context. Since the functions are plotted on an arithmetic probability scale, a linear relationship indicates normality. The cloze procedure obviously departs from normality while Shepard technique is close to it. Further investigation of the data indicate that unless a particular cloze unit is filled exactly in the first few emissions of words, it becomes increasingly unlikely that it will be filled. It is obvious that for the unilateral condition the distributions are quite dissimilar.

The first estimates of the statistical redundancy of the language were made by Claude Shannon (1961). Shannon used a letter-guessing technique. He asked subjects to guess the next letter following a context of varying length. He would then inform the subject whether or not he was right. The subject would continue guessing until he had guessed the correct letter or the printer's space. From the number of guesses required to obtain the correct letter Shannon calculated the redundancy (or uncertainty) at that point. Figure 3 reproduces Shepard's calculations of word uncertainty using his rate of word production method as compared

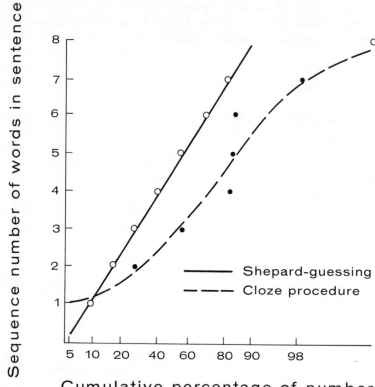

Figure 2.
A comparison of Shepard guessing scores and cloze procedure scores

Table 1. Rho correlations
for scores obtained by unilateral word and letter guessing,
and by bilateral word and letter guessing

	Uni-word	Bilat-letter
Uni-letter	.39	.50
Bilat-word	.10	.15

Fifty deletions; 40 words preceding context
for unilateral condition—40 words preceding
and following context for bilateral condition.

with Shannon's letter-guessing method. The fit is fair. Table 1 is a summary of calculations of the relationship of letter and word uncertainty measures for unilateral and bilateral direction of context. The highest relationship is between the guessing of letters whatever the direction of context. There is a modest relationship between unilateral word and letter guessing situations. The Shepard data in figure 3 is for unilateral letter guessing-bilateral word guessing. While not represented in Table 1, our calculation, *rho* for this dicotomy is .52. There is little relationship indicated between bilateral word guessing and bilateral letter guessing and between bilateral word guessing and unilateral word guessing. We

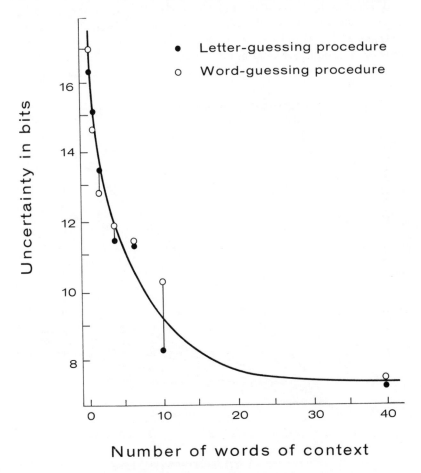

Figure 3. Uncertainty about a missing word
as a function of the amount of context (R. Shepard)

have other data which indicate that these may be orthogonal measures. Tachistoscopic studies also indicate different patterns of perception for letters in isolation and letters in words. The ability to predict these units from context also seems to require different processes.

Shepard extracted a large sampling of language segments from the *New York Times* and presented these segments of varying size context to subjects. His context sizes are indicated on the right side of figure 4. A separate empirical curve was plotted for each of the seven amounts of context supplied. For the context of size 1, he alternated the context word so that it appeared alternately to the right and to the left of the target word. The grammatical categories were allowed to vary randomly over the various contexts. The results are the consistent relationship of figure 4.

Figure 5 is a set of curves we generated by using Shepard's word-guessing technique for continuous language passages. Sentences of the same immediate constituent structure were surrounded by the lengths of

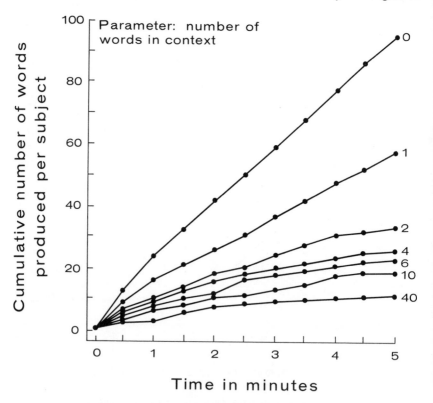

Figure 4. Number of words produced per subject up to each half-minute subdivision of the five-minute period (R. Shepard)

context indicated on the right side of figure 5. The word in each sequential position in the sentence was then deleted and eight subjects assigned randomly to each word position (see also Weaver and Bickley, 1966). The curves of figure 5 are obviously different from those of figure 4. Context has a very erratic effect. A separate empirical curve was again plotted for each of the six amounts of context supplied. There are a number of reversals, i.e., longer context is less constraining than shorter context. Also, most of the curves in figure 4 are approaching asymtotes at 40

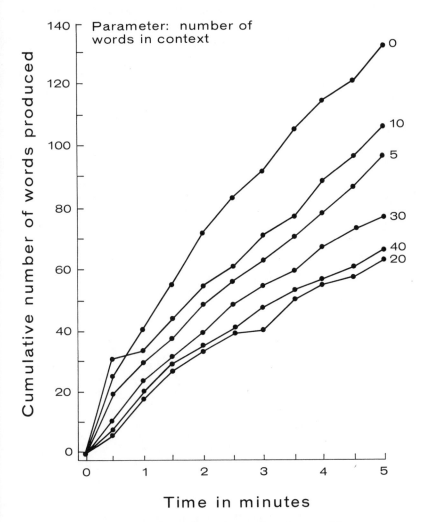

Figure 5. Number of words produced per subject
up to each half-minute subdivision of the five-minute period

words context. This is not true with figure 5. At all levels of context word production is continuing to increase. Shepard notes in his paper that he does not consider context to be the only controlling factor in language production. It is apparent from our data that effects of context tend to be overwhelmed by other factors operating in the linguistic situation.

   This is particularly apparent in figure 6. Here the rate of production in words per minute is compared to two theoretical curves devised by Shepard. Shepard's data, derived from guessing deletions in randomly selected language segments of varying length context, give a decent fit to

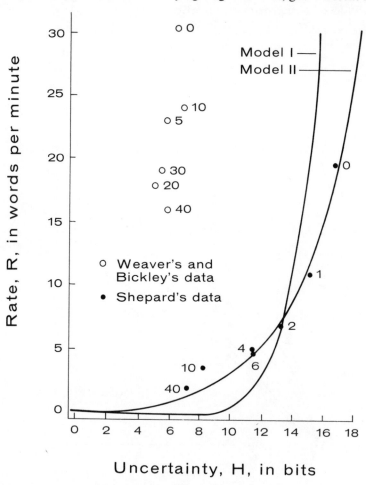

Figure 6. Rate of producing words as a function of uncertainty. Numbers on plot represent the size of context (R. Shepard)

Model II. Our data gathered from continuous language passages of particular linguistic form show no consistent dependence of rate of word production on length of context. Also, our data does not even approximate a fit to either Model I or II.

Model I: $H = \log_2(R/p)$

Model II: $H \cong \log_2(R/p)$
$$+ s/(1-s)\{(p/R)[R/P + 1/(1-s)]\log_2[(1-s)R/p+1] - \log_2 e\}$$

Model I constants: $p = 0.0007$, $s = 0$
Model II constants: $p = 0.12$, $s = 0.69$

Generally, our data shows that when the normal language situation is analyzed, a number of variables enter into determining the response of subjects which entirely subvert the factor of context. These variables have not been isolated to the extent that consistencies may be shown to exist. One may assume that human language production is lawfully determined but we are far from specifying the nature of that lawfulness.

REFERENCES

Carroll, J., Wilds, A., and Wilds, C. "An Investigation of Cloze Items in the Measurement of Achievement in Foreign Languages," in *A Report on Research Conducted under a Grant from the College Entrance Examination Board* (Laboratory for Research in Instruction, Graduate School of Education, Harvard University, Cambridge, Massachusetts, 1959).

Rankin, Earl F., Jr. "An Evaluation of the Cloze Procedure as a Technique for Measuring Reading Comprehension," doctoral dissertation, University of Michigan, 1957.

Shannon, C. "Prediction and Entropy of Printed English," *Bell System Technical Journal*, 30:50–64.

Shepard, R. "Production of Constrained Associates and the Informational Uncertainty of the Constraint," *American Journal of Psychology*, 76:218–28.

Taylor, W. "Application of 'Cloze' and Entropy Measures to the Study of Contextual Constraint in Samples of Continuous Prose," doctoral dissertation, University of Illinois, 1954.

Weaver, W., and Bickley, A. "Constraint on Sentence Elements of Context External to the Sentence," paper presented to the Southeastern Psychological Association, New Orleans, Louisiana, April 1966.

Structural-Lexical Predictability of Materials
Which Predictor Has Previously Produced or Read

The present study dichotomizes English language materials into structural and lexical parts in order to examine the relationship of the written production of language, and reading to these constructs.

The assumption is, that the very frequent words of the language are the major organizational parts of the language. That is, structure is defined as the commonality which allows a member of a language community to "know," to a degree, what to expect when a communication attempt occurs, even before the language sequence begins. If this is a tenable categorization one should be able to show that structural units are more predictable between interpreters than lexical units. Since language within the interpreter has potentially different communication channels than language between interpreters, one would expect a subject to be able to predict his own, previously produced, lexical units as well as he predicts his own structural units.

The cloze procedure, a language deletion technique developed by Taylor (1954), was used to construct measures of predictability of structural and lexical units. The terms structural and lexical were first applied to the cloze procedure by Rankin (1957). He used the terminology and concepts of the linguist Fries (1952) to delineate what Fries calls structural and lexical "meaning." Rankin's argument maintains that "any-word" cloze (an nth word deletion) would sample the more frequent function words at a greater rate than lexical words (in Rankin's study, nouns and main verbs) and thus would measure structural meaning to a greater extent than lexical meaning when the subjects subsequently filled in the exact word removed from the language passage. Conversely, deleting only nouns and main verbs would sample lexical meaning more than structural meaning when subjects replaced the words. Structure is therefore confounded, to an indeterminable degree, with the lexical. The procedure for selecting structural units in this study was an attempt to reduce this confounding.

It has been demonstrated in previous studies using the cloze procedure that structural deletions are more predictable than lexical deletions under

(Co-authored with A. C. Bickley.) Published originally in the Proceedings of the Seventy-fifth Annual Convention of the American Psychological Convention, 1967, 289–290. Reprinted with the permission of the American Psychological Association.

the reading condition (Rankin, 1957). It has been assumed this is because there is high frequency of occurrence and restricted numbers of types in the categories of words making up the structural deletions. For this reason one would expect only a small difference, if any, in the ability of subjects to supply structural cloze units whether the subject had written or read the passage previously.

In contrast, lexical categories are open, and any particular member of a category has a low frequency of occurrence. There is much room for variation. One would expect differences between structural and lexical categories on these bases. In the light of these differences between writing and reading it is not likely that large differences would be found in responses to structural deletions. One would hypothesize that most of the differences in the treatments are in the lexical dimension.

METHOD

The two groups assigned to the writing modality treatment were instructed to produce written stories to two TAT cards (No. 2 and No. 17GF). They were given spirit-duplicator master, ruled with two-inch horizontal lines in columns, on which to record their responses. They were instructed to print.

As soon as these two groups had finished, their productions were duplicated, shuffled, and assigned at random to the groups receiving the reading treatment. All groups were told before they began their respective tasks that they would be asked to recall later what they had written or read.

Cloze tasks were prepared from the stories which the writing modality groups had produced. The following categories were selected for the structural deletion because of the high frequency of successful cloze completions by subjects in Coleman's (in press) extensive study of cloze scores obtained with various word classes. Every fifth structural unit was deleted and replaced by an underline, twelve spaces long.

On another set of stories duplicated from the same producing groups, all words were identified which had not been included in the structural categories. These were designated lexical words. Every fifth word was deleted and replaced by a standard underline.

The subjects were 56 sophomores randomly selected from 152 sophomores enrolled in introductory psychology courses at Campbell College. The subjects were randomly assigned to treatments. Two days after receiving the experimental treatment (writing modality or reading modality) the subjects were presented with the cloze tasks. They were instructed to attempt to fill in the exact word which had been in the blank,

Table 1. Cloze completion percentage of word classes

Word class	Example	Percent completion[a]
Verb (copula)	is	76
Article	the	74
Possessive pronoun	his	58
Modal auxillary	could	75
Not	not	76
Coordinating conjunction	and	65
Preposition	from	67
Do	do	85
There	there	75
Wh-words	where	86
Subordinating conjunction	since	55
Particle	go in	61
Address	Mrs.	79
To	to go	90
Pronoun	you	72
Sounds	bam	95

[a]Selected from Coleman (in press).

and reminded that they had written or read the passage before. Only the first fifty deletions in each paper were scored in order to equate the total possible response score.

RESULTS

A two-way analysis-of-variance was computed on the data. Results were as follows: deletions (structural-lexical) $F = 10.85$, $df = 1$, $MS = 335$; modalities (reading-writing) $F = 13.85$, $df = 1$, $MS = 418$; interaction $F = 11.21$, $df = 1$, $MS = 341$. Error was $df = 52$, $MS = 30.77$. All effects were significant at the .05 level. The cell representing the reading group completing lexical units was the source of practically all the variation.

DISCUSSION

The writer is able to reproduce his own lexical items to a greater extent than the reader can reproduce the same lexical items. However, the reader can reproduce the writer's structure as well as the writer himself. This implies that, in the case of structure, writers and readers of the language possess identical language elements and highly similar probabilities of the occurrence of those language elements in particular contexts.

It is interesting to consider these findings in relation to the constructs of the linguist Saussure (1959). Saussure divides the concept "language," as used in English, into two concepts which he designates by the French words *"la langue"* and *"la parole." La langue* is an abstraction. It is all the possible communication acts which potentially could be carried out by all individuals separately within a particular language community. *La parole* is language acts initiated by a particular individual. Saussure contrasts these concepts at several points, e.g., designates *la langue* as receptive and passive; *la parole* as executive and active.

Psychologically, as Saussure defines it, *la langue* has no reality. There seems to be no separate provision for those aspects of the language *(la langue)* which a particular individual can interpret as distinct from aspects of language (again *la langue*) which he cannot.

The results of this study seem to contradict certain implications of these constructs and to support others. The writer of stories in response to TAT cards is exhibiting *la parole*. The fact that structural and lexical meaning are similarly controlled by the producer fits Saussure's concepts. When one considers the interpretive side, points of contradiction arise. *La langue* is defined by the characteristic that no individual in a language community possesses it. It is the sum of all individual language possessions. Contradictorily, from the present study one infers a language subsystem (the structural) which allows a particular language user to possess *all* possibilities in that subsystem. This is not to say that every language user actually possesses the total distribution, but rather that, in principle, this is possible. The other subsystem (the lexical) is unobtainable in its entirety by any one member of the language community, not because of its enormous size alone, but, in principle, because of basic denotative and connotative contradictions. Denotatively, for example, the same individual cannot assign two contradictory sense impressions to the same object simultaneously. In association studies, iodine is reported by some subjects as "red" and by other subjects as "brown" (Underwood, 1956). One does not conceive of iodine as "red" and "brown" simultaneously in this language community. Connotatively, the word "dog" cannot arouse panic and calm contemplation in the same individual simultaneously. Both reactions, however, may be exhibited consistently by different members of the language community.

Hockett (1963) lists the characteristic of "plural subsystems" as one of the universals of language. Whatever the nature of the constructs by which linguists delineate the categories, there is a ubiquitous emphasis on an enormous number of content elements, mapped onto a small number of meaningless, but message-differentiating, elements. This study demonstrates a differentiation in psychological responses to two of the widely used linguistic categories.

REFERENCES

Coleman, E. B. "Developing a technology of written instruction: Some determiners of the complexity of prose." In E. Z. Rothkopf and P. E. Johnson, *Verbal Learning Research and the Technology of Written Instruction.* NY Teachers College, Columbia Univ., pp. 155–204.

Fries, C. C. *The structure of English.* New York: Harcourt Brace, 1952.

Hockett, C. F. The problem of universals in language. In J. H. Greenberg (ed.), *Universals of language.* Cambridge: The Massachusetts Institute of Technology Press, 1963. Pp. 1–22. Reprinted in Hockett, *The View from Language: Selected Essays, 1948–1974.* Athens: The University of Georgia Press, 1977. Pp. 163–186.

Rankin, E. F. Jr. An evaluation of the cloze procedure as a technique for measuring reading comprehension. Unpublished Ph.D. dissertation, University of Michigan, 1957.

Saussure, F. de. *Course in general linguistics.* (Trans. by C. Bally & A. Sechehaye.) New York: Philosophical Library, 1959.

Taylor, W. L. Application of "cloze" and entropy measures to the study of contextual constraint in samples of continuous prose. Unpublished Ph.D. dissertation, University of Illinois, 1954.

Underwood, B. J., & Richardson, J. Some verbal materials for the study of concept formation. *Psychological Bulletin,* 1956, 53, 84–95.

Affective Correlates of Reading Comprehension

Few students of language have denied that affect plays a part in the acquisition, retention, and comprehension of language. Rankin (5) reported that extroverts (who are characterized as having greater impulsivity than introverts) scored lower on precloze tests of reading comprehension than did introverts. Since this difference was not apparent on postcloze tests, Rankin concluded that the "erratic responses" of the extroverts on the precloze test were responsible for this result. Rankin also found that "manifest anxiety" affected cloze scores. The cloze tests were related to anxiety because high anxiety subjects were "threatened" by the "initial difficulty of the items" (4).

Kingston and White (1) and White, Kingston, and Weaver (8) investigated the relationship of judgments of the concept *self* to judgments of the concept *protagonist* (of a story) by means of the Osgood Semantic Differential (SD). Subjects were divided into high anxious and low anxious, using the 16-PF second-order "anxiety" factor scores. Among high anxious subjects, predictions of the general semantic meaning of the protagonist (evaluation, activity, and potency) could be made as well as predictions of the subject's concept of *self* (evaluation and potency). Among low anxious subjects, only self-concept variables (potency and activity) were predictable from personality factors.

In the same study, extroverts and introverts were identified on the criterion of the second-order factors of the 16-PF. Subjects with relatively high second-order factor scores on "extroversion" projected "tangibility" into protagonist's ratings and "activity" into their own self-concept measures. Introverted subjects projected "anxiety" onto the protagonist as well as "evaluating" their own self-concepts.

Osgood (2, 3) postulates a kind of "meaning" related to connotation and proposes that the Semantic Differential (SD) indexes this meaning. The SD required the construction of a "semantic space" by having subjects judge concepts on a scale composed of bipolar adjectives. There is nothing in this technique which prevents concepts having widely varying denotative meanings from falling in the same semantic space, or, conversely, nothing to cause concepts of very similar denotation from falling in widely differing semantic spaces. Furthermore, there is no

(Co-authored with W. F. White and Albert J. Kingston.) Originally published in the *Journal of Psychology*, 1968, 68, 87–95. Reprinted with the permission of the Journal Press.

assurance that the use of this procedure exhausts the domain "connotation of language." Nevertheless, the Osgood instrument has exhibited the power to index underlying affective components of language and deserves careful consideration in a study of affect and cognition.

Measures of cognition are often categorized by intended function—e.g., achievement, intelligence—or by type of item—e.g., multiple-choice, essay. The cognitive tasks of this study are of the deleted work variety—commonly called cloze tests. Postcloze tests are administered after the reading of a passage from which the deletion is drawn and are thus similar to achievement tests. It is much more difficult to decide how precloze tests should be categorized. They depend upon general background knowledge of the subject and upon his ability to utilize the redundancy inherent in language. They correlate relatively high (in the 70s) with standard test of intelligence (7).

HYPOTHESES

A number of predictions were made about the relationship of cognition (as measured by the cloze procedure) and affect (as measured by the 16-PF second-order factors and the judgments of *self* and *protagonist* concepts on the Semantic Differential). These were as follows:

1. Precloze tests, the 16-PF, and the SD-self will share a dimension definable as "anxiety."
2. Precloze tests will be less predictable by high anxiety subjects than will postcloze tests.
3. Precloze tests, postcloze tests, the 16-PF, and the SD-*self* will share a dimension definable as introversion-extroversion.
4. Precloze tests will be less predictable by introverted subjects than by extroverted subjects.
5. The *protagonist,* as measured by the SD, will be better predicted by low anxious than by high anxious subjects.
6. The *protagonist,* as measured by the SD, will be better predicted by the introverted than by extroverted subjects.
7. Precloze tests will be more closely related to sentences of the story which reflect affect: i.e., which contain "affect-ladened" words.

METHOD

Subjects

The subjects were 80 senior division, undergraduate, female students enrolled in eight sections of an educational psychology course.

Procedure

Tests were given in the following order: precloze, SD-*self,* 16-PF, postcloze, SD-*protagonist.* Subjects read the passage, "I Starved for Science" (6), just before taking the postcloze and SD-protagonist tests. All subjects were tested during the same two-week period. Three testing sessions were used. Subjects were told that the experiment was designed to study language, not to appraise or study their personalities. An attempt to motivate subjects more fully was made by informing them that the results of the experimentation would be discussed with them.

Analysis

The 16-PF was scored in the routine manner and the raw scores factor analyzed. Six second-order factors appeared in the analysis. Although the components varied somewhat from Cattell's findings, it was felt that the analysis was close enough to Cattell's to use his designation in naming the factors.

The Semantic Differential was factor analyzed separately for *self* and *protagonist concepts.* Three factors were found in both analyses. These were identified as being similar in structure to Osgood's "activity," "potency," and "evaluation" factors. The factor scores from these analyses were used throughout the study.

RESULTS

The first four hypotheses were not supported by the data. No marked relationships were observed among precloze tests, 16-PF second-order factors, and the Semantic Differential within the same system. Variable interactions were noted when a principle components analysis was applied to the data (see Table 1).

Factor II in the analysis of the principle components was defined by the SD-self activity factor and introversion-extroversion second-order factor of the 16-PF. In an attempt to determine the relationships of the three SD-self factors and the six 16-PF second-order factors, a canonical correlation was obtained between the two sets of variables ($R = .60$, $p<.01$). While the SD-self activity coefficient was .97, the introversion-extroversion (16-PF) factor was −.81. The remaining coefficients were relatively low, ranging from .05 to .37.

Hypotheses 5 and 7 were tested by a canonical correlational analysis between the three SD-protagonist factors and the 16-PF second-order factors. One of the canonical correlations ($R = .41$) approached a significant level ($p < .10$), but no correlation was significant at the chosen .05 level of confidence.

Table 1. Principle components factor analysis of precloze, postcloze, 16-PF, SD-Self, and SD-Protagonist

Variable	I	II	III	IV	V	VI	VII	VIII	IX	X	XI	h^2
Precloze												
Struc-concept 1								57				.54
Struc-concept 2		48							40			.65
Lex-concept 1									80			.71
Lex-concept 2					76							.75
Struc-affect 1		76										.69
Struc-affect 2							56					.60
Lex-affect 1									67			.60
Lex-affect 2		68										.64
Postcloze												
Struc-concept 1	45										54	.72
Struc-concept 2	47											.67
Lex-concept 1	66											.68
Lex-concept 2	76											.75
Struc-affect 1	39		45								50	.79
Struc-affect 2	75											.61
Lex-affect 1	67											.63
Lex-affect 2	53							47				.72
Semantic Differential												
Self-activity		79										.70
Self-potency							78					.73
Self-evaluation				39								.70
Protag-potency										57		.61
Protag-evaluation											−73	.67
Protag-activity										−74		.78
16-PF												
Factor I				−89								.83
Factor II		−83										.74
Factor III				40	50							.76
Factor IV								77				.75
Factor V						40	−64					.72
Factor VI			82									.76

Note: Loadings below .39 are not considered in the analysis.

Hypothesis 7 was not sustained in the form in which it was stated. There were differential effects of cloze results from sentences chosen to sample "affect."

To explore the data from promising hypotheses, other analyses were made. A step-wise regression was applied to cloze test responses and SD-protagonist measures. Results are found in Tables 2 and 3.

Table 2. Step-wise regression analysis
of the activity (SD-Protagonist) factor as a dependent variable;
cloze tests as independent variables

Order of cloze variable entering	Cumulative multiple R	Cumulative multiple R-square
Postlex concept	.15	.02
Postlex affect	.28	.08*
Prestruc concept	.29	.09
Prelex concept	.31	.10
Prelex affect	.32	.10
Prestruc affect	.32	.10
Poststruc affect	.32	.10
Poststruc concept	.32	.10

*Significant at .05 level.

The activity factor, which tends to dominate all the relationships between SD-self and the 16-PF, exhibits a tenuous correlation to the postlex affect test (Table 2). In Table 3 two postcloze tests, which were deletions of sentences selected because of an apparent absence of affect meaning, were related to the SD-protagonist, evaluation factor.

Relationships between cloze tests and SD-self measurements appear to be more predictable than SD-protagonist and cloze test variables (see Tables 4 and 5).

The activity factor of the SD-self dimension is predictable from the entire battery of cloze tests in the analysis. Potency appears to relate selectively to those cloze tests which were constructed from sentences introspectively judged to contain "affect words."

A step-wise regression analysis was applied to the second-order factor scores of the 16-PF as dependent variables and the cloze test scores as independent variables.

Table 3. Step-wise regression analysis
of the evaluation (SD-Protagonist) factor, as a dependent variable;
cloze tests as independent variables

Order of cloze variable entering	Cumulative multiple R	Cumulative multiple R-square
Poststruc concept	.29	.08*
Postlex concept	.33	.11*
Prestruc affect	.34	.12
Poststruc affect	.35	.12
Prelex affect	.36	.13
Prestruc concept	.36	.13
Postlex affect	.37	.13
Prelex concept	.37	.14

*Significant at .05 level.

Table 4. Step-wise regression analysis
of the factor activity (SD-Self) factor, as a dependent variable;
cloze tests as independent variables

Order of cloze variable entering	Cumulative multiple R	Cumulative multiple R-square
Poststruc concept	.26	.07*
Prestruc affect	.34	.11*
Postlex concept	.39	.15*
Prestruc concept	.42	.17*
Postlex affect	.44	.18*
Poststruc affect	.44	.19*
Prelex concept	.44	.20*

*Significant at .05 level.

Neither anxiety nor extroversion-introversion were observed to have any relationship to cloze tests, yet the second-order factors III and IV predicted cloze test scores. A single, well-defined postcloze test factor was identified, which included all postcloze test conditions: structural, lexical, concept-affect, and subtests 1 or 2.

The Semantic Differential ratings on the concepts of *self* and *protagonist* did not share significant variance.

Table 5. Step-wise regression analysis of the potency (SD-Self) factor, as a dependent variable; cloze tests as independent variables

Order of cloze variable entering	Cumulative multiple R	Cumulative multiple R-square
Prestruc concept	.19	.04
Poststruc affect	.31	.09*
Prelex affect	.38	.14*
Prestruc affect	.39	.15*
Postlex affect	.40	.16*
Prelex concept	.41	.17

*Significant at .05 level.

DISCUSSION

There was no manipulation of the data which indicated that a general affective factor was operative in all the instruments used. In no analysis did the cloze tests, the 16-PF second-order factors, and the Semantic Differential appear in one system of relationships. There were, however, binary relationships between a number of pairs. These findings seem to indicate that affect does not readily appear as a general component underlying all types of affective and cognitive measurement. Valid measurements of affect seem to require specification of a relatively small domain. Even the Semantic Differential, which usually is taken to mean all things to measurements affect-wise, does not exhibit generality in this study. Rather it appears as a specific affect measure related to specific cognitive conditions.

The most stable binary relationship found was between the cloze tests and the SD-*self* "activity" factor. Perhaps a type of "temperament" variable may be involved here which allows highly active subjects to attend more effectively to long stretches of rather boring material.

The "potency" factor of the SD-self was predicted by cloze tests of "affect." The "affect" cloze was constructed, introspectively, to contrast with "conceptual" cloze. The affect cloze sentences were of the type "Some of the men began to get bald," and "We let little doubts and worries get the best of us." So-called "conceptual" sentences were of the type "This fat was used in cooking," and "Some postponed part of their college work." When cloze deletions were carried out on this kind of material, all "affect" tests—pre and post, structural and lexical—were involved in the prediction of "potency." "Conceptual" tests were not involved. The expectation was that subjects would be more inhibited on "affect" tests than on "conceptual" tests and, thus, performance would suffer. The opposite seemed to be true. Subjects scored much better on "affect" tests than on "conceptual" tests. Again an explanation may be that the so-called "conceptual" tests were just too dull to keep attention going until the tasks were completed. A check on incomplete items however revealed no more items were omitted on the conceptual cloze than on the affect cloze.

When we turn to the SD-protagonist, the first impressive result was that no precloze test predicts the Osgood factors for the protagonist. Since at this point in the study the subjects have not read the passage in its integrated form, and have seen only randomly ordered sentences sampled from the passage, containing 20 percent deletion of words, one would be hard-pressed to explain the relationships if they appeared. This result should also be considered in light of the prior finding with the SD-self, where pretests are as effective as posttests in predicting. Success with pretests in relation to the SD-self, then, are convincingly separated from success with pretest in relation to the SD-protagonist. One is encouraged to interpret the SD-self–cloze result as depending upon subject variables regarding his own person, while interpreting the SD-protagonist–cloze results as depending upon subject variables when the subject is indeed considering the character of the story which the experimenters presented.

No relationships were found between the 16-PF "anxiety" and "extroversion-introversion" factors and the cloze tasks. Cloze tests were predicted, however, by the second-order factors which Cattell calls "tough poise" and "independence." All cloze tests supplied variance positively related to the "tough poise" factor. In the case of the "independence" factor, the variance was supplied by postcloze tests only, and the high postcloze scores were negatively related to the positive end pole of the "independence" factor. This might be explained as a "rigidity" effect, with more dependent subjects tightly bound to doing the task "right," even though it might not be intrinsically rewarding.

As Kingston and White (1) have noted before, there is a substantial relationship between the two major 16-PF factors and SD measures. For this particular sample the relationship between the activity dimensions of the SD-self and the extroversion-introversion dimension of the 16-PF was particularly strong. The relationship between the 16-PF "anxiety" and "extroversion-introversion" second-order factors and the SD-protagonist measure has been consistent in other studies of this nature and it is probable that only the limited number of subjects employed in this study may underlie the failure of this relationship to attain statistical significance at the .05 level. It should not be surprising that relationships between a "personal" anxiety and a "personal" extroversion-introversion are more weakly related to affective judgments of the "main character" of a story than are SD-self concepts.

As may be seen by studying the tables in this study, a relatively small amount of variance, on the order of 10 to 20 percent, is attributable to affective influences on cognition. This implies that errors of measurement in the instruments used to examine these relationships must be reduced as much as possible, or else the error variance will easily obscure the treatment effects. A number of cloze categorizations were combined in this study in order to insure higher reliability.

SUMMARY

A study was performed to examine the relationship between the cloze procedure (as a measure of reading comprehension) and affect measures (the Semantic Differential and the 16-PF). The three measures did not appear in one system of relationships. A number of binary relationships between the cloze procedure and the affect measures did appear, however.

It was concluded that the affect component in cognition is more specific than is generally assumed. Further studies are underway examining this specificity in detail.

REFERENCES

1. Kingston, A. J., Jr., & White, W. F. The relationship of reader's personality components to semantic meanings perceived in the protagonist of a reading selection. *Reading Res. Quart.,* 1967, 2, 107–116.

2. Osgood, C. E. Studies on the generality of affective meaning systems. *Amer. Psychol.,* 1962, 17, 10–28.

3. Osgood, C. E., *et al.* Analysis of the connotative meanings of a variety of human values as expressed by American college students. *J. Abn. & Soc. Psychol.,* 1961, 62, 62–73.

4. Rankin, E. F., Jr. An evaluation of the cloze procedure as a technique for measuring reading comprehension. Unpublished Doctoral dissertation, Univeristy of Michigan, Ann Arbor, Michigan, 1957.

5. _____. Reading test reliability and validity as a function of introversion-extroversion. *J. Devel. Reading,* 1963, 6, 106–117.

6. Simpson, E. A. Better Reading Book. Chicago, Ill.: Sci. Res. Assoc., 1962.

7. Taylor, W. L. Cloze readability scores as indices of individual differences in comprehension and aptitude. *J. Appl. Psychol.,* 1957, 41, 19–26.

8. White, W. F., Kingston, A., Jr., & Weaver, W. W. Affective dimensions in the connotative meaning in reading. *J. of Psychol.,* 1967, 67, 227–234.

A Cross-Validation Study of the Relationship of Reading Test Items to Their Relevant Paragraphs

Weaver and Bickley (1967) and Bickley, Weaver, and Ford (1968) have shown (using a stratified sampling of paragraphs taken from standard reading comprehension tests) that certain test items which supposedly show how well subjects have read the accompanying reading paragraphs were answered as well by subjects who did not have the paragraph to read as subjects who had the intact paragraph to read. This study is a comparison of items that are dependent upon reading a passage prior to their successful completion as opposed to items which have a very loose relationship to the accompanying reading paragraph.

Ostensibly, the rationale of reading comprehension tests is that the subjects reads a paragraph and answers the test items presented because he has read the relevant paragraph. The definition of reading in English and English (1958) implies that a reading passage allows the author of the passage to communicate with a reader, and this communication is the reading process. The reading passage, then, should control the reader's behavior. It seems that if items can be answered without the reading of their relevant paragraphs, the subject is bringing information to the situation and to some degree this information rather than the reading paragraph is controlling the reading process. Although this information pool may be correlated with whatever skills are required for reading the paragraph, nevertheless, there is no one-to-one relationship between the paragraphs and answering certain kinds of test items.

PROCEDURE

In the two studies mentioned above, a blackout procedure was used to vary paragraph-reading conditions as treatment variables. Blackout involves masking particular parts of the reading paragraph and then presenting the items to subjects under these conditions. One blackout treatment involved deleting the entire reading paragraph and instructing subjects to fill in the multiple-choice blanks. Under this treatment subjects filled in many more of the particular test items than would be expected by chance. On the other hand, there were items which were filled in by very

(Co-authored with A. C. Bickley and F. G. Ford.) Originally published in *Perceptual and Motor Skills,* 1969, 29, 11–14. Reprinted with the permission of the publisher.

few subjects under these conditions. In this study items were chosen from standardized test paragraphs on which subjects had previously performed well without the reading paragraph. These items were matched with items from the same paragraph on which subjects had not performed well without the reading paragraph. Forty items were selected for each test. This formed the dimension of "more" and "less" relatedness to the reading paragraph. The other categorization was reading paragraph "present" or "absent."

One hundred forty-eight subjects were assigned randomly to one of the four treatment conditions. There were 37 subjects in each group. Treatments were as follows: (1) Reading paragraph present; More paragraph relatedness; (2) Reading paragraph present; Less paragraph relatedness; (3) Reading paragraph absent; More paragraph relatedness; (4) Reading paragraph absent; Less paragraph relatedness. Although the same items obviously could not be used for the relatedness treatment, the items were drawn from a common source, i.e., the same number of samples of each condition were represented within each paragraph.

The subjects were introductory psychology and educational psychology students at the University of Georgia, Athens, and at Campbell College, Buies Creek, N.C. The subjects were predominantly sophomores and juniors. Instructions were given to the no reading-paragraphs group emphasizing the experimental nature of the task in order to minimize the effects of the "face invalidity" of the task. The subjects given the reading paragraphs were also presented the material as involving experimentation and attempts were made to maximize motivation. The subjects were presented the materials in their regular classrooms. Randomization was effected by presenting all four treatments to individuals in each intact class.

RESULTS

Means, standard deviations, reliabilities, and the sum of the raw scores on each treatment are presented in Table 1. A two-way analysis of variance with fixed factors was performed (cf. Table 2). Both main effects and the interaction were significant at the preset .05 level.

The differential response to items of certain types is confirmed. When the nature of the particular items which are easy to complete without the reading paragraph is examined, one finds items which contain factual information: items which might appear on a test like the "Information" subtest of the Wechsler. On the other hand, items which are difficult to obtain correct responses for without the reading paragraphs are almost always indirectly related to the information in the reading paragraph;

Table 1. Means, standard deviations, and split-half reliabilities

Tests	M	SD	r(K-R-20)
Reading paragraph, less relatedness	23.5	12.8	.89
Reading paragraph, more relatedness	18.4	13.6	.87
No reading paragraph, less relatedness	18.4	3.3	.84
No reading paragraph, more relatedness	9.0	3.6	.83

Table 2. Summary table: analysis of variance

Source	SS	df	MS	F	P
Item dependency	2,195	1	2,195	169.2	.05
Paragraph condition	1,675	1	1,675	129.1	.05
Interaction	260	1	260	20.0	.05
Within groups	1,868	144	12.97		
Total	5,998	147			

they seem to require the operations of induction or deduction, i.e., logical operations, in order that the subject be able to complete the item correctly.

It seems that the sort of thing which is happening in the reading test is that the range of difficulty is produced by first giving so-called easy items which come from a common pool of information which many subjects have already attained. Essentially this information presented in the paragraph is redundant and, while it undoubtedly enables the subject to be more precise in his responses, it is not necessary for many of the items. The difficult items involve an entirely different set of mental operations. These items come from a set of items which are related to reasoning processes and which only depend peripherally upon the actual information in the reading paragraph. However, the reading paragraph, though insufficient, is necessary. The items depend upon meanings implied by the reading paragraph, but they cannot be answered without "reading between the lines" and imposing further rational processes upon the materials.

Although the interaction value in this study reaches statistical significance, this occurs because of the greater decline in mean from the reading to non-reading condition of the more relatedness treatment as compared to the smaller decline in mean from the reading to non-reading condition of the less relatedness treatment. In other words, with the materials used here there is a difference between having or not having a reading paragraph even in the less relatedness to reading paragraph condition, but this effect is much more pronounced in the more relatedness to reading paragraph condition.

There is a further interesting question, which we intend to investigate, of whether or not there are different factor structures involved in the presentations of these different item types. Studies are underway using different kinds of concepts of testing reading ability which attempt to separate the factor that seems to be related to the actual information which individuals bring to the reading situation from the information that subjects must deduce from the explicit facts in the reading passage.

REFERENCES

Bickley, A. C., Weaver, W. W., & Ford, F. G. Information removed from multiple-choice item responses by selected grammatical categories. *Psychological Reports,* 1968, 23, 613–614.

English, H. B., & English, A. C. *A comprehensive dictionary of psychological and psychoanalytical terms.* New York: David McKay, 1968.

Weaver, W. W., & Bickley, A. C. Sources of information for response to reading test items. *Proceedings of the 75th Annual Convention, APA,* 1967, 2, 7. (Abstract)

The Effect of Reading Variation and Punctuation Conditions Upon Reading Comprehension

This is a study of the effect upon reading comprehension of reading variation (silent reading, reporting the last word of each sentence read aloud, and reading aloud) and punctuation condition (all of the reading passage punctuated, or none of the reading passage punctuated). Reading comprehension was measured by (a) a noun cloze test; (b) the sum of individual test item latencies; (c) the total required to read the stimulus passage; and (d) the total time required to take the oral test.

THE PROBLEM

Reading Variation

Oral reading and silent reading have been considered to involve different processes. Oral reading has been shown to be slower than silent reading (Huey, 1908), and to result in poorer comprehension (Gilbert, 1940). Oral reading involves a productive operation imposed upon an interpretive process. It can be demonstrated that some individuals can read orally, with proper intonation and stress, material which they cannot understand. On the other hand there is no clear separation of the two tasks. Some people reading aloud seem to understand as much as when reading silently, and most people understand what they read orally to some degree. The difficulty with silent reading for the experimenter is that he cannot apply direct measurement to the reading: he must take his measurements of the total time of the act, or he may measure after the reading act is completed. Oral reading, on the other hand, lends itself to a constant monitoring of the reading act. Here, the relationship of oral to silent reading is studied using several comprehension measures.

Punctuation Conditions

In the reading display, punctuation serves as a cue for intonation and stress. It would seem that if all punctuation is removed from a passage the subject should have to depend to a much greater degree upon his internal organization of the proper sentence patterning. It also seems reasonable

(Co-authored with C. C. Holmes and R. J. Reynolds.) Originally published in the *Journal of Reading Behavior,* 1970, 2(1), 75–84. Reprinted with the permission of the National Reading Conference.

to hypothesize that comprehension will suffer if comprehension is tied to understanding structure.

Measuring Reading Comprehension

Operationally, reading comprehension is generally defined by (a) a subject reading a passage; (b) the subject is asked questions about that passage; and (c) answers the questions with a match to a keyed "right" answer. Weaver and Bickley (1968) have shown that the first part of this chain of events cannot be assumed, i.e., steps *a* and *c* can be carried out successfully at a rate greater than chance without having the reading passage available for reading. However, standard reading tests of comprehension constructed with the above assumptions have been the most widely used measures of comprehension. Cloze tests, such as those used in this study, have correlated highly with comprehension as measured by these multiple-choice reading tests.

Latency Measurement

The measurement of psychological functions using the time required to perform that function has a long, complex history. It is obvious from observing individuals attempting to complete cloze units orally that different latencies exist related to the type of verbal unit with which the subject is dealing. Goldman-Eisler (1961) has shown that short and long pauses in extemporaneous speech are correlated with the ease of completion of cloze units and that the number of words filled in by the subjects at particular cloze units are related to ease of cloze completion. It would seem to follow from studies like these that information intrincity is related to the time which subjects require to complete cloze units.

PROCEDURE

Subjects

Eighteen volunteer undergraduate students from introductory psychology courses at the University of Georgia were used as subjects. Four paragraphs of varying difficulty were presented to them in a preestablished arbitrary order. All subjects were introduced to the task by practicing on the oral, reading, punctuated condition, and receiving the test on that condition. (Bormuth, Passage 13 was used for practice.)

Materials

Paragraphs numbered 11, 12, 16 and 20 were selected from Bormuth's (1966) materials. This set of materials had been calibrated for difficulty by having subjects guess every word in a reading passage and using the mean percentage success of guessing as an index of difficulty. The materials were scaled from 1 (easiest) to 20 (hardest). Each subject received all 4 stimulus passages.

Weaver and Bickley (1968) have shown that nouns carry most lexical information in sentence units. All nouns in the passages were identified and every 5th noun deleted, until 20 nouns were deleted in each of the four paragraphs.

Method

The 18 subjects were assigned randomly to one of six conditions as follows: Oral reading, punctuated; oral reading, unpunctuated; reading final word in sentence, punctuated; reading final word in sentence, unpunctuated; silent reading, punctuated; silent reading, unpunctuated. The test was a cloze test over the reading passages. The test was punctuated, and was always read aloud by the subject in whatever reading condition to which he was assigned. The entire procedure was recorded on a standard Wollensak tape-recorder. For the silent reading and the one word reading conditions the examiner indicated when the subject began and ended his reading of each passage. Latency scores were obtained from the recorded tape using a stop watch accurate to one tenth of a second.

Analysis of the Data

Because of the reputed increment in difficulty levels of the paragraphs employed, each paragraph was treated as a level with each of the dependent variables held to be independent assessments of the effects of level. The repeated measures design, similar to trend analysis, was employed as the analysis technique. Reading and punctuation effects were considered to be fixed; levels of difficulty (paragraph context) were held to be randomly assigned. Edwards (1968) provides a conceptual paradigm and a computing algorithm for the analysis. Reference to the analysis of variance tables indicates that two error terms are utilized in analyzing the treatment effects. Error term (a) refers to the error associated with the fixed effects of reading and punctuation; error term (b) is the appropriate error term for all elements of the variance containing a component of the random variable difficulty (paragraph context).

CRITERIA

The dependent variables used to tap the validity of Bormuth's difficulty levels are (1) total test score, (2) total cloze item latency, (3) total reading time, and (4) total test latency. Total test score was defined as the number of cloze items scored correctly by the subject. Total cloze item latency was defined as the sum of the latencies for each cloze item over the entire set of items for each paragraph. Total reading time was taken as the time required to read a paragraph under one of the six treatment constraints. Total test latency was defined as the time required to read the target paragraph under treatment constraint after deletion for cloze.

RESULTS

Analysis of the data by the repeated measures variance analysis indicated a significant effect for context difficulty over three of the four tasks examined. Total cloze score, total item latency, and total reading time each were affected by difficulty level. A main effect of reading variation appeared on the total cloze score variable as well as an interaction between conditions of reading and punctuation (see Table 1).

Table 1. Analysis of variance of total cloze scores

Source	Sum of squares	df	MS	F	P
A (reading)	50,250	2	25,125	3,941	.05
B (punctuation)	7,347	1	7,347	1,152	n.s.
AXB	134,028	2	67,014	10,512	.01
Error (a)	76,500	12	6,375	—	
C (difficulty)	278,875	3	92,958	36,311	.01
AXC	7,584	6	1,264	<1	n.s.
BXC	5,208	3	1,736	<1	n.s.
AXBXC	15,916	6	2,652	1,035	n.s.
Error (b)	92,167	36	2,560	—	
Total	667,875	71			

Examination of the means for trials of cloze scores indicates that the trend of the difficulty level suggested by Bormuth (1966) is not upheld for these data (see Table 2). The expectation that Paragraph 11, purported to be easiest, should have the highest cloze score while Paragraph 20 should have the lowest, was found untenable. This finding was further substantiated by using item latency as a measure of difficulty. Latency was affected by difficulty level (see Table 3), but again the difference in means was not in the expected direction (see Table 4).

Two other indices of difficulty were utilized to tap the validity of Bormuth's difficulty levels: total reading time and total test time. Reading

Table 2. Means of cloze items for four levels of paragraph difficulty

Paragraph	Mean	Rank of mean	Expected rank
11	11.11	2	1
12	6.83	4	2
16	12.00	1	3
20	10.55	3	4

Table 3. Analysis of variance of total item latency

Source	Sum of squares	df	MS	F	P
A (reading)	1993.79	2	996.89	1.11	n.s.
B (punctuation)	459.05	1	459.05	<1.	n.s.
AXB	1347.18	1	673.59	<1.	n.s.
Error (a)	10749.43	12	895.78	—	
C (difficulty)	1151.13	3	383.71	3.39	.05
AXC	788.49	6	131.41	1.16	n.s.
BXC	380.20	3	126.73	1.12	n.s.
AXBXC	1324.72	6	220.78	1.95	n.s.
Error (b)	4066.04	36	112.94	112.94	
Total	22260.03	72			

Table 4. Means of item latencies
for four levels of paragraph difficulty

Paragraph	Mean	Rank of mean	Expected rank
11	34.07	3	1
12	39.95	1	2
26	28.89	4	3
20	36.20	2	4

time was found to be related to condition of reading as well as to difficulty level (see Table 5). Reading aloud was found to be more time consuming than either of the other reading conditions. Level of difficulty, while significant, was found to be as divergent from the expected trend as either of the preceding measures, with the ranking of the trial means exactly paralleling that of the total cloze score. The final measure of difficulty, total test time, was found to be unrelated to the purported levels of difficulty. While the ordering of trial means was found to be aberrant from expectation based on Bormuth's ordering, the differences were not significant.

Table 5. Analysis of variance of total reading time
as an index of difficulty

Source	Sum of squares	df	MS	F	P
A (reading)	6529.39	2	3264.69	8.745	.01
B (punctuation)	645.99	1	645.99	1.730	n.s.
AXB	217.77	2	108.88	<1.	n.s.
Error (a)	4479.79	12	373.31	—	
C (difficulty)	3343.40	3	1114.46	16.473	.01
AXC	470.99	6	78.49	1.160	n.s.
BXC	491.70	3	163.90	2.422	n.s.
AXBXC	652.74	6	108.79	1.608	n.s.
Error (b)	2435.39	36	67.65	—	
Total	19267.16	71			

DISCUSSION

Bormuth (1966) suggests that the cloze procedure might be used to determine readability levels for language units at word and sub-word levels. It would seem from this that one could infer that larger language unit aggregates such as collections of words of the same part of speech should lend themselves to ranking by the cloze procedures. This study indicates that various measures of parts of language passages rank the difficulty of the passage in different orders. Not only were the passages not ranked in Bormuth's order by the cloze measures, but the latency measures did not rank the passages in the same order as the cloze procedure and they also differed among their rankings. The difficulty rankings did not interact with the other variables although one would expect that if reading aloud is more difficult than reading silently, the more difficult the passage the more pronounced the effect.

Reading silently allowed significantly higher scores on the cloze comprehension measure and significantly lower scores on total reading time. The reading aloud condition and the reading aloud one word at the end of the sentence condition have very similar effects. The imposing of the verbal production task has about the same inhibiting effect upon comprehension as reading aloud. It is not clear whether this is an effect of the production itself, or whether it is an effect of the place in the sentence where the production is required. Furthermore, a motor indication of the position of the reader in the sentence should be less inhibiting than the verbal production.

The interaction between reading condition and punctuation condition is unexpected. Silent readers of punctuated material score higher than silent readers of unpunctuated materials, but one-word readers of unpunctuated materials score higher than one-word readers of punctuated materials. It is possible that the task requirement that the subject report the word at the end of each sentence, better focuses the attention of the subjects on the structure of the sentence, while the task requirement in the comparable condition that the subject produce the word at the end of the sentence in punctuated material allows the subject to concentrate on producing the required word only, thus missing to some extent, perhaps, the structure of the sentence and the precision of its message.

This study, though carried out on a small population, leads to a number of experimental problems which are being investigated. There is the possibility that there were no differences in the punctuation condition because all of the tests were punctuated and no matter what condition was assigned a subject he always ended with a punctuated, oral test. Latencies of test items were taken on all items. A better measure might be latency on right items (or on wrong ones). Total reading time proved a promising dependent measure, agreeing with the cloze test findings in all but the reading by punctuation interaction. The possibility of developing a task which approximates the silent reading task, but allows the experimenter to locate the position of the reader in the text failed here, but indicated above are modifications of the technique which have promise.

SUMMARY

Levels of difficulty of paragraph context were analyzed relative to Bormuth's scaling for difficulty paradigm. Differing levels produced different results on cloze and latency tasks but not in the fashion expected from Bormuth's scalings. Level of difficulty consistently was demonstrated to be in contradistinction to the levels suggested. Reading process variations were found to be generally consistent with previous findings. Interaction between reading process and punctuation was found as a function of cloze deletions and discussed as a constraint on both message and precision of comprehension.

REFERENCES

Bormuth, John. "Readability: A New Approach." *Reading Research Quarterly* 3:79–132, Spring 1966.

Edwards, Allen. *Experimental Design in Psychological Research.* New York: Holt, Rinehart, and Winston, 1968.

Gilbert, Luther. "The Effect on Silent Reading of Attempting to Follow Oral Reading." *Elementary School Journal* 40:614–21, April 1940.

Goldman-Eisler, Frieda. "The Predictability of Words in Context and the Length of Pauses in Speech." *Journal of Communication* 11, 2:95–99, June 1961.

Huey, Edmund. *Psychology and Pedagogy of Reading.* New York: The Macmillan Company, 1908.

Weaver, Wendell, and Bickley, A. Charles. "Structural-Lexical Predictability of Materials Which Predictor Has Previously Produced or Read." *Proceedings, 75th Annual Convention, APA.* 289–290. 1967.

Weaver, Wendell, and Bickley, A. Charles. "Information Removed from Multiple-Choice Item Responses by Selected Grammatical Categories." *Psychological Reports* 23:613–614, Fall, 1968.

Information-Flow Difficulty in Relation to
Reading Comprehension

Since the days of Thorndike (1917) reading has been regarded as a "thinking" process. Comprehension has been considered as representing the major dimensions in which thought is manifested. Davis (1944) found that comprehension correlated highly with inductive and deductive reasoning tasks. Others, also, have demonstrated that reading comprehension correlated positively with thinking or with reasoning (Harootunian, 1966, Hage & Stroud, 1959). In contrast rote learning and paired associate learning have generally been considered to represent comparatively simple and less complex mental operations. English and English (1958, p. 291), define rote learning as "memorizing in which the tasks as seen by the learner requires no understanding but merely the reproduction of words or other symbols in the exact form in which they were presented." Other psychologists, however, view rote learning as more complex. Underwood (1964) and Miller (1958) apparently regard rote learning as akin to concept formation. Such views reflect the idea that rote learning is more complex than previously thought. It does seem clear, when one considers the volume of materials which can be processed in a given period of time, that rote memorization is not easily accomplished by the organism.

One of the major limitations on human information processing is the size of the input. Immediate memory capacity is constrained severely by the length of the input segment (Miller, 1956). A tape recorder has no difficulty storing large volumes of input, because it has no intermediate processing stages before access is gained to the memory storage unit. The human organism, in contrast, must select, rearrange, and modify information because it has two or more buffer storage units, each with different input-output characteristics, between input and final memory storage (Hunt, 1963). Input to memory in the human, then, must flow through a number of stages not designed for direct input-output processing. For example, the input is processed in short, unequal segments. This is indicated by such a reading phenomenon as the "Eye-voice span" where different portions of a continuous text are processed at different rates (Miller, 1951). In such instances there is a tendency to

(Co-authored with Albert J. Kingston, A. C. Bickley, and W. F. White.) Originally published in *Journal of Reading Behavior,* 1971, 1(4), 41–49. Reprinted with the permission of the National Reading Conference.

"chunk" the input, i.e., to recode it into larger "meaningful" units more congruent with the internal organization of the organism than was the original input (Miller, 1956). The list of probable steps in human information processing undoubtedly could be extended. The picture that emerges is one of enormous complexity in the processing stages through which information interchange flows within the organism. Giving the organism instructions to process data in a certain manner, e.g., exactly duplicate the input with output, does not decrease the complexity of the information exchange.

There is great likelihood that the rote learning process will correlate highly with other information processing and that learning differentials and relations to "understanding" will appear in rote learning processes as well as in problem-solving situations. In the rote learning situation subjects must retrieve information as well as store it. However, in certain rote learning tasks, e.g., paired associations, the subjects are instructed to retrieve only part of the input. These kinds of tasks point to the fact that input-output operations require retrieval as well as storage, and that with retrieval different problems are involved than those concerning storage. Rote learning involves at least two problem sets—problems involving input-storage, and problems involving retrieval-output.

In a subtest of the MLAT, subjects must translate from English numbers to nonsense syllables after they have learned the English-nonsense pairings by rote. Weaver and Kingston (1963) have called this process rote memory, flexible retrieval. It is believed that reading is somewhat similar to this type of processing protocol and should, therefore, correlate with rote learning variables.

This study explores certain of the relations between a reading comprehension measure, accuracy of communication measures (the cloze tests), association and rote learning tasks, and personality and attitudinal variables.

PROCEDURE

Subjects were fifty-three sophomores in Educational Psychology classes at the University of Georgia who had been involved in experiments concerning affective variables in reading and volunteered to continue the study by taking the Modern Language Aptitude Test (MLAT) and the Davis Reading Test (DRT). Previously they had taken the Cattell 16 PF, the Semantic Differential, and two cloze measures. They were given the standard instructions on all instruments used.

Two cloze tests were constructed from the reading passage, "I Starved for Science" (Simpson, 1962) by deleting every nth word of two separate stratified samples of the reading passage. One cloze test was designated "precloze" and was given to the subjects before they read the Simpson passage. The other called "postcloze" was given after the reading. The sum of the exact duplicates of deleted items was used as the score.

Subjects were also presented two identical rating scales of bi-polar adjectives and asked to rate the concept "Self" on one and the concept "Protagonist of the story" on the other. Responses to the two concepts were factor analyzed separately. The factors identified as Potency, Evaluation, and Activity emerged from the analysis contributing 64 percent (for Self) and 60 percent (for Protagonist) of the total cumulative variance. Factor scores on each of the three general semantic meanings were computed for both concepts for each of the subjects.

The second-order factor scores of each subject on the 16 PF were computed from the formulas in the Cattell (1962) manual. Cattell names the factors anxiety, extroversion-introversion, tough poise, and independence, and those terms are used here.

RESULTS

The total battery of tests given with means and standard deviations computed are reported in Table 1. Zero-order correlations are reported in Table 2.

Table 1. Means and standard deviations of tests used in the study

Davis Reading	40.28	13.50
Precloze	34.26	5.19
Semantic Differential Self Potency	16.77	2.92
Semantic Differential Self Evaluation	16.51	1.27
Semantic Differential Self Activity	16.83	1.95
Postcloze	35.38	6.91
16 PF Anxiety	5.54	1.74
16 PF Introversion-Extroversion	6.60	2.08
16 PF Tough-Poise	5.26	1.63
16 PF Independence	5.38	1.93
MLAT I	30.26	9.60
MLAT II	22.11	4.17
MLAT III	14.19	7.04
MLAT IV	27.49	8.04
MLAT V	18.77	5.54
SD Protagonist Potency	15.83	2.15
SD Protagonist Evaluation	17.02	2.02
SD Protagonist Activity	1.11	.32

Table 2. Correlations for all tests used in the study

Tests		2	3	4	5	6	7	8	9	10	11	12	13	14	15	16	17	18
							Correlations											
1.	Davis Reading	.28	.04	−.11	−.11	.46	−.10	−.00	−.13	.07	.34	.36	.49	.44	.22	.11	.27	−.08
2.	Precloze		.25	−.09	−.28	.44	.10	.20	.06	.13	.41	.43	.22	.38	.44	.22	−.04	−.02
3.	SD Self Potency			−.22	−.14	.18	−.29	.30	.13	.09	.18	.12	.11	.17	.28	.32	−.06	−.28
4.	SD Self Evaluation				.14	−.22	.20	−.07	−.13	.00	−.27	−.32	−.23	−.14	−.02	.07	.34	.05
5.	SD Self Activity					−.21	.09	.09	.08	−.27	.05	−.08	−.07	.04	.01	−.13	−.03	.06
6.	Postcloze						.02	.11	.06	.13	.60	.59	.27	.34	.47	.18	−.10	−.04
7.	16 PF Anxiety							−.36	−.41	−.08	−.09	−.09	−.07	−.14	.00	−.28	−.14	−.21
8.	16 PF Introversion-Extroversion								.52	.05	.07	.13	−.02	.07	.11	.34	.24	.05
9.	16 PF Tough-Poise									.21	.13	.10	.05	.03	.14	.06	.05	.26
10.	16 PF Independence										−.07	.03	.18	.05	.08	−.08	−.04	−.16
11.	MLAT I											.51	.37	.39	.47	.10	−.01	.01
12.	MLAT II												.43	.43	.50	.15	−.06	.05
13.	MLAT III													.56	.40	−.08	.01	−.12
14.	MLAT IV														.35	.00	.00	−.10
15.	MLAT V															.14	−.12	−.09
16.	SD Protagonist Potency																.11	−.11
17.	SD Protagonist Evaluation																	−.06
18.	SD Protagonist Activity																	

The basic regression analysis uses the Davis Reading Test as the criterion and is presented in Table 3. All variables in the study are present in the analysis. The spelling clues subtest of the MLAT (essentially a vocabulary measure) enters as the largest predictor, accounting for 24 percent of the variance. The semantic differential—protagonist: Evaluation is next in size, followed by the words-in-sentences subtest of the MLAT, a test which is thought to be related to grammatical sensitivity (Carroll, 1959).

Table 3. Significant variables in the step-wise regression analysis using the Davis Reading Test as the dependent variable

Order of cloze variable entering	Cumulative multiple R	Cumulative multiple R-square	Increase in R-square
MLAT III	.49	.24	.24
SD Protagonistic-Evaluation	.55	.30	.07
MLAT IV	.58	.35	.04

As a further analysis, two sub-problems were run using the Davis Reading Test as the criterion variable. One run excluded precloze test and postcloze test; the other run excluded the 16 PF second-order factors. The run with precloze and postcloze test out remained the same. However, when the 16 PF is left out, the postcloze test replaces the semantic differential—protagonist: evaluation in entering with the second largest variance.

Step-wise regression analyses were also run using precloze test and postcloze test as criterion variables. In each case, some one of the five subtests of the MLAT enters first, representing the major variance contribution. For the postcloze criterion, the Davis Reading Test always contributes a significant part of the variance. When the precloze test is the criterion, this is not true.

DISCUSSION

The results of this study provide further evidence for the interrelationships of rote learning processes and so-called higher level mental processes. The best predictors of reading comprehension and post-cloze scores are sub-tests of the MLAT which require the subject to learn by rote material with which he has little or no previous familiarity (in the sense of being able to relate the materials to semantic meaning). The response task which is required, however, forces the subject to revamp the input-storage in some manner, in order to produce the output specified by the examiner. The complexity of the process may be visualized by speculating about the conditions that would have to be imposed upon the input-storage required of the human. Obviously, nothing less than a complex information-manipulating program which would allow major rearrangements of the storage would suffice.

Another important consideration is that although the intent of the examiner is to have the subject store in a one-to-one relationship the input data, a retrieval instruction is given in many instances which requires responses not in one-to-one relationship with input, that is, even in most studies where rote learning is required and flexible retrieval routine is expected of the organism. In fact, it is this retrieval instruction which directs the information-flow within the organism, so that data input in one form, may be output in another. Even in rote learning situations, then, retrieval must be flexible in most cases.

The above arguments may be documented from a logical analysis of the form of input and output. It is reasonable to argue further, using known characteristics of organismic processing of information, that there is no such thing as rote learning, rote retrieval. All human data processing, except perhaps the digit span type tasks, requires several stages of memory storage with different storage consolidation and decay times and with different interference characteristics. Even when retrieval is specified in terms of output, the presence of the data in various stored states which must be combined to make up the ultimate output obviates the use of rote as anything more than a superficial comment upon the congruence of observable input-output forms of the data.

When the model of human information processing is considered in this light, it is not surprising that so-called rote processes correlate highly with concept formation processes and problem solving processes. All of these constructs designate certain routes of information-flow or certain "programs" or "plans" (Miller, 1957) for dealing with a particular type of information processing. The correlations probably lie in the functional similarity of all information processes within the organism.

REFERENCES

Carroll, John B. *Modern Language Aptitude Test, Manual.* New York: The Psychological Corporation, 1959.

Cattell, Raymond B., and Eber, Herbert W. *Handbook for the Sixteen Personality Factor Questionnaire.* 1967 Edition (with 1964 Supplementation.) Champaign, Illinois: Institute for Personality and Ability Testing, 1962.

Davis, Frederick. "Fundamental Factors of Comprehension in Reading." *Psychometrika* 9:185–197, September 1944.

English, Horace B., and English, Ava Champney. *A Comprehensive Dictionary of Psychological and Psychoanalytical Terms.* New York: David McKay, 1958.

Hage, D. S., and Stroud, J. B. "Reading Proficiency and Intelligence Scores, Verbal and Non-verbal." *Journal of Educational Research* 52:258–62, March 1969.

Harootunian, B. "Intellectual Abilities and Reading Achievement." *Elementary School Journal* 66:386–92, April 1966.

Hunt, Earl B. "Simulation and Analytic Models of Memory." *Journal of Verbal Learning and Verbal Behavior* 2:49–59, July 1963.

Miller, George A. "Free Recall of Redundant Strings of Letters." *Journal of Experimental Psychology* 56:484–91, 1958.

Miller, George A. *Language and Communication.* New York: McGraw-Hill, 1951.

Miller, George A. "The Magical Number Seven, Plus or Minus Two: Some Limits on our Capacity for Processing Information." *Psychological Review* 63:81–97, March 1956.

Miller, George A., Galanter, Eugene, and Pribram, Karl H. *Plans and the Structure of Behavior.* New York: Henry Holt, 1960.

Thorndike, Edward L. "The Understanding of Sentences: A Study of Errors in Reading." *Elementary School Journal* 18:98–114, October 1917.

Underwood, Benton J. "Rote Learning." *Categories of Human Learning.* (Edited by Arthur W. Melton.) New York: Academic Press, 1964.

Weaver, Wendell W., and Kingston, Albert J. "A Factor Analysis of the Cloze Procedure and Other Measures of Reading and Language Ability." *Journal of Communication* 8:252–261, December 1963.

Vertical and Horizontal Constraints in the Context Reading of Sentences

A competent reader of English reads sequentially from the first to the last word in the sentence. In our typography this requires a left to right eye movement. The eye movements of readers long have intrigued psychologists. However, the significance of eye movements lies in the fact that while fixating on parts of words, whole words, or groups of words, the reader "inputs" the linguistic unit as he derives meaning from the print. Eye movement fluency generally is regarded as symptomatic of reading competency, but the process can be interrupted and disrupted by distorting the words being read, e.g., a misprinted word, or by changing the structure of the sentence so that the order of the words being read violates the subject's internalized rules of grammar, e.g., name my is John. Similarly the deliberate deletion of a word and the substitution of a blank, as in the cloze procedure, or some other type of mutilated sentence, elicits behavior from the reader not ordinarily noted. Thus, if a sentence, which contains a deleted word (marked by an underline) is presented to a subject who has been instructed to supply the word which he best thinks fits the blank, the response of the subject may seem to be affected by certain characteristics of the sentence itself. For example, the word class of the deleted word, the position of the deleted word within the sentence, or the amount of context preceding or following the deletion appear to function as constraints which partially act to affect the word a subject supplies from his repertoire. These constaints are spoken of in this paper as horizontal constraints.

In addition to these horizontal constraints there are constraints which operate over the distribution of words that have the privilege of occurring at a particular word class deletion. Shepard (1963) has shown that vertical constraint and horizontal constraint interact. If language passages are selected at random and a target word deleted at random (ignoring word form class) the vertical distribution decreased with the length of the horizontal distribution (i.e., the sentence context). Goldman-Eisler (1961) has shown that as the vertical distribution increases (the potential

(Co-authored with Albert J. Kingston and James A. Dinnan.) Originally published in the *Journal of Reading Behavior*, 1971, 3(2), 39–43. Reprinted with the permission of the National Reading Conference.

distribution) the ability of subjects to fill in the exact word deleted from the sentence, at that point, decreases. Just as certain aspects of horizontal constraints operate independently (sequential redundancy, for example), aspects of vertical constraint occur independently of horizontal constraints. These vertical constraints have been studied most often under the label "association studies" and have been completely divorced from their relationships to natural language. Horizontal and vertical constraints apparently function in "context" reading, for the highly able reader seems to be aware of not only the specific textual setting of a word, but also associates the inputs with previously learned concepts and verbal learnings.

This study, then, is based upon the assumption that the completion of a deleted language unit at a particular point in a sentence is based upon sequential—syntactical relations at that point (the horizontal constraints), upon the associational relationships exhibited by the distribution of words with a privilege of occurring at that point (the vertical constraints), and upon the interaction between the two types of constraint. The following experiment was designed for the purpose of measuring these relationships.

PROCEDURE

A group of forty upper division college women were administered ten sentences. Each sentence consisted of a sentence with a single, deleted word. Words deleted included nouns, adjectives, verbs, and adverbs; thus all deletions were lexical deletions. The subjects were asked to supply all possible words they could think of that made sense in each deletion. Three minute periods were assigned for each sentence. For each subject five of the sentences were presented with the first word of her previous list included as her first word in the production lists. In the other five sentences the last word of her former production list was included on the second stimulus word list. That is, each subject received five tasks in which her first response was supplied as the first word of her three minute production list and five sentences in which her last response was supplied as the first word for her second production list. Thus each subject was cued by her first and last response for filling in the rest of the words she could think of in three minutes. The data were analyzed to determine the number of exact duplicate responses in the two lists and the position of that response in the list (first half of list or last half of list). The total number of responses (the verbal fluency for both lists) was also determined.

RESULTS

The total sum of fluency scores for the subjects showed no significant differences (chi-square test) between the production of the subject when no stimulus word was presented in the position of the deleted word and when the first word from the subject's own association list was placed in the position of the deleted word and when the last word from the subject's association list was placed in the position of the deleted word. The investigators believed that production under the deletion unit would lead to greater fluency than production under the deletion unit when words were inserted. They also believed that the insertion of the last word from the subject's association list (previously obtained) would lead to a smaller production than the insertion of the first word from the subjects' lists. This did not prove to be true.

The major analysis is presented in contingency tables for the reverse list and the forward list.

Table 1. Contingency table for first and second list
for reversed association lists*

		Second list				
		First	Part	Last	Part	Total
		O	E	O	E	
First list	First part	453	424	148	177	601
	Last part	269	298	154	125	423
	Total		722		302	1024

*$\chi^2 = 16.28$**, p $\leq$ .001

Table 2. Contingency table for first and second list
for forward association lists*

		Second list				
		First	Part	Last	Part	Total
		O	E	O	E	
First list	First part	429	395	137	171	566
	Last part	215	249	141	107	356
	Total		644		278	922

*$\chi^2 = 25.13$**, p $\leq$ .001

Both forward and reverse association contingency tables show significant chi-squares (Reversed = 16.6 and Forward = 24.6) at the p = .01 significance level.

It may also be seen from these contingency tables that the first list shows the stronger relationship between items on the first list appearing first on the second list and items on the first list appearing last on the second list. Nevertheless there is obviously also a statistical difference between the relationships of the front and the back part of the second list. Items which are on the first part on the second list occur more probably from the first part of the first list, and items which are last on the second list occur more probably from the last part of the first list. It may also be shown that this relationship holds up when the contingency table for each list is broken down sentence by sentence. There is no essential difference between these sentence contingency tables and the overall contingency tables which are presented here.

The most obvious general effect is that there is no difference in supplying further fill-ins between an empty cloze blank and a cloze blank filled in with one word, whether that word is taken from the first or the last of a prior association list of the subject based on the same sentence passage. Although it is true that there is no difference in the characteristics of a list which follows a word last on a subject's association list and a word first on a subject's list, nevertheless, there is a great deal of difference in the characteristics of the association list produced. There are obvious cases where associations are produced to fit particular categorical perception units. For example, an individual filling a blank where an appropriate unit to fill in might be "Russia," also might include a long list of other countries. It seems likely that in such cases the serial association list, i.e., nations or countries, serves as the constraining factor and functions as a more powerful stimulus control for the production of words than do the original sentence constraints. On the other hand when categories change it may be that at this point the subject again must review the sentence and align the new category so that he can supply a word which fits the particular cloze unit. It seems logical, then, to conclude that both vertical constraints, indicated by the association effect, and horizontal constraints, represented by the sentence context, are operating under these particular conditions. It should be noted that this particular phenomenon is apparent only when a productive operation is imposed, in the midst of a reading operation. Whether or not vertical constraints are modified or whether they even operate in the normal reading situation is indeterminant from this study. The fact that there seem to be few pauses in oral reading behavior except for phrasing and breathing would argue against vertical constraints functioning as important controllers of the oral reading process. On the other hand, the fact that even the best readers show consistent eye regression patterns when the eye is photographed in silent reading might argue that vertical constraints are important in obtaining "meaning" from written passages.

This study appears to indicate that a skilled reader does indeed receive information from the constraints of the sentences he reads. It also demonstrates that the responses of the competent reader under situations such as presented here at least, are somehow constrained by the responses he makes while reading. Probably both horizontal and vertical restraints are important in the comprehension of competent readers.

REFERENCES

Goldman-Eisler, F. Hesitation and information in speech. *Information Theory, Fourth London Symposium.* London: Butterworths, 1961.

Shepard, R. N. Production of constrained associates and the informational uncertainty of the constraint. *The American Journal of Psychology,* June, 1963, 76, 218–228.

Experiments in Children's Perceptions
of Words and Word Boundaries

Teachers of reading, particularly teachers of beginning readers, tend to use the "word" as a major goal in reading pedagogy and for judging pupil progress. Constantly we see and hear references to word recognition, word attack skills, and sight vocabulary whenever reading is discussed. Interestingly little is known about how a beginning reader learns to recognize words or, for that matter, what a word actually is. It is difficult to reconcile the linguist's deliberate shunning of the concept "word," for he seemingly prefers terms such as phoneme and morpheme, with the proclivity of the reading teacher and psychologist to use "word" as an analyzable language unit (Weaver, 1966; Weaver, 1967). At any rate "words" represent comparatively elusive units of study particularly in oral language and even analytical philosophers have had difficulty in adequately defining the term. Because reading specialists apparently view words as so important to reading, the study of how children learn to distinguish words in both aural and written form should be helpful in understanding how children learn to read.

Karpova (1966) examined the ability of children aged three to seven to identify the number of words in a spoken sentence. The subjects were asked to tell the number of words they heard, and later to tell the ordinal position of words, i.e., which word was first, which word was second, etc. As a result of this study, Karpova hypothesized three stages of development: the youngest children used the sentences as "unified" wholes; older children were able to isolate the main action of the sentence upon repeated questioning by the examiner; a few older children were able to discriminate most of the words although they had difficulty with prepositions and conjunctions. Reid (1966) interviewed five girls and seven boys, five years of age, to discover what they thought about reading. Among her findings was the fact that the five year olds showed a very poor understanding of the categories of "word" and "sound." Downing (1970) extended this study by presenting a non-human noise and four human utterances ranging from a single vowel phoneme to a complete

(Co-authored with Albert J. Kingston and Leslie E. Figa.) Originally published in *Investigations Relating to Mature Reading,* F. P. Greene, ed. The Twenty-first Yearbook of the National Reading Conference, 1972. Reprinted with the permission of the National Reading Conference.

simple sentence to subjects aged four to five years. The subjects were instructed to say "yes" if what they heard was a word and "no" if what they heard was not a word. None of the children were able to identify a word as an adult would. McNinch (1970), as part of a broader study, constructed a so-called Aural Word Representation Test which required the subjects to duplicate the number of words heard by placing an appropriate number of foam rubber cubes equivalent to the number of words they thought they heard. He found a positive correlation between the AWR given in October and a standard end-of-year reading achievement test.

If one considers the philosophical studies of the concept "word" it is apparent that the treatment of the concept by linguists is not shared by most philosophical positions. Merleau-Ponty argues that the word has meaning, that a familiar thing appears indeterminant until we recall its name, and that the thinking subject is in a kind of ignorance of his thoughts until he has spoken or written them (Charlesworth, 1970). Among analytical philosophers the word as a meaningful unit has a high status (Hospers, 1967). Others argue that the word has a substantial character: one can hit a person with a word as well as with a weapon, and that at the beginning of conceptualization the word is considered an attribute of the thing itself (Blackmur, 1952; Burke, 1957; Werner and Kaplan, 1963).

The question of word boundaries had not received extensive examination from either philosophers or psychologists. Cowgill (1963) in a discussion of universals in diachronic morphology admits that in his study of word boundaries he was over-influenced by the printer's space of the text he used. He hypothesized that the identification of words is primarily a grammatical problem. Greenberg (1963) reached the same conclusion as a phonological problem.

In a study of children's discrimination of word boundaries in written language Meltzer and Herse (1969) sought to determine whether or not first grade children could locate the boundaries of written words in sentence form. They found that while most children identified some boundaries, there were many words the children could not identify using the criterion of the printer's space. The assumption here is that the identification of words is primarily a mechanical unitizing problem.

THE EXPERIMENTS

In order to test the general hypothesis that first grade children do not understand the nature of a "word," a series of experiments were conducted which are briefly reported here.

Experiment One

This study replicated the Meltzer and Herse (1969) study but expanded the independent variable by using three distinct types of reading selections. The subjects were 45 first grade pupils, upper-lower and lower middle class, randomly selected from 150 pupils enrolled in a rural, northeast Georgia school. There were three experimental conditions.

The basal reader condition. This consisted of 15 sentences or phrases selected from the Pre-primer and Primer editions of the basal reader series used at the school. The sentences or phrases ranged in length from a minimum of two words per sentence to a maximum of six words per sentence. Three sentences were presented at the beginning of the list in order to instruct the subjects, and these sentences were not scored or used in the final analysis. Each sentence was typed, using a Primary typewriter, on 1″ by 8″ strips of paper.

The second-order approximation to English condition. Nonsense words were formed using the basal reader material as a source. A letter was located in a random position on a page. This letter was then located at its next appearance in the text and the letter next to it recorded. This letter was then searched for next in the text and the letter next to it recorded. Constraint was imposed upon this approximation by fixing the length of the pseudo-words equal to the length of the words in the first experimental condition. These pseudo-sentences or phrases were also typed on individual strips of paper.

The adult novel condition. Sentences were selected from an adult novel. The number of words per sentence was held constant to match the number of words per sentence in the other two experimental conditions. The number of letters per word was greatly increased. These sentences were then typed on strips of paper.

The subjects were obtained from their classrooms individually, given a pair of scissors, and asked to cut the strips of paper where ever they thought a word occurred. There were 15 subjects in each experimental group. The first three sentences administered to each subject were used to illustrate and to make sure the subject understood and could perform the cutting task. The order of sentences in each condition was randomized for each subject.

In analyzing the results the scoring criteria developed by Meltzer and Herse (1969) were adopted. These were:

Type A error—divided word at tall letter.
Type B error—divided word elsewhere than at tall letter.
Type C error—combined two words.
Type D error—combined letters with no regard to space.

Type E error—equated words and letters.
Type F error—other combinations.

In analyzing the responses it was noted that a number of errors did not fit the criteria. Such errors were placed in the other combinations category.

For each subject the different types of errors as well as the frequency of each type of error was recorded. (Tables available from authors upon request.) The total number of errors for all subjects was then calculated and means, variances, and standard deviations computed (see Table 1).

Table 1. Means, variances, and standard deviations of errors
for various materials in experiment one

Materials	Means	Variance	Standard deviation
Basal reader	5.27	58.21	7.63
Second-order approximation to English	6.53	84.14	9.17
Adult novel	20.80	991.71	31.49

A significant difference was found between the Adult Novel task and both the Basal Reader and the Second-Order Approximation tasks. An F-value of 5.64 was attained.

Table 2 shows the errors attained using the Meltzer-Herse system of classification. It can be noted that a number of different types of errors were found.

Table 2. Total frequency of errors over all three conditions
(values indicate number of times a particular type of error occurred)

Conditions	No errors	Divided at tall letter	Divided elsewhere than at tall letter	Combined two words	Combined letters with no regard to space	Equated words and letters	Other types
Basal reader	4	5	5	43	6	2	3
Second-order approximation to English	2	6	12	52	12	0	1
Adult novel	1	80	75	84	47	2	9

The most common error was that of combining two or more words. For the basal reader and second-order approximation conditions this was the major source of error and the combining errors were generally restricted to combining two words of which one word was a one-letter word, for example: "I said," "I can," "and I." On the other hand there were some instances when combinations such as: "said, 'No,'" "get the," and "is not," were observed. This type of error carried over to the adult novel material condition where a number of other word combinations were introduced, for example: "lowered his," "her foot impatiently," "what you," "his knee," and "even more pronounced." The combinations here seem to be a result of a failure to perceive any word meaning, in addition to the fact that the printer's space was not recognized as a word boundary cue. The adult novel material brought out high frequencies of all the Meltzer and Herse categories except the "equating the letter and word" category and the "other" category. There was great confusion about word boundaries; some of them were divided at ascenders and some at descenders, and some at neutrals. There also was the error of putting together parts of two words, i.e., the last letters of one word and the first few letters of the next word, for example: "mo/re pr/onoun/ced."

It should also be observed that there is no difference in the response to basal reader materials which were constructed from materials which the subjects covered in their classrooms, and a second-order approximation to English equated to the word length of the basal reader materials. The error patterns in the second-order approximation materials is essentially the same as that of the basal reader materials with the preponderant error being a combination of two words, in most cases one of the words consisting of a one-letter word, for example: "vex i," "iro s," "i ner," and "c apro."

It would appear from the results of this experiment that recognizing the printer's space as the separator of words is secondary to perceiving that a particular linguistic unit represents a meaningful entity. The reason for the performance in the case of long words is obscured because length of the word and the ability to perceive words as meaningful units are correlated—the longer the word the more difficult is its comprehension. In this case therefore there may be a regression to a more primitive level of perception and analogies drawn to the basal reader situation where words of six and seven letters in length are rare. This "stimulus-bound" perception would then also account for the performance on the second-order approximation materials. Here the length of the pseudo-words are the same as that of the basal reader materials. And the behaviors toward the two kinds of materials are essentially the same. Thus, the developmental trend observed by Meltzer and Herse (1969) was not found in our data.

Experiment Two

In experiment two, the materials used were taken from an aural word representation task presented originally by McNinch (1970). The stimulus consisted of three short trial sentences and sentences or phrases at each length from two to six words per sentence or phrase.

There were three experimental conditions. The subjects heard the examiner read the sentences to him; the subjects were presented with the sentences typed with a primary typewriter on strips of paper; and the subjects heard the sentences read to them via a tape recording. Each subject was given a number of wooden cubes and was instructed when he heard or read a sentence to place the number of cubes equivalent to the number of words in the sentences before the E. The dependent variable was the number of cubes successfully placed.

As shown in Table 3, the highest scores were obtained over the visual presentation. This "reading" condition also had the most constricted spread of scores as shown by the standard deviation. (Tables illustrating these data showing analyses by frequency of errors available upon request.)

Table 3. Means, variances, and standard deviations for conditions one, two, and three in experiment two

Conditions	Mean	Variance	Standard deviation
Aural	7.33	25.27	5.03
Visual	12.07	6.87	2.62
Taped	6.20	12.40	3.52

A simple, one-way, randomized design, analysis of variance was computed. The F-value was significant beyond the .05 level of confidence.

Table 4 is a summary of successes and errors of all subjects in judging the number of words in a sentence or phrase. The most important consideration is the columns labeled Times Below and Times Above the correct number of words in the stimulus. In the reading aloud and taped conditions the number of words were consistently underestimated while in the reading condition, which had many fewer errors, the number of words in the stimulus were overestimated.

It seems that for these young subjects that amalgamation of units is characteristic. Subjects however reading the same materials seem to have many more cues to the word unit as revealed by their greater success in

Table 4. Summary of successes and errors in sentences
of all subjects in experiment two

Conditions	Number correct	Number incorrect	Times below	Times above
Aural	95	130	119	11
Visual	166	59	16	43
Taped	78	147	115	32

counting the correct number of words and when they commit an error the tendency is to perceive more units than those defined by the printer's space rather than less.

Experiments Three, Four, and Five

The results of experiments one and two as well as the work of Reid (1966) and Downing (1970) and others led us to suspect that one source of difficulty that children encountered in recognizing word boundaries was due to their faulty concepts concerning the nature of a "word." Careful study of philosophical, linguistic, and reading literature reveals that the construct "word" is a vague term. Unfortunately time and space limitations preclude an adequate discussion of just how ambiguous the term is.

Experiment three tested the children's ability to identify human words and human sounds. A tape consisting of common words and common human utterances was prepared. A group of 15 randomly selected first graders were asked to identify the sound they heard as either a word or not a word. Experiment four consisted of 10 compound words and 10 two word pairs, presented on a tape to another group of 15 first graders. The subjects were asked to identify what they heard as either one word or two words. Some of the "sounds" used in experiment three were: hum; ahem; mmm; tsk; oh. Some of the words used were map; amen; shoot; street; banquet. For experiment four some of the compound words were policeman; skyscraper; baseball; quartermaster. Some of the two word pairs were: ball game; two wheeler; dump truck; fire engine.

As shown in Table 5, the children as a group had some difficulty in telling the difference between human words and human utterances and recognizing compound words from two words.

The fifth experiment consisted of twelve taped sentences which contained both sounds and words. Fifteen first graders randomly selected were asked individually to tell how many words they heard in each sentence. Examples of the task were: (Snore) (Snore) Daddy is asleep; Listen to the teapot (Whistle); (Arf) (Arf) went the dog.

Both human and inanimate sounds were used and the position of the sound in relationship to the sentence was varied. Unfortunately this task was too difficult for these subjects. It seemed apparent however that many children had difficulty in not only remembering what they heard and counting the number of words, but also confounded noises and sounds with the words in context.

Table 5. Means, variances, and standard deviations
for the Word-Sound Test and the Compound Word Test

Test	Mean	Variance	Standard deviation
Words	6.67	4.29	2.07
Sounds	7.33	1.00	1.00
Total (words & sounds)	14.00	5.00	2.24
Compound words	5.40	8.86	2.98
Two-word pairs	6.73	7.36	2.71
Total (compound & two-word pairs)	12.13	10.86	3.30

CONCLUSION

These five experiments demonstrate quite conclusively that first grade children lack precise concepts concerning the nature of a "word." Apparently in oral language the concept is not a major barrier either to speaking or listening. In reading, however, word recognition is an essential and fundamental skill. Perhaps the difficulties of certain children in learning to read may stem from the problem they have in distinguishing words. It also is possible that young children may attend to word units when they begin instruction in reading. Until that time there apparently is little need to concentrate on separating words from their context. As noted in experiment one, however, this does not mean that learning the printer's space is the primary requisite for unitizing words. After all, the concentration in reading instruction is not upon identifying word boundaries, but upon perception of words themselves. It is also impressive that once children learn the conventions for identifying word units in reading (an ability which comes with the mastery of reading skills) it is apparently an easy transfer to break up the aural phonological stream into word units. These first graders however, do not exhibit this easy transfer which is apparent in older children. It is possible then that this is because they are still erratic in their perception of both meaning and the function of the printer's space, and therefore do not have a firmly grounded reading perception of words from which to operate on the phonological stream.

One final speculation seems to be in order, although these experiments did not address themselves to this question. As one observes children grappling with the types of tasks presented here, one can only wonder about the nature of the "word" as a unit of language. Linguists who as a group prefer to work with oral language tend to shun the construct "word." These studies tend to show that for young children at least the word does not seem important. Perhaps sounds become words only in written form, and perhaps even in written form they are not too important.

REFERENCES

Blackmur, R. P. *Language as Gesture*. New York: Harcourt, Brace, and World, 1952.

Burke, K. *The Philosophy of Literary Form*. New York: Vintage Books, 1957.

Charlesworth, J. H. Reflections on Merleau-Ponty's phenomenological description of "word." *Journal of Philosophical Phenomenological Research*, 1970, 30, 609–613.

Cowgill, W. A search for universals in Indo-European diachronic morphology. In J. H. Greenberg (Ed.), *Universals of Language*. (2nd ed.) Cambridge: The MIT Press, 1963.

Downing, J. Children's concepts of language in learning to read. *Educational Research*, 1970, 12, 106–112.

Greenberg, J. H. Some universals of grammar with particular reference to the order of meaningful elements. In J. H. Greenberg (Ed.), *Universals of Language*. (2nd. ed.) Cambridge: The MIT Press, 1963.

Hospers, J. *An Introduction to Philosophical Analysis*. Englewood Cliffs: Prentice-Hall, 1967.

Karpova, S. N. Osoznanie slovesnogo sostava rechi rebenkom doshkol'nogo vozrasta (The preschooler's realization of the lexical structure of speech). Voprosy. Psikhol. 1955, 4, 43–55. Abstracted by D. I. Slobin, in F. Smith & G. Miller (Eds.), *Genesis of Language*. Cambridge: The MIT Press, 1966. Pp. 370–371.

McNinch, G. H. W. The relationship between selected perceptual factors and measured first grade reading achievement. (Doctoral dissertation, the University of Georgia) Ann Arbor. University Microfilms, Order No. 71–3756. *Dissertation Abstracts*, Feb. 1971, 31, 3965A.

Meltzer, N. S. and Herse, R. The boundaries of written words as seen by first graders. *Journal of Reading Behavior*, 1969. 1, 3–13.

Reid, J. F. Learning to think about reading. *Educational Research*, 1966, 9, 56–62.

Weaver, W. W. Units of measurement and units of language. Paper presented at the symposium on *The technology of written instruction*. New York: Columbia University, 1966.

Weaver, W. W. The word as a unit of language. *Journal of Reading,* 1967, 10, 262–268.

Werner, H., & Kaplan, B. *Symbol Formation.* New York: John Wiley and Sons, 1963.

Feasibility of Cloze Techniques
for Teaching and Evaluating
Culturally Disadvantaged Beginning Readers

To date, most studies of the learning problems of culturally disadvantaged children have been concentrated on inner city or urban populations. It has been known for many years, however, that children who reside in economically substandard rural areas also are disadvantaged when compared to the typical middle class school population. This condition has been amply demonstrated by manuals of published standardized intelligence tests, for the norms of the tests tend to reflect the lower mean scores attained by rural school children. One difficulty shared by both inner city children and rural disadvantaged pupils is that their patterns of oral language are different from standard English. These differences are so great, in many cases, that first grade teachers are concerned about the "fit" between the language used by their pupils and the language employed in the typical basal reader. Such differences have been noted in both structure and vocabulary of different students (1, 4).

Recent renewal of interest in the so-called language experience approach to beginning reading instruction is based upon a realization of the difficulties engendered by the use of materials written in standard American with children who do not normally speak or hear standard language outside of the classroom (6, 7).

An additional problem with the typical culturally disadvantaged pupil is the difficulty of motivating him so that he becomes actively involved in the teaching-learning situation. The use of the child's own language, and the presentation of experiences with which he is already familiar in reading instruction tends to increase his interest in the school-presented learning tasks.

In the study reported here the technique of using teacher-learner prepared material was employed. Unlike previous methods of instruction, however, these materials were presented in a measurement setting. Also, efforts were made to begin an examination of the manner in which the oral language code is transduced into the written language code by the

(Co-authored with Albert J. Kingston.) Originally published in the *Journal of Social Psychology*, 1972, 82, 205–214. Reprinted with the permission of the Journal Press.

beginning reader—information which the typical readiness test and the basal reader achievement tests fail to provide.

It was hypothesized that certain forms of the cloze procedure and tasks based upon the deleted language format could be modified to achieve this goal with beginning readers. These techniques, then, could be used with both oral and written language to furnish baseline data. From these data it is hoped that a degree of specification of a child's oral language abilities prior to beginning reading will be possible. Measurement would then be possible along the same relevant dimensions whether made before the child learns to read or after he masters certain fundamental skills. It also seemed that cloze type tasks, because of their game-like challenge and their "guessing" aspect, might serve to motivate children who might not be highly interested in basal reader stories.

THE PROBLEM

The present study was undertaken to examine the feasibility of the use of cloze and cloze-like tasks with culturally disadvantaged first grade pupils. Because all of the children serving as subjects in this study were completely unfamiliar with cloze-like tasks, the use of cloze tasks was incorporated into the instructional sequence in reading, with the aid of the teachers involved.

The efficiency of the cloze tasks in charting reading achievement was examined by comparing the predictive power of the cloze tasks with the predictive power of achievement tests supplied by publishers of the basal reader series used. The criterion for reading achievement was a standardized reading test given at the end of the first grade.

SUBJECTS

This study involved children of several small rural schools where other, more extensive federal programs were in operation, but where research, as such, was considered an activity of highly dubious value. There was no opportunity to provide comparison groups in the schools where the research treatments were going on. In the light of studies by others (3) who are skeptical about the possibilities of applying the cloze procedure to these lower age levels, it was felt that this correlation evidence merited distribution. Distribution seemed especially important, since the schools in which the data were collected involve children, large proportions of whom are characterizable as economically and culturally deprived.

The subjects used were 182 first graders in rural, white elementary schools in Georgia and North Carolina. About half of these subjects were used to obtain reliability data on the instruments used in the study. Another eight subjects were dropped from the study because of incomplete data due to absences during the testing period or withdrawal from school. Seventy-four subjects from six classrooms make up the population of the regression analysis reported here.

PROCEDURE

The subjects were introduced to the cloze procedure during their regular reading lessons. A regular activity of the class had been making up stories and having the teacher write these stories on the chalk-board. This activity was extended by deleting, arbitrarily, a lexical item and having the children supply all the words they could think of which would complete the passage and still "make sense." Each word contribution was discussed and its relationship to context explored in the discussion. Children (there were very few) who did not participate in this exercise, were grouped and, at other times, were shown the passage originally written on the chalk-board and then were given a visual clue to the missing word—e.g., a picture of a horse for the deleted word "horse." Pupils were then encouraged to supply other words which might "make sense" in the context of the deletion.

A new procedure was begun which moved along with the chalk-board exercises. The stories the children produced as a group were typed, using a primary typewriter, and at subsequent reading sessions these stories were presented to the children. Stories constructed by children in other classes at the same grade level also were presented to the children for reading. After a period of exposure to the typed materials as complete reading exercises, deletions were made in the materials.

While the above instruction was proceeding over a two or three week period, the children were shown books with certain words left out and with pictures substituted for the deleted words. For slower learners materials were constructed which began with pictures for all deleted items. The number of pictures presented in the deletions was gradually decreased as the children advanced in proficiency. After they became adept at supplying one word to fill the blank, the children were encouraged to search for other words which "make sense" in the same slot.

After working with the materials as described above for about a month, group sessions were held where the teacher read stories aloud which they had produced while the children read them silently. The children were then presented deleted versions of the stories and the stories were reread by the teacher. At first only two or three words were deleted in an entire 100–200 word story, but it soon became apparent that with materials they themselves had produced, the children had no difficulty supplying words from a regular mechanical deletion procedure. The children next were given versions of stories they had produced in class but had not seen in print before. They were asked to read silently and fill in the blanks in the deleted versions which followed the reading. They were instructed to attempt to write the word whether they could spell it correctly or not. Words which had the first letter correct were scored as correct. Actually, this technique proved adequate for measurement purposes, but it caused the teachers so much anxiety to see so many "word-parts" counted as correct that the multiple-choice format was designed.

The Lee-Clark Readiness Test was administered from −1 to 1 weeks from the beginning of school. The Ginn Pre-Primer test was given by the schools approximately halfway through the school year. All cloze tests (as distinguished from the practice exercises) were given in February and March. The Ginn Primer Test was given in April. The California Achievement Tests were administered by the teachers in the school. The experimenters instructed the teachers during the subject practice phase of the experiment in the administration of the tests.

INSTRUMENTATION
"Any-Word" Cloze

This test is constructed by deleting mechanically every nth word: e.g., every 5th word or every 10th word in a language passage. For example, the sentences, "This is Lucille. Lucille belongs to a farmer. She pulls the farmer's plow and works very hard in the field," would appear as follows with a 5th word deletion: "This is Lucille. Lucille _____ to a farmer. She _____ the farmer's plow and _____ very hard in the _____." A 10th word deletion would appear as follows: "This is Lucille. Lucille belongs to a farmer. She _____ the farmer's plow and works very hard in the _____."

On all cloze tasks used as measurement devices with first graders the child read the intact passage (as in the sentence example above) before he was required to complete the cloze units. Under these conditions it has been shown that the total number of exact replacements of the word in the original passage correlates well ($r = .75$ to $.85$) with measures of vocabulary, reading comprehension, and intelligence (10). First grade pupils were presented the 50 items in this cloze test in five sessions of 10 items each. There was no time limit. Test-retest reliability for this test was .78.

Multiple-Choice, Structural Cloze

"Any-word" cloze, described above, often has been designated structural cloze, following Fries' (5) categorizing of language into a structural-lexical dichotomy. Since an any-word deletion samples more of the frequently occurring words of the language, generally function words, and these words contribute more to the structure of the language than to its semantic content, an any-word deletion is considered to measure structural meaning—in Fries' terms. In the any-word format, the deleted word is replaced by a standard-length underline; in the multiple-choice format here, each word to be deleted is paired with a distracter of the same grammatical class. After every five cloze deletions the 10 words are listed across the page, under the relevant material, in a random order. This format provided a test-retest reliability on the task of .91.

Lexical Cloze, Multiple-Choice

The other element of Fries' (5) dichotomy is lexical meaning which he believes carries the content of the language message. In this study, words were first classified as noun, main verb, or adjective. Then a 5th word deletion was carried out on nouns, main verbs, and adjectives only. As above each word to be deleted was paired with a distracter of the same grammatical class and the multiple-choice format arranged. This format provided a test-retest reliability of .76.

Ginn Pre-Primer Achievement Test

This is a test designed to accompany the Ginn Basal Reading series. One of its purposes is to "provide a permanent record of each child's reading development" (9). No reliability or validity data are reported in the test manual. A test-retest reliability of .70 was obtained locally. The test is intended to measure vocabulary and comprehension as separate constructs. In this study only the total raw score is used due to low reliabilities of the part scores.

Ginn Primary Achievement Test

This is a higher level test in the same series as the Pre-Primer test described above. Its purposes are the same (9). No reliability or validity data is reported. Test-retest reliability obtained locally was .90.

Lee-Clark Reading Readiness Test

This test was designed "to provide the teacher with an objective basis for identifying children who are ready to receive reading instruction" (8). Split-half reliability for the total score is given as .87 for first graders.

Since the first two part scores (of four parts) are speeded tests, this reliability is inappropriately measured. A test-retest reliability obtained locally gave a reliability value of .82.

California Achievement Tests

This battery includes general achievement measures in the areas of reading, arithmetic, and language with reported reliabilities on the Lower Primary test used in this study computed only on second graders. The Kuder-Richardson formula 21 reliabilities are Reading .93; Arithmetic .93; and Language .87 (11). A separate test-retest reliability was computed locally on a sample of first graders. Total reading score test-retest reliability was .84. Part score reliabilities were much lower. Only total raw scores are used in this analysis.

Aural-Reading Cloze

This cloze deletion was the same as for "any-word" cloze. Instead of having the children read the passage silently, however, the teacher read the passage aloud while the subjects read the material silently. A pause of approximately 30 seconds was made by the teacher at each cloze blank. Test-retest reliability was .85.

RESULTS

Raw scores were used in all analyses. A step-wise regression analysis, with the use of the California Reading Test as the criterion variable and all of the other tests (with the exception of the California Arithmetic Test and the California Language Test) as predictor variables was the basic statistical analysis performed. Subproblem analyses were also run, with the use of the California Reading Test as criterion variable and all other tests as predictor variables, and with the Ginn Primary Reading Test as criterion variable and all other tests as predictor variables with the exception of the California Reading, Arithmetic, and Language Tests.

The step-wise regression was computed with the use of the UCLA Biomedical Computer Program, BMD02R. The basic analysis (see Table 1) shows that *Lexical Cloze, Multiple-Choice* is the best single predictor of the California Reading Test scores. *Any-Word Cloze,* however, in spite of its high correlation with *Lexical Cloze, Multiple-Choice,* adds a relatively large amount of prediction. Other tests add significantly more and more predictive power, but since the percentages of increase in predictive power are low, and since the step-wise regression algorithm probably squeezes the data too dry anyway, those increases will not be commented upon.

Table 1. Step-wise regression analysis
excluding California Arithmetic and Language Tests—
California Reading Test dependent variable

Variable entering	Multiple R	Multiple R-square	Increase in multiple R-square	Order of entering
Multiple-Choice Cloze (Lexical)	68	46	46	1*
Straight Cloze	73	53	08	2*
Lee-Clark Readiness	75	56	03	3*
Ginn Primer	76	57	01	4*
Aural-Reading Cloze	76	58	01	5*
Ginn Pre-Primer	76	58	00+	6*
Multiple-Choice Cloze (structural)	77	59	00+	7*

* Sig. F at .01 level.

When the California Arithmetic Test and the California Language Tests are added to the predictor pool, *Any-Word Cloze* and *Lexical Cloze, Multiple-Choice* still hang together and contribute a relatively large increase to the prediction. In this case California Arithmetic is so closely related to California Reading (for a number of reasons—reading and arithmetic are related through a general verbal factor, they were given at the same time, etc.) that the arithmetic test is the best predictor of the reading. This probably would not have been true if the arithmetic test had been given in February, as were the cloze tests (see Table 2).

When the criterion variable is the Ginn Primary Reading Test, Aural-Reading Cloze entered first as the best predictor. Any-Word Cloze, again, adds predictive efficiency. The readiness test contributes small amounts of statistically predictive efficiency, but in all cases this contribution is smaller than that of certain types of the cloze tests (see Table 3).

The correlation table illustrates the cloze relationship between most of the variables (see Table 4).

Descriptive statistics of the tests used are present in Table 5.

DISCUSSION

This study represents an attempt to grapple with two thorny problems which face reading teachers. First, it is difficult to appraise effectively the development of reading ability in beginning readers because of the present lack of a common measurement dimension. Even a casual examination of readiness measures and primary grade reading achievement test reveals considerable differences in design format and content.

Table 2. Step-wise regression analysis including all measures—
California Reading Test as dependent variable

Variable entering	Multiple R	Multiple R-square	Increase in multiple R-square	Order of entering
California Arith.	72	52	52	1*
Straight Cloze	77	60	08	2*
Multiple-Choice Cloze (lexical)	79	62	02	3*
California Language	80	64	02	4*
Lee-Clark Readiness	80	64	00+	5*
Ginn Primer	80	65	00+	6*
Multiple-Choice Cloze (structural)	80	65	00+	7*
Aural-Reading Cloze	—	—	—	not entered
Ginn Pre-Primer	—	—	—	not entered

* Sig. F at .01 level.

Second, although it is commonly stated that the first grade child's oral language capabilities serve to limit, in some fashion, his success in beginning reading skills, little is known about the manner in which oral language either facilitates or hampers the course of reading development. Other things being equal, the first grade child with the highest measured intellectual abilities also possesses the greatest language proficiency. When one realizes, however, the complexities of the language measures

Table 3. Step-wise regression analysis
including only cloze and readiness test as independent measures—
California Reading Test dependent variable

Variable entering	Multiple R	Multiple R-square	Increase in multiple R-square	Order of entering
Aural-Reading Cloze	67	45	45	1*
Straight Cloze	71	50	05	2*
Ginn Pre-Primer	73	53	03	3*
Lee-Clark Readiness	74	55	01	4*
Multiple-Choice Cloze (lexical)	75	56	01	5*
Multiple-Choice Cloze (structural)	75	57	01	6*

* Sig. F at .01 level.

Table 4. Correlational coefficients of first graders
on various tests of cognitive achievement

Test	1	2	3	4	5	6	7	8	9	10
1. California Reading	—									
2. California Arith.	72									
3. California Language	62	56								
4. Multiple-Choice Cloze (structural)	63	60	62							
5. Multiple-Choice Cloze (lexical)	68	68	56	76						
6. Straight Cloze	64	58	60	75	63					
7. Aural-Reading Cloze	62	66	57	87	73	76				
8. Lee-Clark Readiness	63	56	42	32	47	50	34			
9. Ginn Pre-Primer	28	28	38	34	32	33	43	08		
10. Ginn Primer	39	32	38	60	57	66	67	19	45	—

commonly employed by the linguists, it is not surprising that the typical first grade teacher has failed to explicate the concept of language proficiency in her approach to teaching the beginning reader. If, however, oral language ability does serve to limit the acquisition of reading skills, effort should be put forth to utilize more directly these abilities in read-

Table 5. Mean, standard deviation, and total possible score for
first graders on various tests of cognitive achievement

Tests	Mean	Standard deviation	Total possible score
California Reading	52	8.64	90
California Arithmetic	57	15.73	90
California Language	34	9.27	85
Straight Cloze	14	4.91	35
Multiple-Choice Cloze (structural)	28	3.72	50
Multiple-Choice Cloze (lexical)	15	3.80	50
Aural-Reading Cloze	16	6.73	35
Lee-Clark Readiness	52	8.72	64
Ginn Pre-Primer	29	3.61	36
Ginn Primer	61	9.44	75

ing instruction rather than simply making subjective judgments, based upon very gross measures, that the child's language is "ready."

Cloze deletions were thought to provide one approach to more directly bridging the oral-writing language gap. The first task was to develop an adequate cloze which could be used with children before they began reading. While no attempt was made in this study to devise an oral language cloze test, children were performing in oral cloze situations in a manner that made it apparent that such measures could be developed. It was demonstrated in this study that first graders could perform on written cloze tests soon after they began reading.

The results of this study indicate that under systematic methods of the sort described, first grade children were able to handle oral and written cloze procedures. Furthermore the technique was highly motivating to the culturally disadvantaged pupils studied. The combination of techniques utilizing the language produced by the children themselves, oral and visual modes of presentation, systematic repetition and reinforcement, and finally oral and silent reading experiences seemed to be highly effective with these pupils. The utilization of materials stemming from the experiences of the pupils themselves introduced in a systematic, sequential way may be one solution to motivating the culturally disadvantaged child and assuring his greater involvement in the learning situation.

SUMMARY

One hundred eighty-two first grade children in rural, white schools in North Carolina and Georgia were taught to complete deletions in the natural language. These completed deletions were then used to study oral and written language performance by the children. It was found that first grade subjects could perform the tasks presented and that the measures offered promise for use in evaluating the relationship of the child's oral language performance to his performance with reading tasks. The six cloze tasks were better predictors of end-of-course standard reading test scores than were the readiness and basal reader instruments.

REFERENCES

1. Bernstein, B. Language and social class. *Brit. J. Sociol.,* 1960, 11, 271–276.
2. ———. Social structure, language and learning. *Educ. Res.,* 1961, 3, 163–176.
3. Bloomer, R. H. Non-overt Reinforced Cloze Procedure Project Report of U.S. Office of Education, #2245. University of Connecticut, Storrs, 1966.

4. Deutsch, M. Social and psychological perspectives on the development of the disadvantaged learner. *J. Negro Educ.*, 1964, 33, 232–244.

5. Fries, C. G. The Structure of English. New York: Harcourt Brace, 1952.

6. Gray, W. S. The Teaching of Reading and Writing. Chicago, Ill.: UNESCO, Scott, Foresman, 1956.

7. Lee, D. M., & Allen, R. V. Learning to Read Through Experience. New York: Appleton-Century-Crofts, 1963.

8. Lee, J. M., & Clark, W. Manual, Lee-Clark Reading Readiness Test, 1962, Kindergarten and Grade 1. Monterey, Calif.: California Test Bur., 1962.

9. McCullough, C. M., & Russell, D. H. Manual and Answer Key for Teachers, Primer Achievement Test (rev. ed.). New York: Ginn, 1957.

10. Taylor, W. L. "Cloze" readability scores as indices of individual differences in comprehension and aptitude. *J. Appl. Psychol.*, 1957, 41, 19–26.

11. Tiegs, E. W., & Clark, W. W. Manual, California Achievement Test, Complete Battery, Lower Primary (Grades 1 and 2). Los Angeles, Calif.: California Test Bureau, 1957.

A SHORT BIOGRAPHY OF
WENDELL WEAVER
AND A LIST OF
ADDITIONAL PAPERS

Wendell W. Weaver was born in Rome, Georgia. Educated in the public schools, he joined the United States Navy as a radioman, serving in the Asian theater from 1943 to 1946. After his discharge from the service he attended the University of Georgia for one year but switched to Oglethorpe University in Atlanta. He graduated in 1950, with majors in philosophy, economics, and history. Immediately recalled to the Navy during the Korean War, he served there from 1950 to 1951. After his release from the service he returned to Georgia and obtained the M.Ed. from Emory University. Later he gathered several years' experience as a teacher and counselor in Polk County, Georgia. With his interest in education now firm, he entered the graduate program at the University of

Georgia and received the Ed.D. in 1961 in counseling and educational psychology. He then joined the faculty of Campbell College in Buies Creek, North Carolina, as professor of psychology and education, to return in 1966 to the University of Georgia as associate and later professor of educational psychology. He remained at Georgia until he died April 7, 1972, a victim of Hodgkins Disease.

At the time of his death he was a member of the graduate faculty at the University of Georgia, the American Psychological Association, the American Educational Research Association, the International Reading Association, and the Southeastern Psychological Association. He also was president of the National Reading Conference. He was married and had seven children.

ADDITIONAL PAPERS OF WENDELL W. WEAVER

"An examination of some differences in oral and written language using the cloze procedure." Doctoral dissertation, University of Georgia, 1961, Ann Arbor, Michigan: University Microfilms 1961, 61–6587.

"Personality theory implied in Christian thought." Paper presented at the biannual meeting of instructors in psychology and religion in Baptist institutions, Southern Baptist Theological Seminary, Wake Forest, N.C., November 1962.

"The nature of knowledge." Paper presented at the annual meeting of the Higher Education Division of the North Carolina Education Association, February 1963.

"Communication, arts, and psychology." Paper presented to the meeting of instructors in education in Baptist colleges, Wake Forest College, Winston-Salem, N.C., April 1964.

"Imitation and education" (with W. C. Gass). Paper presented at the annual meeting of the South Atlantic Philosophy of Education Society, Virginia State College, Petersburg, October 1965.

"Counselor, teacher, and the problem of information." Paper presented at the joint meeting of the North Carolina Psychological Association and the North Carolina Academy of Science, Davidson College, March 1965.

"Affective dimensions in connotative meaning in reading" (with W. F. White and A. J. Kingston). *Journal of Psychology,* 1967, 227–234.

"Recent developments in readability-appraisal" (with A. J. Kingston). *Journal of Reading,* 1967, 11, 44–47.

"Reading research critically" (with A. J. Kingston). *Journal of Reading,* 1967, 10, 338–341.

"Constraint on sentence elements of context eternal to the sentence" (with

A. C. Bickley). Paper presented at the annual meeting of the South-eastern Psychological Association, New Orleans, La., April 1966.

"The relevance of learning theories for English education programs." Paper presented at the annual meeting of the National Council of Teachers of English, Boulder, Colo., March 1968.

"The use of black-out techniques for the study of grammatical categories" (with A. C. Bickley). Paper presented at the American Educational Research Association, Chicago, Ill., 1968.

"Information removed from multiple-choice item responses by selected grammatical categories" (with A. C. Bickley and F. G. Ford). *Psychological Reports,* 1968, 23, 613–614.

"Spatial dimensions in reading comprehension" (with W. F. White and A. J. Kingston) in J. A. Figurel (ed.) *Reading and realism.* Proceedings of the Thirteenth Annual Meeting of the International Reading Association, 1968, pp. 677–681.

"A study of randomizing sentences within paragraphs on reading test results" (with A. C. Bickley and F. G. Ford). Paper presented at the annual meeting of the Southeastern Psychological Association, Roanoke, Va., 1968.

"Correlations of error rate in the pronunciation of WISC vocabulary items" (with L. E. Hafner). *Journal of Reading,* 1970–71, 3(2), 27–31.

"Psychological and perceptual correlates among fourth graders" (with L. E. Hafner and K. Powell). *Journal of Reading Behavior,* 1970, 2, 281–290.

"Units of measurement and units of language" (published under the title "Discussion of Professor Neal F. Johnson's paper") in E. Z. Rothkopf and P. E. Johnson (eds.) *Verbal learning research and the technology of written instruction.* New York: Teachers College Press, 1971.

"The letter preferences of college women" (with A. J. Kingston and L. E. Figa) in P. L. Nacke (ed.) *Diversity in mature reading.* Boone, N.C.: National Reading Conference, 22nd Yearbook, 1973, 131–136.

AUTHOR INDEX

SUBJECT INDEX